MICHAEL J. WINSTANLEY

# The shopkeeper's world

## 1830–1914

Manchester University Press

To my parents

© MICHAEL J. WINSTANLEY 1983

*First published in 1983 by*
Manchester University Press, Oxford Road, Manchester M13 9PL
*and* 51 Washington Street, Dover, N.H. 03820, USA

*British Library cataloguing in publication data*

Winstanley, Michael J.
  The shopkeeper's world 1830–1914
  1. Retail trade – England – History
  I. Title
  381'.1'.0942        HF5429.6.G7
  ISBN 0–7190–0728–3

*Library of Congress cataloging in publication data applied for*

*Photoset in Garamond by* Northern Phototypesetting Co., Bolton
*Printed in Great Britain*
*by* The Alden Press, Oxford

# CONTENTS

# ILLUSTRATIONS

# ACKNOWLEDGEMENTS

This volume would not have been possible without the initial assistance of the Social Science Council which financed a broadly-based 'oral history' project at the University of Kent, 1974–7 during the course of which all the interview material for Part III was collected. I owe a debt of gratitude to Theo Barker for his encouragement and extensive comments on an earlier draft, to John Whyman, joint project supervisor, for his assistance with some details, and to Roger Scola and John Walton for helpful ideas and material. Needless to say, for errors of interpretation and detail that remain I bear sole responsibility. I should also like to thank Tony Carr of Shropshire's Local Studies Library for alerting me to a rich photographic archive and providing details of its contents; Charles Pyke of Lancaster for the loan of material relating to his business; Maureen Humphries for help with the original transcription; Mandy Charlton for typing some of the draft; Jim Styles for assistance with photographic reproductions and John Banks of the Press for being so patient and understanding during the book's conception period. Above all, I must thank all those individuals listed in the text who allowed me into their homes to record their memories. Although I have edited and re-arranged the order of the recollections, without them this work would not have been possible.

For permission to reproduce photographic material I would like to thank the following: Shrewsbury Museums (7, 11, 13, 16); Shropshire County Museum Service (Ludlow Museum) (14, 17); Lancaster City Museum (5, 15); Dover Public Library (8); Douglas West collection, Whitstable (21); Charles Evernden (10, 23); James Medhurst (6); Charles Marks (20); Ellen Bryan (22); Dora Fenney (24); Edward Carpenter (25). I have been unable to trace the source for No. 12.

# INTRODUCTION

This book represents a first foray into a well-trodden historical jungle in search of a largely ignored race: the motley collection of shopkeepers, the vital links in the chain between producers and consumers. The 'middle class' in more senses than one, they were from the eighteenth century, when they and other middlemen first made their impact felt, the focus of popular hatred from below and mild scorn and condescension from above. Historians in search of the middle class (assumed to be manufacturers), or even the elusive working class, have frequently stumbled across the nineteenth-century shopkeeper in their explorations but have passed on, relegating him to the role of onlooker or dependant in the historical process. Much of the early chapters is based on the scraps of information they have let fall in their books or on their few attempts to study the retailer in detail. I am indebted to them for the groundwork they have provided although I have not always been able to accept their conclusions. No doubt my own preliminary sketch of shopkeepers' activities and values will in turn be challenged.

I have four fundamental themes in this book. First, I am convinced that shopkeepers hold a key to our understanding of much nineteenth-century political history. We have never looked for them and consequently we have never found them but they are there nevertheless and their importance is not diminished by our oversight. They can be found in many reform movements in the period and were increasingly active in local politics, concentrating their energies in the area where power lay in what was essentially a decentralised state.

Secondly, I have endeavoured to show that the projected stereotype of the committed individualist, irretrievably wedded to a dogmatic, classical, *laissez-faire* economic, political and personal philosophy is a false one. Underneath this veneer lay a more pragmatic, hard-headed businessman less hidebound by ideology than would first appear. Indeed, this champion of free competition generally operated in an imperfect market, protected by natural barriers to entry, geographical situation, collusion — informal at first but progressively written into contracts with manufacturers — and finally government controls. This theme I have demonstrated by concentrating on retailers' reactions to competition around the turn of the century from co-ops, multiples, department stores and an increasingly important army of small shopkeepers, all of them examples of 'unfair' competition in the established traders' eyes.

Arguably these newcomers made insignificant inroads into the retail market before 1914 and did no more than cream off the increasing purchasing power of the working classes, providing complementary not competitive services to that of the established, substantial shopkeeper but the latter's concern was both understandable and real. Outright opposition, however, the stance adopted towards the 'monopolistic' multiples and 'socialistic' co-operatives, was not feasible in the campaign against the small shopkeeper. He posed as the exemplary individualist, a scaled-down version of the successful tradesman whose prosperity he apparently threatened. The dilemma this created for the allegedly committed champions of *laissez-faire* and free trade was indeed a difficult one. Some practised what they preached and adapted their businesses to meet the competition but there were significant efforts to come to restrictive, collective agreements and to enlist the aid of the government in their fight for 'fair' trade and a 'fair' profit, their equivalent of the trade unions' demand for a 'fair day's wage'. These moves were adroitly disguised behind an ideological veneer which suggested that they were fighting for the very thing they opposed – the operation of a free market. This does not mean that they were consciously ideologically dishonest; many no doubt failed to appreciate the contradictions in their position or were able to explain them away to their own satisfaction. Historians, however, should not be so gullible as to believe that such men were motivated by the individualist, entrepreneurial ideals that they professed or that their public utterances were an accurate reflection of their real intents. We must remember that we are dealing not with theoreticians or philosophers but with pragmatic businessmen whose chief, but not only concern, was to obtain adequate returns on investments of time and money. The shopkeepers' convincing sales talk, his justification for his activities, must be taken with a large pinch of salt.

Thirdly, I have emphasised the diversity of the retail trade and the dangers of relying solely on broad catch-all terms like 'shopkeeper' when referring to those engaged in it. This did not preclude the possibility of common ground between them based usually on the commitment to low taxation and to achieving the most favourable conditions for the maximisation of profit, but there were as many divisions within this middle class as there were in the working class. There were – and still are – gulfs between the skilled craftsman/retailer and the straightforward unskilled shopkeeper; between the large concern and the small; city, town, suburban and rural dealers; proprietors and managers; high-class, mixed and working-class traders. I have specifically highlighted two. In the first two sections I have stressed the important gap, that was only slowly filled, between the shopkeeper of some capital and the small self-employed shopkeeper: the not so *petite bourgeoisie* possessing considerable capital and enjoying a high return on it, and the *petite, petite bourgeoisie* barely above the level of their working-class customers. The former I have referred to in a variety of ways since there seems to be no accepted nomenclature for them: private/substantial/established/large traders/tradesmen/retailers/shopkeepers or, in the early sections, shopocrats. The latter are simply small or corner shopkeepers. Unqualified references to shop-keepers usually include them both and are intended to distinguish them from the new race of managers spawned by the co-ops, multiples and department stores.

Finally, I have portrayed the varying personal experiences of specialist retailers around the turn of the century, depicting the uneven nature of retail development, the different threats each faced and the daily routine of shop life. The case studies have been chosen to represent a cross-section of the private sector. Grocers were substantial tradesmen widely tipped as the most likely species to become extinct with the evolution of new types of shops. Butchers, operating in an expanding market, maintained traditional skills but also faced threats to their prosperity and independence. Small shopkeepers who relied on family labour are represented by the greengrocer. Saddlers were craftsmen decimated not so much by new competition or mechanisation but by the later collapse in the demand for their products. A department store in miniature, the village shop apparently enjoyed a local monopoly but was, in fact, open to competition from unexpected quarters. Finally, there are pawnbrokers, a law unto themselves, generally at loggerheads with the rest of the retail community but thriving in pre-1914 years. I have, except in the case of the village shop where documentary evidence survives, used edited oral interviews in their entirety presenting them as individual case studies to allow readers to draw their own conclusions from them although I have pinpointed some of their more significant features in the preface to each extract. The value of these interviews to the book lies not just in the detail they provide but in the ideas and questions they generate for further research. Why was skilled retailing able to survive so long after the arrival of the multiples, co-ops and branded proprietary goods? Why the excessive emphasis on service and deliveries as opposed to price competition? Why such long hours? What role did the family play in shops and what consequences did child employment have on upbringing, education and career prospects? How often did the working class actually pay the advertised price for the goods they bought? Clearly, relying as they do on childhood recollections, the interviews present only a counter-high view of shop life and they contain no references to the public world of the shopkeeper described elsewhere, but in the absence of other reliable sources on his private life they are still valuable. Without them we have nothing.

PART I

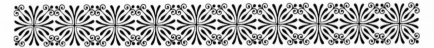

# Victorian retailing: a changing world

# CHAPTER 1

# Tradesmen and shopkeepers

## Was there a retailing revolution?

Asked of the period before 1850, this question has aroused considerable controversy. One school of thought has emphasised the importance of new features: the emergence of wholesalers, the speedy adoption of price competition, advertising, window displays and cash selling, and the spread and significance of shops themselves especially those catering for the working classes. Its critics have insisted that the pace of change was leisurely and that retailing remained essentially 'pre-industrial'. Both sides would agree, however, that the foundations of an increasingly complex distributive sector had already been laid before the end of the eighteenth century. The existence of a wide range of middlemen has been shown by Westerfield's authoritative study and by a number of social and political historians examining food rioters' hostility towards dealers and engrossers during times of high prices.[1] Joan Thirsk and T. S. Willan have emphasised a developing consumer goods market while a local study of three Cheshire towns has revealed a large number of fixed retail outlets in high-class trades like grocery, drapery and jewellery.[2] The resourceful Younger Pitt earned the reproach of such shopkeepers by taxing them in 1784.[3] The presence of late eighteenth-century shops adds weight to the view that it was 'an increasingly broadly based and in the long run continuous and expanding home market', especially among the 'middling ranks' of society which laid the foundations for Britain's accelerating economic growth but the range and extent of subsequent change in retailing itself remains less clear.[4]

The high priest of the revolutionary school of thought is still J. H. Clapham who flew in the face of conventional wisdom on the subject as long ago as 1926.[5] More recently articles by Janet Blackman on grocery developments and David Alexander's pioneering study of *Retailing in England in the Industrial Revolution* have been widely interpreted as providing support for Clapham's case.[6] All suggest that there were marked declines in the skilled nature of retailing, in the amount of capital required and in competition based on product differentiation and that these resulted in a substantial increase in shop numbers and fierce price competition by the middle decades of the century. James Jefferys, however, has argued that 'modifications in structure and method had been relatively slight' by 1850 and that the distributive system still 'bore the marks of a pre-industrial economy', a line subsequently followed by Dorothy Davis.[7]

This disagreement is really about emphasis rather than about the actual features of the retail sector, the common ground between the two sides being far greater than is generally appreciated. Jefferys's picture is a far from static one. He points to a decline in local self-sufficiency and the role of fairs; a 'corresponding increase in the role of marketing and *particularly of fixed-shop retailing* (my italics); and the increasing importance of wholesalers and other intermediaries in groceries, textiles and coal trades where 'the chain from the producer at home or overseas to the consumer was a long one ... Many different types of intermediaries – agents, jobbers, factors, wholesalers, dead meat salesmen, bummarees in the fish markets, cheesemongers, butter factors and so on – played a part and a profitable part inside and outside the central wholesale markets in equating supply and demand'. Furthermore he concedes that 'some of the shops in the larger towns', especially drapers in London, were adopting large window displays although such devices were still frowned on by many established tradesmen. He insists, however, that the basic structure of retailing had not been 'fundamentally changed'; small-scale units still predominated, knowledge, skill and capital were at a premium, open markets remained important, higgling over price persisted, competition was restrained. The relative stability of this early Victorian picture he contrasts with the changes in organisation and operation later in the century, especially the emergence of large scale co-operatives, multiples and department stores.[8]

Clapham agreed with much of this. Bazaars, or primitive department stores, and multiples had only 'just made their appearance' by 1850. Co-ops had yet to spread outside a small corner of textile Lancashire. Fairs survived and were important for livestock and foodstuffs with direct producer-consumer links being maintained away from the large towns. The itinerant chapman or pedlar, perhaps working more for a principal than on his own account, remained an important figure. Bakers were only just beginning to appear in the North. Craft retailing was still prevalent everywhere. The 'trades in home-grown foodstuffs had changed less than those in clothing materials'.[9] Clearly the old and the new co-existed and any transformation of retailing was only partially complete by 1850.

3

But was there progress 'everywhere, fast' or was it a 'comparatively leisurely rate of change'?

### The slow decline of self-sufficiency

It is clear from stray housebooks, diaries and autobiographies which have survived from the period and from later oral recollections that many families from a broad spectrum of society continued to rely on their own resources for some basic necessities remaining semi-independent of the market economy. This consequently restricted the growth of the retail sector.[10]

Country dwellers obviously enjoyed most opportunities. 'Home farms' or large kitchen gardens were able to supply the landed class with perishable foodstuffs: fruit and vegetables, eggs, poultry, meat and milk. Although the material would be bought, many clothes, especially the lady's and the children's, were made at home by the lady's maid or nanny. Hairdressing, shoe repairing and other services were performed by domestics. Wealthy people's shopping usually involved the bulk purchasing of non-perishable provisions or the acquiring of expensive luxury items: furniture, *objets d'art*, jewellery, fashionable attire.[11] Labourers also relied on home produce. Wood provided a free fuel source in some areas. Cottagers with a little capital invested in a pig, came to arrangements with local millers, farmers or butchers to help in its rearing or pooled resources to form 'pig clubs' based on shared ownership of the animal by several families. Chicken, goats, rabbits (domestic or poached), garden birds, even hedgehogs all supplemented – indeed in some cases seem to have formed the major part of – the labourer's diet. The practice of domestic baking of bread only died out slowly in the north of England. Further south gleaning for flour persisted into the twentieth century. Although the degree of rural self-sufficiency undoubtedly declined it has remained an integral part of daily life.[12]

Town dwellers had to rely more on the market but there was still scope well into the present century for 'making do', relieving them of recourse to retail outlets. Early Victorian, densely packed housing developments were devoid of gardens but this does not seem to have deterred first and second generation settlers from keeping livestock to supplement their meat supplies. It was possible in many towns to walk into the surrounding countryside to take advantage of 'free' sources of food and fuel. As in the country, women's and children's clothes were rarely bought unless at second-hand sales, being either home-made, modified hand-me-downs or recut gifts from wealthier relations or those in service. Discarded clothing was cut up for rag mat floor coverings. Bed linen comprised unbleached calico sheets made up at home.[13] This self-help was good

4

household management born of necessity rather than indoctrination from above. The alternative was not reliance on shop supplies but simply going without. Until urban workers enjoyed incomes sufficient to enable them to dispense with such makeshifts, a trend only obviously evident from the 1870s, then significant mass retailing development was impossible; most substantial shops relied on the 'better class' of custom for the bulk of their trade.

## Markets and itinerants

A low, unstable level of working-class demand meant that few retailers, even food dealers, were willing to invest heavily in fixed shop premises. Fairs, markets and hawkers consequently retained their importance for most perishable produce and small household utensils.[14] Of the three, fairs proved the least adaptable to an urban environment and declined rapidly, their wider roles as job centres, livestock markets and social occasions being usurped by a variety of alternative channels and institutions, their very existence being questioned by moral reformers. Markets, however, were flexible enough to make the transition from the rural or small country town environment to the larger urban centres and remained important throughout the nineteenth century. They were familiar to, and consequently more easily accepted than shops by the migrant populations of the early towns. Their expenses were minimal; if stalls were not provided by the market owner they could be assembled with little effort or outlay by the traders themselves. Open stalls allowed ample space for display of goods and reduced advertising costs to a minimum. Prices could be arrived at by bargaining. Hours could be tailored to suit local needs. If trade fell away in one town or was insufficient to provide the stallholder with a living, then he could increase his turnover by travelling to nearby centres whose markets were held on different days. It was by such manoeuvring that Michael Marks, as late as 1883, accumulated sufficient capital to expand into his chain of Penny Bazaars, the forerunners of the highly successful Marks and Spencer variety stores.[15]

Market trading, therefore, flourished. Direct producer/consumer contact remained in the smaller towns, middlemen were more common in cities, but everywhere 'the local town market was the family's main source of food'.[16] Perishables formed the bulk of the trade, with butchers occupying the majority of market stalls in Liverpool and Manchester in the 1830s and 1840s. Greengrocers were also increasingly common in these decades and there were also fishmongers, poulterers and butter and cheese dealers and a sprinkling of dealers in household goods for which there was no established demand. All these dealers only gradually expanded into fixed shop premises when the volume of business warranted such a move, usually from the third quarter of the century.[17]

Accommodating the army of stallholders caused considerable headaches for local authorities. Customary market sites proved inadequate and stalls spread along adjoining thoroughfares causing inconvenience and congestion. Various solutions were adopted ranging from attempted repression and strict control through far-sighted efforts to cater for the obvious requirements of traders and customers, offsetting the cost of improvements by charging stallholders substantial rents or by increasing local rates. In Liverpool the corporation erected the handsome, covered St John's Market as early as 1822, installing gas and water supplies. There were similar later improvements in other places like Manchester, Leeds, Birkenhead and Birmingham.[18] By 1891 just over half of the country's markets were wholly or partially under cover and, significantly, those with the best facilities were in the newer industrial and commercial towns of the North and Midlands where one might have expected their role to have declined more rapidly in the face of developments in shop retailing.[19] In London, too, customary weekly street markets flourished unchecked by local authorities.[20] Markets, therefore, remained an important, colourful and, as we shall see, contentious component of the retail scene throughout the century.

Itinerant traders were also important, enjoying low operating costs and calling on customers over wide areas. Official sources seriously understate the numbers involved which probably continued to rise steadily until the third quarter of the century. They ranged from the Cheap Jack, the 'Prince of Hawkers', usually a man of some substance possessing a winter base in town and a horse and cart, selling hardware and crockery, down to the virtual beggar who carried a few pins or some thread to avoid prosecution for begging and to provide introductions to prospective benefactors.[21] They sold almost anything that could be easily transported on their back or in a cart: furniture, cooking utensils, crockery, perishable and dry foodstuffs especially tea, cloth, haberdashery, hosiery. As the century drew to a close those in towns were increasingly confined to marginal sectors offering cooked foods, muffins, hot chestnuts, cooked meats and baked potatoes ('Warm your hands and fill your belly for a ha'penny'). The less reputable provided services: umbrella menders ('mush fakers'), mat repairers ('tiger hunters'), scissor grinders, cane chair repairers, glaziers.[22] Like marketing, therefore, itinerants were ideally suited to areas of the economy where demand was low or unstable and they continued to fulfil a useful role well into the nineteenth century.

## Islands of change: London and the drapery trade

The survival, indeed the expansion of essentially pre-industrial itinerant and market trading suggests that shop trading was restricted to certain products and social classes. However, viewing the period before 1850 as a period of rapid and significant change might still be justified if it can be shown that such shops as existed were expanding their operations, exhibiting signs of becoming purely retail outlets as opposed to workshops where production or processing was also carried out or adopting such novel competitive devices as price displays, window dressing or advertising.

There is little to support the view that such changes were indeed widespread; virtually all the evidence on them relates to the less respectable sector of the London drapery trade.[23] That such practices existed here several generations before they emerged elsewhere should not surprise us; the metropolis's enormous population, its wealth and, consequently, its very large demand for all products, far outstripped any other city's. All this encouraged the sub-division of labour, the early and strong emergence of middlemen and aggressive marketing policies. The capital's access to a wide range of food and consumer goods was also unparalleled; road, coastal shipping and later rail networks all converging on it. As the country's major entrepôt, London possessed sophisticated facilities for dealing in bulk while its commercial institutions were capable of providing necessary funds for enterprising tradesmen on a scale unknown elsewhere. That the cloth trade in particular should be in the van of progress here is also not unexpected. Clothes were important status symbols and fashion-conscious, emulative Londoners over a broad social spectrum supported the country's largest market for them. Entry into this potentially lucrative business was also relatively easy, the exceptionally early development of factory production in textiles and the clear separation between manufacturer and retailer that subsequently emerged reducing the amount of skill or knowledge required well below that needed in other trades. Recruits required just enough working capital to purchase stock or convince suppliers to advance credit or goods, not a difficult task in an industry prone to crises of overproduction. As evidence presented to the Select Committee on Manufactures in 1833 shows, therefore, what Alexander has called the 'unmistaken characteristics of modern retailing' – advertising, price wars, cash as opposed to credit trading, the employment of unskilled labour, eye-catching window displays and large 'monster shops' – were to be found in London although still largely confined to lower-class establishments in Whitechapel and Shoreditch.[24] Just as the factories of Lancashire and Yorkshire attracted widespread attention in the period because they were novelties, atypical of the

7

majority of industry, so, too, did 'Contemporaries who commented on the radical changes in the retail trade refer mainly to the drapery trade'.[25]

## A leisurely rate of change

Evidence of such dramatic developments elsewhere, whether in manufacturing or retailing, is less forthcoming. Recent reassessments of Britain's early industrialisation have stressed the slow emergence of factory production and the limited application of steam power and machinery in sectors of the economy not related to textiles or heavy industry.[26] In 1850 'Britain was not yet an 'industry state . . . Many trades and industries were more familiar with handicraft method and outworking than with power-driven machines and factories'.[27] The description of Britain as the *workshop* of the world was an apt one. Only in the last quarter of the century was there a transformation in the production, processing and retailing of most consumer goods and foodstuffs.

The implications of this for retail development are considerable, strongly implying that the producer/retailer survived in many trades or, as a minimum, that shopkeepers relied on specialist, hand-made products from craft outworkers which could be distinguished by quality as well as price. Pressure to change traditional shop practices was not great. It was evident, concludes Alexander, only in London and 'perhaps a hundred cities and towns at the most' before 1850. Resistance from shopkeepers meant that even here pressure was not immediately translated into 'impersonally competitive norms' which were scarcely heard of over 'much of the countryside'.[28] It is clear that 'shopcraft skills' and specialist knowledge of products retained considerable importance and that these, combined with substantial capital requirements, continued to restrict entry into many trades and ensured the survival of, at best, competition based on product and service differentiation, and at worst, monopoly or collusion. Significantly the number of specialist tradesmen listed in commercial trade directories did not increase appreciably during this period.

Although his range of stock broadened considerably the grocer was still primarily a 'purveyor of luxuries to the rich' dealing in imported products which, since they were still liable to tariffs, were consequently expensive: tea, coffee, sugar, spices, dried fruits, 'Italian goods'. As his title suggests, he was a dealer in bulk, in grosses, and the term was not applied to small general shopkeepers. Wholesalers in the large cities and ports, increasingly responsible for supplying the provincial grocers, were gradually taking over some of the initial cleaning, sorting, grading and packing but the majority of the processing including the crucial blending, labelling and weighing remained the grocer's responsibility.

Other food traders also retained considerable processing roles. Except in London where a few brought carcases from wholesalers, butchers slaughtered and dressed their own meat. Bakers and confectioners transformed a variety of ingredients into bread, pastries and sweetstuffs, relying on the quality of their merchandise, not just its price, to secure sales.

Unmechanised craft production in the hands of either the retailer himself or wage-earning outworkers employed by him continued to characterise, among others, the clothing (as opposed to the cloth) trade, furniture and hardware distribution. Although the manufacture of metal goods and cutlery was increasingly concentrated in Sheffield and the Midlands, the ironmonger retained an important, skilled service role. Tailors, milliners and dressmakers dominated the clothing business mainly offering personalised garments but with a restricted number of 'off-the-peg' items. The footwear trade relied heavily upon independent boot and shoe makers, admittedly resorting, in some cases, to assembling ready-made components. Cabinet makers, upholsterers, saddlers, jewellers, clock and watchmakers – all these and others managed to retain substantial elements of a skilled artisan tradition, their retail premises doubling as workshops. Despite the much publicised plight of the handloom weavers, most skilled men of moderate means benefited considerably from, and were largely responsible for, the expansion of trade and prosperity which characterised early industrial Britain.[29]

### Tradesmen and shopkeepers

The uneven nature of development, combined with the different markets which traders operated in, discourages any easy generalisations about the level of competition in retailing or the prosperity of those engaged in it. Skill did not necessarily bring affluence and security to those dealing primarily in a working-class market. As we shall see this was certainly true for the small, general shopkeeper but it also applied to some specialists: bakers, tailors, cloggers, boot and shoe makers. Where demand was more stable and less price-elastic, saddlers, clock makers, upholsterers, dealers in most household products, most grocers and some butchers undoubtedly did well, but breaking into the better-class market successfully required capital as well as skill. Extensive premises were needed for workshops, the storage and safekeeping of materials or for living quarters especially if living-in apprentices were employed. The purchase or renting of such places in overcrowded town centres, the cost of equipping them, purchasing stock and materials, paying rates, all necessitated a hefty initial capital outlay of several hundred, possibly several thousand pounds. Theoretically this could be accumulated by apprentices or journeymen from their wages but much of it seems to have been inherited or obtained from kin, friends or money lenders. Few of the tradesmen documented by Alexander started in business with less than £100. Most of them had much more.[30] Unless a lowly individual was blessed with wealthy friends or patrons as was the case with the famous radical draper Francis Place in the 1790s, there was little hope of breaking into this select circle. Trade depressions or poor management might result in individual tradesmen coming to grief but competition from hordes of newcomers would not seem to have been a major problem.

Most specialist shopkeepers relied heavily, but not exclusively, on the more affluent groups of society for their business. In all but a handful of cities this middle-class demand was rarely able to support more than few such tradesmen. This, combined with the effective barriers to entry which existed ensured that their numbers rose only slowly in the first half of the century.[31] Such a position was not conducive to free competition; in fact, it was fertile ground for local collusion, for the persistence of a 'live and let live attitude' noted by Alexander with limited competition based on product differentiation and service rather than price.[32] Grocers emphasised the uniqueness of their teas. Butchers prided themselves on the quality of their meats. Jewellers, cabinet makers, saddlers, and a variety of craftsmen appealed on the attractiveness and durability of their distinctive products. Competition that was potentially damaging to profit margins does not appear to have been rife in the retail trade; the low percentage mark-ups tradesmen claimed in public can hardly be regarded as reliable indicators of their true position. Complaints of 'unfair competition' were largely confined to the cities, especially London. Over much of the country tradesmen remained, despite the gradual adaptation to changing demands, a wealthy minority of far from insignificant or marginal members of the community, able to enjoy the fruits of an expanding market without facing 'excessive' competition which they were later to encounter. In Chester, in 1815, it was not uncommon for any tradesman to leave wealth of between £100 and £500 at death while many, especially mercers, drapers, grocers, corn and cheese dealers, druggists and ironmongers were all capable of leaving in excess of £1,000.[33] The position was much the same half a century later, John Vincent's analysis of wills proving that tradesmen were capable of amassing just as much as, if not more than, the majority of manufacturers and farmers.[34] The world of such 'shopocrats' was a comfortable and secure one, offering real prospects for social and material advancement. In 1812, for example, one Macclesfield linen draper, John Swanwick, promoted himself to the ranks of the landed proprietors, buying country estate at Brereton in south Cheshire.[35]

Tradesmen such as these increasingly objected to being referred to simply as 'shopkeepers'; they preferred a specialist description. As Raymond Williams has pointed out, words change their meaning, develop different nuances over time. 'Industry', for example, only really came to be applied to the process of manufacturing in the early nineteenth century.[36] Similarly the word 'shopkeeper' in trade circles and the pages of commercial directories was increasingly reserved as a term which was applied to small, general retailers who lacked capital or standing. In the eighteenth century it did not have such definite connotations. It had been applied freely to all in retailing whether they produced the goods they sold or not, implying nothing about the size of the business. As men of some substance all shopkeepers had been accorded a certain, clearly defined, amount of respect and authority in society. The mercer and wine merchant Abraham Dent of Kirkby Stephen acted as churchwarden, poor law overseer and surveyor of highways. He also voted in county elections.[37] The intemperate but regularly repentant Georgian diarist and shopkeeper Thomas Turner mixed freely with farmers, clergy and local people of middling ranks.[38] In Chester the wealthy traders, urban gentry and merchants dominated town life.[39] Shopkeepers, however, were still some way down the social ladder. Although their prosperity was tempting, Jane Austen's young heroines intuitively rejected them as eligible marriage partners. They were simply not 'gentlemen' with the correct breeding and background.[40] Adam Smith's reference to England as a 'nation of shopkeepers' reflects both their importance and the mild contempt which the upper class felt for them.[41] Clearly, however, these 'shopkeepers' were very different from the small neighbourhood dealers of the following century.

The word, of course, has continued to be used to refer to all in trade but from the early nineteenth century it has been increasingly prefaced by descriptive terms – 'lesser', 'small', 'large' – as a recognition of the fact that smaller, less reputable retailers existed as well. Richard Cobden made it clear that he specifically sought support from the 'respectable and wealthy shopkeeper', the 'shopocracy', in his fight for Manchester's incorporation as a borough in 1838.[42] In the same year the socialist Bronterre O'Brien stressed the gulf that existed between the ordinary, impoverished shopkeeper whom he regarded as 'politically honest' and 'to whom we are not hostile', and the other 'shopkeeper . . . the animal we call a "Shopocrat" which means a shopkeeper or capitalist'.[43] Respectable drapers like Edward Flowers objected to the 'offensive appelation of shopman' being applied to his trade.[44]

The increasingly specialist meaning of the term, however, is most clearly manifested in the pages of commercial trade directories from the 1820s. Large tradesmen, especially provision dealers and grocers, gradually ceased to be

11

double-entered under a specialist heading and as a shopkeeper as the latter description came to be applied to small general retailers only.[45] The substantial dealer's obvious desire to be included in these *trade* directories as a recognised, specialist tradesman on a par with the merchants and manufacturers listed there clearly caused considerable headaches for the compilers, who had to resort to an elaborate system of cross-referencing to avoid labelling them simply as 'shopkeepers'. Parsons, responsible for the directory section of Baines's *History, Directory and Gazetteer of the County Palatine of Lancaster* (1824), notes before his listing of Liverpool tradesmen, 'It will be found from the Notes inserted immediately under the Titles that reference is frequently made from the head under inspection to others of a somewhat similar nature'. Readers looking for 'Grocers and Tea Dealers' were referred to 'Tea Dealers' as well. Under 'Corn and Flour Dealers' they were advised to look up 'Flour Dealers' where it was made clear that the previous category had also included bakers but that further similar traders could be located under 'Provision Merchants' where some were asterisked as 'Ham and Bacon Dealers', others as 'Flour Dealers'. No tradesmen were listed twice although clearly many fell across several categories and none was labelled as a shopkeeper. This term was reserved for the few small retailers who appeared in the alphabetical list of residents none of whom reappears in the trades section or in the catalogue of principal streets and their occupants.[46]

### The small shopkeeper

There was a massive expansion in the number of unclassified, general 'shopkeepers' and 'dealers in groceries and sundries' listed in trade directories from the early 1820s so much so that in most towns by mid-century they easily comprised the largest single category and usually outnumbered all other traders put together. The apparent rapid growth of such small shops stocking a wide range of products – provisions, household sundries, cloth and clothing, groceries – has been documented in detail by Alexander.[47] Their existence suggests that the working classes did not rely entirely on markets and itinerants for their supplies and seems to undermine several views expressed so far in this study. It implies that a period of training and hefty capital sums were not necessary preconditions for entry into retailing and that competition, and consequently threats to position of the larger tradesmen, should have increased.

Let us deal first with the speed of the expansion of small-scale shopkeeping. While supporting Alexander's view that 'In the general shopkeeper category the evidence for growth of retail shops is very strong'[48] Roger Scola's study of Manchester's experience sheds doubt on his emphasis on the rapidity of that

12

growth only from the 1820s. He shows, by examining local non-commercial directories, that small shops existed in considerable numbers by the last decade of the eighteenth century. Indeed, on the basis of this he concludes that Manchester was better served for food shops than it was in the 1840s, despite Alexander's evidence to the contrary; 'If we use a crude measure of population per outlet, the ratios of one outlet to approximately 150 people in 1800 and 1811 are not again achieved until after 1850.'[49] Clearly the early commercial directories of the 1820s covering large geographical areas and concerned primarily with substantial tradesmen simply omitted small shops in their listings. Pigot's *London and Provincial New Commercial Directory for 1822–3*, used by Alexander in his calculation, lists no 'shopkeepers' for the Manchester area yet Scola's study reveals that over four-hundred small food shops alone existed at least ten years earlier.

The unreliability and extreme selectivity of Pigot's 1822 work is further highlighted by comparing his figures for Bolton with those provided by Baines's county directory just two years later. It is difficult to believe that they are describing the same town.[50] Pigot grossly understates the extent of retail development at this time. Only from the early 1830s when he published regional directories did he begin to include 'shopkeepers' among his categories. The figures therefore give a totally false impression of the speed of expansion of such shops. The picture is not one of a massive, unexplained acceleration in numbers from the 1820s which might well have seriously worried larger tradesmen, but of a relatively slow growth over a much longer period barely in line with population growth but with occasional surges during periods of boom.

Far from presenting a threat to the substantial tradesman, except in terms of the public image of retailing, such shops provided a complementary service supplying the irregular, unstable but expanding working-class market. Through them the larger retailer could also participate indirectly in this trade. The specialist wholesaler was a rare bird outside the cities and did not deal anyway in the small quantities required by the corner shopkeeper. Consequently the latter's stock was bought from the larger flour dealers, grocers, provision dealers, dealers and drapers.[51] The small man took all the risks if he paid in cash; if he did not he was perpetually in debt to his larger competitor. Not until working-class demand expanded sufficiently in the last quarter of the century did specialist wholesalers emerge dealing directly with the small shop and many town centre traders lost this valuable sideline.

The larger tradesmen also possessed a direct foothold in the working-class market. A detailed analysis of bankrupted traders' debts has revealed that a substantial proportion of grocers, drapers and even ironmongers, unwisely in

13

**Tradesmen and shopkeepers listed in Bolton**

| *Pigot's London and Provincial New Commercial Directory for 1822–3* (from Alexander, pp. 247–8) | *Baines's History, Directory and Gazetteer of the County Palatine of Lancaster, 1824* | |
|---|---|---|
| 6 Booksellers | 7 | (including printers and librarians) |
| 7 Chemists | 11 | |
| 8 Boot and shoe makers | 55 | (+28 cloggers) |
| 11 Shoe warehouses | 5 | |
| 4 Clothes dealers | 7 | |
| — Milliners/Dress makers | 55 | |
| — Tailors | 49 | |
| 13 Linen drapers | | |
| 9 Linen & woollen drapers | 32 | (unspecified drapers, haberdashers, hosiers) |
| 6 Woollen drapers | | |
| 3 Glass and china dealers | 3 | |
| — Earthenware dealers | 6 | |
| — Confectioners | 7 | |
| 43 Bakers and flour dealers | 71 | (see also shopkeepers) |
| 5 Corn and flour dealers | 6 | |
| — Butchers | 35 | (not all market traders) |
| — Fishmongers | 3 | |
| — Fruiterers/Greengrocers | 2 | |
| 18 Grocers/Tea dealers | 30 | |
| 5 Tea dealers | 13 | (see also grocers, tobacconists) |
| — Poulterers | — | |
| — Shopkeepers | 102 | |
| — Cheesemongers | 5 | |
| 1 Cutlers | 2 | |
| — Hardware dealers | — | |
| 5 Ironmongers | 5 | |
| — Musical instrument dealer | 3 | |
| 4 Curriers, Leather sellers | 5 | |
| 5 Saddlers | 7 | |
| 5 Tobacconists | 7 | |
| — Perfumier and Hairdressers | 16 | |
| — Drysalter | 2 | |
| 7 Pawnbrokers | 14 | |
| 5 Tallow chandlers | 3 | |
| — Toy and Jewellery dealers | 4 | |
| — Watch and clock makers | 9 | |
| — Cabinet makers and upholsterers | 10 | |

their cases, loaned small but not inconsiderable sums to customers, between forty-six and thirty-five per cent of the total money owing comprising sums less than £1. These men, it should be emphasised, were men of considerable capital, operating from premises usually valued at over £200, holding £200 to £400 of stock, paying annual rents and rates in excess of £50.[52] The small under-capitalised shopkeeper was unable to match the credit facilities which the tradesman, backed by his capital and more secure middle-class custom, could offer. If he did so he was likely to fall victim to recurrent depressions in trade unless his suppliers backed him. Nor could he rely yet on picking up trade by siting himself well away from the larger town shopkeepers. The close, tightly packed nature of urban development meant that the vast majority of shops were potentially 'local', situated within a few hundred yards of the central market area in most towns in the 1820s, within easy reach of the mass of people who were not yet dispersed through layers of suburban residential zones.[53] The private trader, despite his high-class trade, also possessed a distinct price advantage. Buying in bulk and resorting to price and quality discrimination, that is, making his profits on sales to less price conscious customers and selling to the working classes at cost, or even below cost price to clear less marketable products, he could persistently under-cut his small rival if he so wished.

Unable to compete on price, convenience, credit or products, lacking independent access to supplies, the lot of the early Victorian small shopkeeper was not an enviable one. Only working-class antipathy to shopping in the larger establishments or possibly the small man's longer opening hours must have allowed him to survive in many cases. Theoretically a ladder to independence and local status for aspiring working men, in practice running a small shop was the resort of unskilled migrants, widows and wives of labourers trying to eke out a living and possibly, as some Oldham evidence suggests, a cushion for blacklisted factory operatives. In the hard decades up to 1850 at least such shopkeeping offered little chance of a 'rags-to-riches' fairy story.

This picture of impoverished, frustrated corner shopkeepers is supported by impressions from a number of other sources. Successive directories reveal a large turnover in personnel. The stray surviving ledger like one for a Sheffield shop of the 1840s run by a labourer's wife reveals a virtually non-existent trade with between two and five customers per day despite stocking a range of goods.[54] The slow painful emergence of the retailing co-ops also emphasised the near impossibility of an individual small shopkeeper raising sufficient capital without outside assistance to compete effectively against established traders and circumvent the need to rely on them. Even skilled, reasonably well paid operatives in the Lancashire textile towns had to *combine* to raise sufficient capital to set up in business, even in a small way dealing initially in a few items, operating from unprepossessing premises. Their combined savings fell far short of the capital invested in premises and stock by the wealthy shopocrats. The original Rochdale Pioneers of 1844 raised £28 and later co-ops managed little, if any, more: Eccles's co-op was started with £31, Bury's with £6 while Accrington's 'pioneers' fell well short of their target of £200.[55]

## Summary

We are now in a position to sketch in the major features of the early Victorian retail scene. Many goods, especially perishable foodstuffs, were still sold by itinerants and market traders. An expanding number of small shopkeepers eked out a bare living servicing the working-class demand for groceries and household goods but they did not present a major threat to the prosperity of the established tradesmen. Skilled or craft retailers involved in processing or producing the goods they sold, and substantial traders carrying expensive or bulky stock dominated many sectors of fixed premise retailing. Such men usually required some specialist knowledge and capital to set up in business. They relied heavily on more affluent sector of society but were able to participate in the less stable working-class market either by direct selling or by supplying small shops with goods for re-sale. Barriers to entry into trade at this level, therefore, remained and this restricted the expansion in numbers of such outlets which in turn enabled those in them to benefit from rising demand. Outside London, and the drapery trade there in particular, cut-throat competition and novel trading methods were rare. Competition revolved mainly around quality and service and, in the small and medium sized towns where numbers were small, there was opportunity for informal collusion. The apparent possibility of progression through the ranks from apprentice to journeyman and ultimately to tradesman, more apparent than real, also enabled them to pass as self-made men, deserving of social respect, even emulation, their success resting, so they liked to believe, on their own qualities of perseverance, character and skill rather than on inherited advantages or good fortune. Like manufacturers and qualified professionals, and for similar reasons, tradesmen consequently felt that they were in a position to demand more social and political recognition.

### Notes to Chapter 1

[1]R. B. Westerfield, *Middlemen in English Business, particularly between 1660 and 1760*. New York, 1915; E. P. Thompson, 'The moral economy of the English crowd in the eighteenth century', *Past and Present*, L, 1971; J. Stevenson, *Popular Disturbances in England, 1700–1870*, 1979, chapter 5.

[2]J. Thirsk, *Economic Policy and Projects: the development of a consumer society in early modern England*, Oxford, 1978; T. S. Willan, *An Eighteenth Century Shopkeeper: Abraham Dent of Kirkby Stephen*, Manchester, 1970; T. S. Willan, *The Inland Trade*, Manchester, 1976; S. I. Mitchell, 'Retailing in eighteenth and early nineteenth century Cheshire', *Transactions of the Historic Society of Lancashire and Cheshire*, CXXX, 1981, pp. 37–60.

[3]S. I. Mitchell, 'Pitt's Shop Tax in the history of retailing', *Local Historian*, XIV, pp. 348–51.

[4]D. E. C. Eversley, 'The home market and economic growth, 1750–1780', in E. L. Jones and G. E. Mingay (eds.), *Land, Labour and Population in the Industrial Revolution*, 1967, pp.

206–59; H. J. Perkin, *The Origins of Modern English Society, 1780–1880*, 1969, pp. 91–6.

[5]J. H. Clapham, *An Economic History of Modern Britain*, Cambridge, 1926, I, chapter 6 esp. pp. 225–6.

[6]D. Alexander, *Retailing in England in the Industrial Revolution*, 1970; J. Blackman, 'The food supply of an industrial town', *Business History*, V, 1963; 'The development of the retail grocery trade in the nineteenth century', *Business History*, IX, 1967, pp. 110–17; 'The corner shop: the development of the grocery and general provisions trade', in D. J. Oddy and D. Miller (eds.), *The Making of the Modern English Diet*, 1976, pp. 148–60.

[7]J. B. Jefferys, *Retail Trading in Britain, 1850–1950*, Cambridge, 1954, pp. 1–5; D. Davis, *A History of Shopping*, 1966, chapter XII.

[8]Jefferys, *Retail Trading*, pp. 3–5.

[9]Clapham, *Economic History*, I, pp. 220–8, 334.

[10]This clearly has implications for 'the standard of living debate' which has largely ignored such unquantifiable aspects. A. J. Taylor (ed.), *The Standard of Living in the Industrial Revolution*, 1975, contains most of the major contributions.

[11]See chapter 4 and interviews with Lord Harris of Belmont (born 1889) and Mrs J. Wray (born 1899), Oral History Collection, University of Kent.

[12]M. J. Winstanley, 'Voices from the past: Kent at the close of an era', in G. E. Mingay, (ed.), *The Victorian Countryside*, 1981, II, pp. 627–32; W. Cobbett, *Cottage Economy*, 1822.

[13]E. Roberts, 'Working-class standards of living in Barrow and Lancaster, 1890–1930', *Economic History Review*, 2nd series, XXX, 1977, pp. 316–17; Kent Oral History Collection, *passim*.

[14]Alexander, *Retailing*, pp. 29–60.

[15]G. Rees, *A History of Marks and Spencer*, 1969, pp. 5–6.

[16]J. Blackman, 'Changing marketing methods and food consumption', in T. C. Barker, J. C. Mackenzie and J. Yudkin, (eds.), *Our Changing Fare*, 1966, p. 37.

[17]R. Scola, 'Food markets and shops in Manchester, 1770–1870', *Journal of Historical Geography*, I, 1975, pp. 153–68; Alexander, *Retailing*, pp. 42–4.

[18]Davis, *Shopping*, p. 253; Scola, 'Food markets', pp. 159–61; Alexander, *Retailing*, pp. 50–9; K. Grady, 'Profit, property, interest and public spirit: the provision of markets and commercial amenities in Leeds, 1822–9', *Thoresby Society*, LIV, 1973–7, pp. 165–95.

[19]Royal Commission on Market Rights and Tolls, P.P. 1890–1, XXXVII, p. 54.

[20]Select Committee of the House of Lords on the Sunday Closing (Shops) Bill, P.P. 1905, VIII, pp. 29ff.

[21]C. Hindley, *The Life of a Cheap Jack*, 1881; W. H. Davies, *Autobiography of a Supertramp*, 1908, chapter XXXI; M. K. Ashby, *Joseph Ashby of Tysoe, 1859–1919*, Cambridge, 1961, pp. 201–2; M. Penn, *Manchester Fourteen Miles*, Cambridge, 1947, pp. 173–5; Alexander, *Retailing*, pp. 61–86; see also chapter 13.

[22]H. Mayhew, *London Labour and the London Poor*, 1861–2, I and II; M. J. Winstanley, *Life in Kent at the Turn of the Century*, Folkestone, 1978, pp. 197–8.

[23]Clapham, *Economic History*, chapter 6; Alexander, *Retailing*, pp. 128–36, 161–4.

[24]Select Committee on Manufacturers, P.P. 1833, VI, pp. 91–4; Alexander, *Retailing*, p. 136.

[25]Alexander, *Retailing*, p. 164.

[26]R. Samuel, 'The workshop of the world: steam power and hand technology in mid-Victorian Britain', *History Workshop*, III, 1977, pp. 6–72; A. E. Musson, 'Industrial motive power in the United Kingdom, 1800–70', *Economic History Review*, 2nd series, XXIX, 1976, pp. 415–39; C. Wilson, 'Economy and society in late Victorian Britain', *Economic History Review*, 2nd series, XVIII, 1965, pp. 183–98; P. Mathias, *The First Industrial Nation*, 1969, chapter 9.

[27]Jefferys, *Retail Trading*, p. 1.

[28]Alexander, *Retailing*, p. 162, 236.

[29]Samuel, 'Workshop', pp. 24–7, 32–9; Alexander, *Retailing*, pp. 110–58; R. Perren, *The Meat Trade in Britain, 1840–1914*, 1978, pp. 39, 104–5.

[30]Alexander, *Retailing*, pp. 198–225, esp. 208–12.

[31]*Ibid.*, Appendix, II; Scola, 'Food markets', p. 156.

[32]Alexander, *Retailing*, pp. 159–63.

[33]Mitchell, 'Retailing in Cheshire', p. 48.

[34]J. Vincent, *Pollbooks: How Victorians Voted*, 1967, p. 38 shows that 25 per cent left in excess of £1,000.

[35]Mitchell, 'Retailing in Cheshire', p. 48.

[36]R. Williams, *Culture and Society*, 1961, p. 1.

[37]Willan, *Eighteenth Century Shopkeeper*, pp. 6, 145.

[38]T. Turner, *The Diary of a Georgian Shopkeeper*, 1925, rpt. Oxford, 1979.

[39]Mitchell, 'Retailing in Cheshire', p. 49.

[40]J. Austen, *Emma*, 1816, chapter 55.

[41]A. Smith, *The Wealth of Nations*, 1776, III, p. 41.

[42]Quoted in D. Fraser, *Urban Politics in Victorian England*, 1976, p. 121.

[43]*Operative*, 18 November 1838, quoted in R. Sykes, 'Some aspects of working-class consciousness in Oldham, 1830–42', *Historical Journal*, XXIII, 1979, pp. 167–79.

[44]E. Flowers, *Hours of Business*, 1843, p. 4.

[45]Scola, 'Food markets', pp. 157–8.

[46]E. Baines, *History, Directory and Gazatteer of the County Palatine of Lancaster*, 1824, rpt. Newton Abbot, 1968, I, pp. 353ff.

[47]Alexander, *Retailing*, pp. 97–9, appendices I and II.

[48]*Ibid.*, p. 98.

[49]Scola, 'Food markets', p. 159.

[50]Alexander, *Retailing*, pp. 247–8; Baines, *Lancashire*, I, pp. 545–56.

[51]Mitchell, 'Retailing in Cheshire', p. 56; Alexander, *Retailing*, pp. 175, 70, 76.

[52]Alexander, *Retailing*, pp. 178, 200–1, 208–9, 215–6.

[53]G. Shaw and M. T. Wild, 'Retail patterns in the Victorian city', *Transactions of the Institute of British Geographers*, IV, 1979, p. 288.

[54]Blackman, 'Retail grocery trade', pp. 115–16.

[55]A. Bonner, *British Co-operation*, Manchester, 1961, p. 50; T. Rigby, *Co-operation in Bury*, Bury, 1905, pp. 12, 14; J. Halsam, *History of Fifty Years' Progress* (Eccles Co-op), Manchester, 1907, p. 24.

# CHAPTER 2

# The politics of pragmatism

Two pieces of legislation in the 1830s gave the urban shopocracy unprecedented political influence. Nationally, as £10 householders, they were enfranchised by the Reform Act of 1832, an attempt by the aristocratic government to win the support of men with moderate property at a time of potential popular unrest. In many borough constituencies they emerged as the largest single recognisable group of voters in a strong position to influence the outcome of the parliamentary election. In 1835 the Municipal Reform Act – its household suffrage provision so hedged about with restrictive exclusions as to disenfranchise the vast majority of the working classes and exclude all but those with over £1,000 or paying £30 per year in rates from the council chamber – thrust tradesmen to the fore locally in the reformed corporate boroughs. In addition to these breakthroughs shopkeepers also wielded power as members and electors of other diverse local government institutions – vestries, Poor Law Guardians, Improvement and Police Commissions, Local Boards of Health – and were numbered among the supporters of many of the political, economic, religious and moral pressure groups which provided the key issues for national debate in Victorian England. Running with the tide of public opinion, helping to forge it, their overall influence was far from negligible. Their general philosophy, more than any other group's, mirrored that associated with the Victorian heyday.

## Radicals and Liberals

The survival of many pollbooks giving details of electors and how they cast their votes in parliamentary elections up to the introduction of the secret ballot in 1872 allows us to ascertain the political sympathies of the enfranchised shopkeepers. For much of this period the small neighbourhood shopkeeper's primitive premises failed to qualify him for the vote; the number of electors in the pollbooks more nearly matched that of specialist retailers in commercial directories than that of the entire retail sector. Even their gradual entry into the electorate, noticeable by the 1850s, did not substantially affect the trading community's political allegiance. The majority of all types of shopkeeper all over the country voted for Whig, Radical or later Liberal candidates.[1] Exceptions to this rule can, of course, be found. Butchers dealing in home-killed meat were often Tory, as too were publicans, both having links with the agricultural interest. In some of the old corporate boroughs where tradesmen had enjoyed considerable power, as freemen, under the unreformed political structure, there was also a residual Tory element. In Liverpool, with its significant Irish Catholic presence, nonconformist traders threw their lot in with the Church party on a slogan of 'No Popery' especially after the Liberals had secured themselves to the cross of disestablishment and the Irish cause after 1868. More than any other group in society, however, retailers represented the backbone of Victorian Liberal England as it was popularly conceived and their grass root pressure and support transformed the party within a decade and a half into the vehicle for the enhancement and enforcement of their ideals. Wealthier manufacturers, merchants and professional men were already drifting towards the Conservative camp by mid-century but tradesmen remained wedded to the individualism and *laissez-faire* policies of Gladstonian Liberalism.

As a significant minority of an electorate otherwise almost equally divided between the major parties their influence could be considerable, helping to ensure Liberal ascendancy in Parliament. The crusader for free trade Richard Cobden was returned as M.P. for Stockport in 1847 not by the textile interest in the town who are generally regarded as his most ardent supporters, but by the retailers' solid voting.[2] Ten years later in Rochdale with the larger capitalists and professionals again leaning towards the Tories, shopkeepers (excluding butchers) voted two to one for Miall, the Liberal candidate. Only 'craftsmen', a much smaller group in the electorate and also containing independent businessmen among their number, came close to matching this loyalty.[3]

Shopkeepers' mid-Victorian Liberalism, like the Liberal party itself, grew out of a long-standing commitment to reform expressed earlier as support for Whig or certain Radical candidates. This championing of parliamentary radicalism can be traced back to the London Corresponding Society of the mid-1790s and to Francis Place, the Radical London draper, who, with fellow tradesmen, succeeded in electing Francis Burdett for the Westminster constituency in 1808. After 1832, when successive Whig governments' records left much to be desired, especially in the field of finance, shopkeepers were the most disillusioned sector of the new electorate and continued to fight under a Radical flag. Fifty-five per cent of Newcastle's shopocracy were Radicals in 1835, a proportion matched in nearby Gateshead and Sunderland.[4] Tradesmen and artisans of moderate means, occupying premises valued at between £10 and £40 per annum, were overwhelmingly Radical in Bath in 1841.[5] The Radicals' unparalleled landslide victory in Oldham's election of 1832 owed much to their solid support as indeed did the popular Radical movement here and elsewhere throughout the 1830s.[6] As John Foster has shown, they and Oldham's small businessmen accounted for all the leaders of the 1830–2 campaign against 'old corruption' in government, spearheading Radical attacks on the Poor Law Amendment Act introduced by the Whigs in 1834, packing the Police Commission and rejecting attempts to increase the size and cost of the force. They provided the 'hysteria' associated with the Anti-Corn Law League, gave lukewarm support for factory reform and rejected increases in church rates. Although there was certainly industrial unrest in the town it is difficult to find the revolutionary working-class political activity Foster has claimed.[7] Although the increasingly violent tone of some of the demagogic Chartist leaders who rallied popular support for parliamentary reform in years of depression led men of property to keep a low profile and even disown the label 'Chartist', nevertheless, the early years of the movement relied heavily on these traditional Radicals in Oldham while they provided the core leadership in the North-East, Bath and to a lesser extent London and Birmingham.[8] In Leeds tradesmen stood as Chartists in local elections and were successful throughout the 1840s.[9] In parts of the country where mass support was lacking they could still be found as supporters of the movement.[10] Their Radicalism spilled over into every avenue of political activity. Shopkeepers and artisans returned Radical candidates in municipal elections after 1835; they packed vestries which were still responsible for many local services as well as church maintenance, all financed by compulsory church rates; they sat as Poor Law Guardians.

Shopkeepers' important and prominent political role is undeniable. Less obvious, at first glance, are the reasons behind their early anti-establishment. Radicalism and subsequent shift to Liberalism. Were they politically free agents? Did they desert their principles?

### Exclusive dealing

Various historians have argued that retailers were not free to cast their votes as they wished; they were vulnerable to pressure from other social groups, especially the working classes who operated a system of exclusive dealing. This involved

21

organised boycotts of shopkeepers whose political views clashed with their own, giving custom only to those who agreed to support their own causes. With open voting in elections the retailers in John Foster's picture of Oldham in the 1830s 'dare not vote otherwise' than for Radical, and therefore by implication, working-class-sponsored candidates.[11] Liberal shopkeepers of the 1850s and 1860s identified by John Vincent were also allegedly victims of non-electors' intimidation exercised through exclusive dealing. 'It is claimed, therefore, that the working class in the larger boroughs, far from being excluded from all voice in government by the franchise of 1832 actually benefited by being saved from bribery and coercion from above while remaining free to practice much the same things from below.'[12] The obvious assumption behind such views is that the working classes, not the shopkeepers, were the true Radicals or later Liberals.

This emphasis on customer coercion, overt or covert, is misplaced. Posters recommending exclusive dealing certainly existed, their purpose being to discourage trade with the minority of Tory tradesmen. The text of the Oldham bill of 1832 makes this clear:

> The enemies of reform are everywhere alarmed at the non-electors adopting exclusive dealing. The nation and your enemies know the immense power of the working classes ... Therefore, workingmen, if you wish well to yourselves, lay out your money with those electors of Oldham who support ... Fielden and Cobbett ... The electors' franchise is a trust to be used for your benefit; and not a right to be used against you.[13]

But who precisely supplied this literature to 'compliant shopkeepers'? It was certainly not the unenfranchised working classes. The Oldham Political Association, the society which had invited Cobbett and Fielden to stand and which was to remain at the head of the Radical movement in the town for the rest of the decade, organised the campaign. Its leaders comprised a surgeon, schoolmaster, employers and tradesmen, the last including one Alex Taylor, flour dealer, later its secretary, who left over £5,000 at his death.[14] This poster campaign was in fact organised by Radical tradesmen and their middle-class allies to attract custom by displaying their natural political loyalties. They were not victims of unspecified coercion and if they were it is unlikely that they would have consented to organise and lead a movement which they did not support. Exclusive dealing was neither necessary nor effective in explaining the Radical landslide; Cobbett and Fielden both had much to offer to the propertied electorate of the town.[15]

The same unease exists about Vincent's wider claims for the later period. Some of the luckless victims of coercion were inexplicably prominent among the original proprietors of Rochdale's Liberal newspaper, *The Rochdale Standard.* Evidence for the effectiveness of trade boycotts relies heavily on allegations from unsuccessful Tory shopkeepers searching for a scapegoat to blame for their business failure. Most damaging of all is the unproven assumption that the majority of the working-class non-electors were Liberal.[16] This was certainly not the case after 1867 when the newly enfranchised electorate in the textile towns where exclusive dealing has been identified manifested strong Tory sympathies. Indeed, it has recently been argued, with some conviction, that it was the working men who lacked an independent political stance, following their employers' leads.[17] The self-employed tradesman would seem to have voted Liberal despite, not because of the political views of many of his customers.

There are other general reservations and criticisms of such claims. Given the recognised national tendency of tradesmen to vote Liberal or Radical such exclusive dealing would have to have been extensively organised and consistently successful. There is no evidence to suggest that it was. Nor is there any reason to suppose that it could be effective. As we have seen, irregular working-class trade was a bonus, not the primary source of income for many specialist, enfranchised shopkeepers and they possessed sufficient capital to weather any short-term political boycott of their shops. Their customers, on the other hand, could not afford to alienate them. As Foster, to suit the artificiality of his argument, later admits, shopkeepers exerted 'very considerable social influence over credit', vital to hard-pressed workers especially in times of depression.[18] Indeed, exclusive dealing has ceased to be of importance for Foster a decade before it is recognised by Vincent.

Equally unsatisfactory is the view that many shopkeepers were influenced from above by their wealthier customers' political affiliations and possible pressure. They certainly voted for men of much higher social status than themselves in parliamentary elections but they did so not because they lacked their own ideas, were deferential or frightened of losing custom. Restrictive property qualifications for M.P.s, and shopkeepers' understandable preference for personal involvement in local politics where much power lay, meant that they both preferred and were obliged to rely on others to present their views in Parliament. These men received their support only if they championed the shopkeepers' causes. As pollbook surveys show, most tradesmen were not swayed by the political loyalties of the local social elite. Even in strong Tory county seats and boroughs like Cambridge they voted on balance for Liberal candidates.[19]

Convoluted explanations of political behaviour relying on influence or economic pressure are both unsatisfactory and unnecessary. Shopkeepers, even under the imperfect electoral system that existed before 1867, voted as relatively

23

free agents; they could not be bought or coerced, they could only be wooed.

### The economics of Radicalism

Why then were such men Radicals or Liberals? Proponents of Radical change were never short of fine rhetoric to justify and account for their campaigns in ideological or abstract terms. Universal suffrage represented the granting of inalienable rights, a recognition of the importance of the individual. Attacks on Parliament or the established church were attacks on corruption, waste, unjustified privilege, monopoly and abuse of power. The burden of taxation was unjust, oppressive, falling particularly hard upon the poor and the revenue raised was used for indefensible purposes – sinecures, pensions and the forces of oppression. Some historians have taken such justifications at face value, believing that Radicals were indeed inspired by principles, involved in disinterested campaigns for justice and freedom. This may have been true of a minority but the majority also had more pragmatic self-interest at heart. As the astute diarist Edwin Butterworth noted of the strident Oldham Radicals, 'Most of them profess extreme regard for certain principles, but whilst indulging in a vast amount of theory, they generally take care to frame their actions as the exigencies of the moment may seem to require.'[20]

Radicalism is an over-used, ill-defined blanket term used indiscriminately during the early nineteenth century and by later historians to refer to any demands for change, some of them diametrically opposed to each other in principle and practice. Most, but not all, revolved around the overhaul of the political system to achieve a desired transformation in the role of government and the nature of society; there any similarities end. Some Radicals looked to a co-operative or socialist society; others hoped for a return to a 'peasant' society based on individual proprietorship. Some demanded that the state take greater responsibility for the welfare of its citizens providing for their basic needs during times of distress; others claimed that the state already did too much and ought to be restricted in its activities. In short, they could agree only on their opposition to what already existed, what was wrong, not what ought to be done. A failure to appreciate this has dogged much discussion of their activities. It explains the rift in the Chartist movement. All Chartists agreed that the government was largely to blame for the ills of society but their solutions to the problem were irreconcilable, apart from agreeing on the need for political reform. The cause of the unskilled workers who flocked to meetings led by the demagogic Feargus O'Connor, Bronterre O'Brien or the Reverend J. R. Stephens in the years of terrible depression had little to do with strong 'Radical tradition' nurtured over the previous decades by erstwhile artisans and shopkeepers. These kept themselves aloof from such proponents of 'physical force' and the solutions they championed, retreating into 'moral force' campaigns, seeking allies among propertied classed also unhappy with Melbourne's government. They emerged after 1850 as staunch Liberals; in the twentieth century they would have been equally comfortable in the Conservative Party of Baldwin or Thatcher. Only by the most imaginative can such men be regarded as working-class leaders, the progenitors of a distinct Labour or working-class tradition.

Hatred of taxation, especially 'taxation without representation' to borrow a phrase from an earlier democratic revolution, is the key to the Radical tradition, to subsequent Liberal hegemony and to shopkeeper politics. Viewed as complex or dry or both, fiscal policy has not been accorded the attention it deserves although the passions which taxation arouses, and has always aroused among the public, ought to have alerted historians to its importance. 'Finance', declared Gladstone, 'is, as it were, the stomach of the country from which all the other organs take their role.'[21] Even the religious, moral and ideological issues frequently portrayed as dominating mid-Victorian politics were ultimately concerned with money. 'Retrenchment' and 'cheap government' are the main rallying cries of disaffected Radicals and the democratisation of parliamentary and local government was seen primarily as a means of ensuring this came about by shifting power to their hands. Significantly, by the 1850s, ardour for further franchise reforms, extending the vote to those who did not pay direct taxes, had cooled, as the various political institutions concerned showed themselves willing to implement the Radicals' policies and incorporate them into accepted, establishment dogma. One generation's Radicals, if successful, becomes the next's establishment.

It is difficult to find a Radical of the first half of the century who did not believe in wide ranging tax reform and reductions. William Lovett, cabinet maker, responsible for the Charter's conception, desired above all else 'cheap and wise government'. John Gast, London shipwright, was converted to Radical politics by the oppressive burden of taxation.[22] The otherwise enigmatic John Fielden appealed to the parsimonious Oldham electorate on the issue; 'The only remedy, therefore, for the sufferings of the people lies in a large reduction of taxation . . . I should vote for the abolition of tithes, of all sincures and pensions not merited by well known public services, the repeal of assessed taxes and tax on malt, hops and soap; and these having been repealed I would support the total abolition of the Corn Laws and I would also support an inquiry into the Debt, with a view to secure its equitable extinction.'[23] Roebuck's appeal to the Radicals of Bath in 1832 was on similar lines, calling for a 'taxpayer suffrage'.[24] Henry

Vincent, campaigning in Ipswich in 1842, called for the abolition of church rates, assessed taxes and the corn laws and for a reduction in expensive armed forces, the abolition of pensions and 'the equating of the National Expenditure to the limits of the People's means of contribution'.[25]

The Radicals' disillusionment with Whiggery in the 1830s is understandable. Although their pressure had ensured that Whig candidates also promised a reduction of taxation, their successive governments failed to achieve this. The New Poor Law of 1834 with its hated and expensive workhouses threatened to raise poor rates in some districts. The Municipal Reform Act included an unwelcome provision for obligatory borough police forces, major items of expenditure for the newly created corporations. Little was done to implement the requirement effectively for several decades. Stamp duty was reduced but not abolished. Little progress was made towards abolishing assessed taxes or church rates. Tariffs on overseas trade remained as did tithes on land. In contrast Peel's financial measures after 1842 and subsequent Liberal government budgets of the 1850s which went some way towards reducing indirect taxes and tariffs and shifting the burden of taxation on to the rich, may well explain the waning of cheap-government Radical pressure for further political reforms. Indeed, they were intended to do just that.

When Radicals achieved political power or representation locally they always attempted to put their theories of cheap government into practice. The famous Oldham group blocked the implementation of the potentially expensive New Poor Law in the town; they prevented an increase in the size of the police force by refusing through the Police Commission to sanction an increase in funds, even going so far as to disband the force entirely in 1831 'conceiving no doubt that economy and retrenchment are highly necessary in every branch of public expenditure'. They packed the vestry to keep church rates down especially after an expensive church rebuilding programme of the 1820s had pushed them up significantly. After the town had achieved borough status, the Shopkeepers' Association, formed in 1850, kept alive this spirit of retrenchment in the face of more progressive groups' attempts to raise rates for municipal improvement.[26] In London vestries in the 1830s tradesmen and small businessmen were active economisers, vehemently opposed to the levying of church rates.[27] In Leeds, as 'Chartist councillors' they formed the second largest group by 1852 and 'could always be counted on voting in favour of keeping expenditure down'.[28] In power after 1835, Bath's Radicals inaugurated a programme of unparalleled austerity which lasted for over ten years, doing nothing about flooding, living on the capital of the old corporation to finance water supply and sanitation provisions, reducing the police force considerably.[29] In Leicester the Radicals sold off long treasured symbols and regalia of civic authority for the sake of economy.[30]

Retailers and their allies, small businessmen and independent artisans, some of them undoubtedly shopkeepers themselves, comprised a significant proportion of all these potentially powerful elected bodies. They were members of all the major municipal corporations. Eighteen of the first sixty councillors elected in Manchester in 1838 were retailers,[31] all the Chartists on Leeds city council were small tradesmen and shopkeepers,[32] while in Birmingham they formed the backbone of the 'Economy Party' in the 1850s and 1860s, their 'short-sighted penny-pinching policies' being 'disastrous for the town'.[33] The obsession which early Improvement Commissioners and Local Boards of Health exhibited with superficial improvements to central thoroughfares, their provision of services like gas used primarily by businessmen and their unwillingness to invest more heavily in public health measures, can be largely attributed to the presence of such men. The increasing parsimony of the Poor Law regime, especially after 1844 when changes in voting qualifications for the Guardians gave the *petite bourgeiosie* even more leverage, and the practice of giving tickets to applicants for outdoor relief to exchange at local shops bear the hallmarks of tradesmen's drives for economy and self-interest.

This drive for retrenchment and low taxes on the part of the Radical or Liberal trading community was both understandable and widespread. Not only did they, as men of moderate means and aspirations, have to pay a larger percentage of their income in tax than wealthier landowners or fundholders, but all taxes reduced consumer spending power, diverting resources to less beneficial purposes – military expenditure, unproductive monopolies or the pockets of the very rich whose marginal propensity to spend was lower than other social groups. Tariffs on imports reduced access to cheap supplies, especially groceries, and raised prices in the shops, further restricting the market; not surprisingly retailers were ardent free traders.[34] Other apparently more innocuous and high-minded pressure groups, led in the main by men of principle, also attracted the pragmatic shopkeepers' support. The Liberation Society's campaign for the end of the Church of England's privileges, led by non-conformist ministers, promised the end of the hated, compulsory church rates. Early district co-ordinators in the movement included retailing and commercial men.[35] Sabbatarians fought shopkeepers' battles on Sunday trading for them, although they also appeared themselves before official enquiries on the subject.[36] Temperance and teetotal leaders could count on their blessing, even their active support at times, since they were fighting the tradesmen's main competitors for the spending power of the working classes – the publican.[37] Diverse moral reformers attacking other 'counter attractions' to the shop – pawnbrokers, street traders, fairs, markets,

27

brothels — were in effect fighting shopkeepers' battles for them. If the tradesman himself is absent from the front ranks of all these movements which raised issues which dominated Liberal politics it was simply because he had found such unexpectedly innocent allies. For him the issues were material not moral ones although the concerns God and Mammon appeared inseparable on many points.

### Political successes

Retailers' Radicalism, therefore, had much in common with the Gladstonian Liberal Party and their support for it contributed significantly to its success and determined the issues which dominated the political arena both locally and nationally. Despite the couching of issues in the language of morality, ideology or religion, the dominant concern of Victorian politicians and their supporters was money; the Liberal Party was, in the words of Lord Aberdeen in 1853, engaged in a 'financial mission'.[38] Significantly it was Gladstone himself, especially during his period as Chancellor of the Exchequer, who most clearly represented the rank and file's desire for cheap government, winning their loyal and devoted support. 'Economy', he wrote to his brother in 1859, 'is the first and great article of my financial creed.'[39] He consistently repeated the view that 'all excess in the public expenditure beyond the legitimate wants of the country is not only a pecuniary waste, but a great political, and above all, a great moral evil'.[40] Instances of his petty-minded thriftiness are legion. In the words of his sycophantic biographer, John Morley, 'Mr Gladstone made thousands eager to follow the public balance sheet and the whole nation became his audience . . . All this made a significant contribution to the national spirit of the time'.[41]

'Cheap government' was a major vote-winner for the Liberals among shopkeepers and small businessmen. Their support did not go unrewarded. After 1853 Gladstone progressively slashed tariffs and assessed indirect taxes, and everything was done to reduce national expenditure. The system of grants to state-aided schools was reformed in 1862 by Robert Lowe's 'Revised Code' to cut costs. The armed forces were reorganised and trimmed to dangerously low levels despite the Crimean experience and Palmerston's support for a strong foreign policy backed up by military might. Administrative reforms were undertaken to reduce bureaucratic waste and inefficiency. The detested church rate was abolished in 1868 and the Liberation Society's momentum was immediately lost. A sinking fund was established in 1866 to reduce the National Debt. Where central government did suggest strong measures involving additional expenditure as in the public health legislation of 1866 and 1872 and the Education Act of 1870, it gave responsibility for funding and execution to local authorities; in most other cases, however, it remained wary of obliging them to act, merely empowering them to do so if they wished. Economy and the interests of the taxpayer, therefore, dominated national government fiscal policy. There was even specific consideration of tradesmen's business needs. Pubs and beerhouses were brought under stricter control by legislation of 1869 and 1872 while the Married Women's Property Act of 1870 allowed shopkeepers to sue married female customers who had previously been able to claim that they had no assets. Attempts to outlaw Sunday trading in 1855 were only abandoned in the face of massive working-class opposition. At no stage, however, did Gladstone or his supporters achieve all they hoped for. The National Debt service charges and expenditure on armed forces remained obstinately higher than intended and income tax consequently continued to be levied, but this and the increased succession duties on inherited wealth introduced in 1853 fell more heavily on the wealthier members of society and those in receipt of unearned income; astute businessmen could evade it by careful accounting.

Locally, too, shopkeepers wielded considerable influence even though the initial, overwhelming Radical successes after 1835, when everything was sacrificed for the sake of economy, were soon moderated. Local government did expand its responsibilities and costs but those intent on using ratepayers' money to improve an area had to tread warily to get their schemes accepted, retain public support and divert potential ratepayer rebellions. This they did by keeping careful accounts to prove that no waste was incurred, by offsetting the costs of non-profit-making improvements with income from municipal undertakings in gas, transport or other services, and by presenting the case for expenditure as a means of raising the value of property or improving the trade of the town.[42] Indeed, it is remarkable how much of the Victorians' 'municipal socialism', like the Labour government's nationalisation schemes after 1945, provided the infra-structure for the efficient operation of private enterprise. Gas, communications and for many businesses, water, were all important assets yet, by their nature, prone to monopoly and abuse under private control. Tradesmen did not necessarily object to the levying of rates when such schemes were at issue or when central redevelopment held out prospects of increased custom. Nowhere was this more evident than in Birmingham. Not only were gas profits used to subsidise the modernisation of the city centre but this itself was largely intended to boost the commercial and trading community's prospects. Slum clearance did not lead to the provision of adequate council housing; it made way for shops and impressive boulevardes. 'I have always held that Birmingham ought to be the metropolis of the Midland Counties . . . To it should come all the principal retail trade of these counties . . . I am sure that every penny which can be spent in Birmingham . . .

will be spent not only to the advantage of the shopkeepers, but of the whole town.'[43] Chamberlain's words hint at the healthy suspicion which domestic ratepayers harboured against the scheme. Shopkeepers in seaside resorts were also keen to use revenue from the rates for their own ends to improve amenities for the visitors on whose trade they relied; this generally aroused opposition from respectable residents whose livelihoods were not so dependent upon the resort and who did not wish to be disturbed by hordes of holidaymakers.[44]

### Conclusions and provisos

Retailers were far from insignificant politically at both national and local levels. With clear ideas of what they required of government which they pursued throughout the nineteenth century and beyond, politicians (of both parties) found it expedient to seek their support. Although their most consistent demand was for relief from taxation and for cheap government we must not be misled into imagining that this was part of a comprehensive, all-embracing commitment to *weak* government and individualist policies. Central or municipal expenditure was acceptable if it was used to boost the value of property or held out prospects of improved trade. There was also nothing inherently 'liberal' or *laissez-faire* about calls for legal restrictions or abolition of certain practices which shopkeepers demmed undesirable: the ending of Sunday trading, limitations on street traders and fairs, controls on publicans and beer retailers. Such moral government could be both cheap and authoritarian and committed Radical individualists like J. A. Roebuck, a hero of the 1830s, were to be branded as traitors to the Liberal cause for their refusal to sanction such use of state power by the 1860s.[45] Like the predominantly Liberal trade unions, shopkeepers also had reservations about the uncontrolled operation of the market. Free trade overseas opening up access to new products and business was acceptable but free competition at home was not welcome or called for. Rather they sought to maintain radius agreements, apprenticeship regulations and local agreements on trading standards. Economic *laissez-faire* stood for an absence of unwanted state restrictions on the businessman's legitimate role of profit making. Contradictions and ambiguities in Victorian Liberalism's creed are more understandable if viewed in the context of the material interests of these loyal supporters. As Radicals or Liberals shopkeepers were pragmatists, not philosophers; they were never shackled by an ideology.

## Notes to Chapter 2

[1] T. Nossiter, *Influence, Opinion and Political Idioms in Reformed England, 1832–74*, Hassocks, 1975, p. 169; T. Nossiter, 'Shopkeeper radicalism in the nineteenth century', in T. Nossiter (ed.), *Imagination and Precision in the Social Sciences*, 1972, pp. 430–4; Vincent, *Pollbooks*, pp. 61–3.

[2] Vincent, *Pollbooks*, pp. 181–2.

[3] J. Vincent, *The Formation of the British Liberal Party, 1857–68*, 1966, Penguin ed. 1972, pp. 152–3.

[4] Nossiter, *Influence*, p. 148.

[5] R. S. Neale, *Bath, 1680–1850: a social history*, 1981, pp. 359–62.

[6] J. Foster, *Class Struggle and the Industrial Revolution*, 1974, p. 54.

[7] *Ibid.*, pp. 58–9, 133–6 (esp. p. 134)154–9, 167, 171–2. I hope to show that Foster's claims for working-class consciousness are not supported by his evidence; for the debate on this see Sykes, 'Working-class consciousness in Oldham'; D. Gadian, 'Class consciousness in Oldham and other North-West industrial towns, 1830–50', *Historical Journal*, XXI, 1978; D. Gadian, 'A Comparative study of popular movements in North-West industrial towns, 1830–50', University of Lancaster, Ph.D., 1976.

[8] Nossiter, *Influence*, pp. 149–55; Neale, *Bath*, pp. 370–9; Gadian, 'Comparative study', chapter VII.

[9] J. F. C. Harrison, 'Chartism in Leeds', in A. Briggs (ed.), *Chartist Studies*, 1959, pp. 91–2.

[10] Briggs, *Chartist Studies*, pp. 157–8.

[11] Foster, *Class Struggle*, pp. 133–4, 53–6.

[12] Vincent, *British Liberal Party*, p. 138.

[13] Foster, *Class Struggle*, p. 53.

[14] *Ibid.*, pp. 134–5, 69. 'Shopkeepers' may have been closely related to the working classes by marriage as Foster argues, but the politically active retailers tended to be wealthier tradesmen with no such connections.

[15] Gadian, 'Comparative study', pp. 112–13.

[16] Vincent, *British Liberal Party*, p. 136.

[17] P. Joyce, *Work, Society and Politics: the culture of the factory in late Victorian England*, Hassocks, 1980.

[18] Foster, *Class Struggle*, p. 238.

[19] Vincent, *Pollbooks*, pp. 87–92.

[20] Gadian, 'Comparative study', pp. 110–11.

[21] Quoted in H. C. G. Matthew, 'Disraeli, Gladstone and the politics of mid-Victorian budgets', *Historical Journal*, XXII, 1979, p. 642.

[22] I. Prothero, *Artisans and Politics in Early Nineteenth Century London*, Folkestone, 1979, p. 77.

[23] A. Marcroft, *Landmarks of Local Liberalism*, Oldham, 1913, pp. 78–9.

[24] Neale, *Bath*, p. 349.

[25] H. Fearn, 'Chartism in Suffolk', in Briggs, *Chartist Studies*, p. 167.

[26] Foster, *Class Struggle*, pp. 59–64, 154–9, 167–70.

[27] Prothero, *Artisans and Politics*, p. 273.

[28] Harrison, 'Chartism in Leeds', pp. 91–2; E. P. Hennock, *Fit and Proper Persons: ideal and reality in nineteenth century urban government*, 1973, pp. 33, 197.

[29] Neale, *Bath*, pp. 365–6.

[30] A. Temple Patterson, *Radical Leicester: a history of Leicester, 1780–1850*, Leicester, 1954, p. 216.

[31] Fraser, *Urban Politics*, p. 121.

[32] Harrison, 'Chartism in Leeds', p. 92; Hennock, *Fit and Proper Persons*, p. 197.

[33] Hennock, *Fit and Proper Persons*, pp. 31–3.

[34] Foster, *Class Struggle*, p. 172. See also Vincent on Cobden's victory at Stockport, 1847.

[35] D. N. Thompson, 'The Liberation Society', in P. Hollis (ed.), *Pressure from Without in Victorian England*, 1974, pp. 218, 229.

[36] J. Wigley, *The Rise and Fall of the Victorian Sunday*, Manchester, 1980, pp. 115–18, 123–4; for this and the reception such proposals met with from the working classes, see B. H. Harrison, 'The Sunday trading riots of 1855', *Historical Journal*, VIII, 1965, pp. 219–45, esp. p. 222.

[37] B. H. Harrison, *Drink and the Victorians*, 1971, pp. 97, 139; *Dictionary of British Temperance Biography, 1828–72*, Society for the Study of Labour History, 1973, *passim*.

[38] J. Morley, *The Life of William Ewart Gladstone*, 1905 ed., I, p. 460.

[39] *Ibid.*, p. 696.

[40] *Ibid.*, p. 687.

[41] *Ibid.*, p. 689.

[42] E. P. Hennock, 'Finance and politics in urban local government, 1835–1900', *Historical Journal*, V, 1963, pp. 218–23.

[43] Hennock, *Fit and Proper Persons*, p. 127.

[44] J. K. Walton, *The Blackpool landlady*, Manchester, 1978; P. S. Peers, 'The development of St Annes-on-Sea as a residential town and watering place, 1874–1914', University of Lancaster unpublished M.A. dissertation, 1979.

[45] A. F. Cruikshank, 'J. A. Roebuck, M.P.: a reappraisal of Liberalism in Sheffield, 1849–1879', *Northern History*, XVI, 1980.

# CHAPTER 3

# Newcomers and 'excessive burdens'

In the half century after 1850 the established private trader's position and methods were challenged in a number of trades by the emergence of new species of shops: multiples, co-operatives and department stores. These were made possible by a transformation of the conditions of supply and demand.

The gradual perfection of the steam ship which opened up foreign markets also tapped new sources of raw materials and, towards the end of the century, the manufactured goods of emerging industrial nations like the United States and Germany. This, combined with the reduction of trade tariffs and barriers, which were virtually non-existent from the 1860s, expanded the variety of goods available to shopkeepers. Rail and, later, tramways and motor vehicles further facilitated the movement of goods and potential customers to the shops. All this gave an impetus to the development of large-scale manufacturing of consumer goods relying on savings from economies of scale to offset the now much reduced transport costs. The position of the producer/retailer was thus threatened as the separation of production from distribution accelerated, the length of the chain of supply increased by the inclusion of middlemen in it; he apparently was destined to be no more than a straightforward salesman. Increased personal mobility undermined previous local monopolies or oligopolies.

Mass manufactured goods, which the producer, not the retailer, took responsibility and credit for, began to appear in increasing numbers. By the 1890s, grocers' journals, which had expanded from the 1860s to keep retailers informed of developments affecting their trade, bulged with advertisements for proprietary products. Factory-made footwear from Freeman, Hardy & Willis or Stead & Simpson was, by the 1870s, hitting the individual shoemaker hard. There were also branded products in clothing, alcoholic and non-alcoholic beverages, smokers' requisites, cigarettes, confectionery, hardware and scores of patent medicines. Competition based primarily on product differentiation was no longer so feasible when shops stocked such branded goods from common suppliers, products which were often cheaper to produce than the skilled retailer's own lines.

Equally significant were the rising purchasing power in the economy and the increasing price elasticity of demand. These developments were brought about in several ways. In the first place, there were more consumers, the population of England and Wales rising from 17.9 million in 1851 to 32.5 million by 1901. Secondly, it was an increasingly affluent population. Certain sections of the working classes, the skilled unionised élite, were gaining ground from the 1850s in the more stable economic climate of the 'Great Victorian Boom'. The majority, despite occasional trade slumps and cyclical unemployment, experienced a substantial rise in real income from the mid-1870s until the end of the century.[1] A broader based white-collar professional, managerial, clerical and commercial middle class also emerged over the same period.[2] Thirdly, the recipients of this income had a high propensity to consume, to spend rather than save, to reduce their dependence on self-sufficiency, improve the quality and variety of their diet and leisure, and amass consumer goods such as pianos ('household gods'), chiffoniers, 'best' clothes, curtains, floor coverings and domestic appliances. 'The social standing of every person within the community was constantly affected by material possessions', recalls Robert Roberts, 'and the struggle for the acquisition and display of objects seemed fiercer than any known in Britain now.'[3] Finally, since most of this increased demand was concentrated in urban areas, there were tremendous opportunities for the enterprising retailer who, if he could find ways of lowering his prices or making his business attractive in other ways, could justifiably hope for a dramatic rise in turnover and in profits as well. Progressive shopkeepers consequently experimented with retailing methods which flew in the face of those cherished by the early-Victorian tradesman and had more in common with the early London drapery trade. What, in a more restricted sense, Peter Mathias has labelled the 'Retailing Revolution' was set in motion.

### The department store

The affluent middle classes were wooed into city centres from the 1860s by new department stores. As their name suggests, these were based on the 'sell everything' principle, displaying a varied selection of manufactured goods under one roof. Many – like William Whiteley's Universal Provider, generally recognised as the first of its kind in Britain – originated as drapers and retained a strong bias towards clothing, especially women's and children's. Others, like

Harrod's, a fully-fledged store by 1868, diversified from grocery.[4] By the Edwardian period there were over two hundred stores in existence situated largely in cities but also to be found in provincial towns or seaside resorts like Southport where there were high concentrations of middle-class residents or visitors.[5] They could reach mammoth proportions. When Selfridge's opened in Oxford Street in 1909 with stock valued at over £100,000, it employed eighteen hundred staff. Whiteley's topped four thousand, Harrod's six thousand by 1914.[6] Obliged by the scarcity and expense of city centre land to expand upwards, they developed into multi-storey monstrosities serviced with lifts, elevators, cash dispensers, modern lighting and heating and decorated without by elaborate designed frontages.[7]

Although originally intended to appeal to all social groups, most stores soon realised that their clientèle were largely concerned with convenience, comfort and quality. The customers they catered for were consequently middle-class. Their policy was to convince the well-to-do, usually female customer that shopping was no longer an unavoidable chore but a pleasurable social activity which took place amidst sumptuous surroundings, in a warm, light environment, freed from the inconvenience of negotiating numerous accounts with individual proprietors, achieved without venturing out into changeable weather or brushing shoulders with lower classes in the streets. 'Our "Stores" ', remarked one writer, 'becomes at once a place for one to take one's friends and to meet one's friends; a fashionable resort, a lounge, an art gallery, a bazaar and a delightful promenade.'[8] Such facilities were not unappreciated. 'Many more people than formerly come to London, and to city centres to do their shopping; they prefer to make their purchases where they can concentrate their forces and diminish fatigue', wrote Lady Jeune in 1896. 'What an amount of trouble and expense is avoided where one can order one's mutton downstairs, buy one's carpet on the ground floor, and deck oneself out in the glory of Worth or La Ferrier on the top floor, to all of which one is borne on the wings of a lift, silent and swift.'[9]

Specialist, high-class, even foreign suppliers like Paris fashion houses probably lost trade to these grand stores but they also threatened private retailers, even those who had previously enjoyed undisturbed local monopolies in their provincial towns. Despite their emphasis on service and comfort, stores remained price-competitive with many such traders. They did not merely entice customers up to the city for the day; they circulated extensive illustrated catalogues and offered efficient delivery services over a wide area.[10] Grocers in Faversham, Kent, 'rather grouched' at Lord Harris having his provisions sent down by train from the Army and Navy Stores.[11] A vicar in Tunbridge Wells in 1888 entreated his congregation to patronise local traders since 'the weight of goods arriving at our local stations for private people exceeds that for the tradesmen'. Brighton's shopkeepers complained that the resort's long-stay visitors had their supplies sent down from London. Throughout the Home Counties and as far afield as Bristol and Leamington Spa there were rumbles of discontent.[12] In effect, although their share of the total retail market was only three per cent by 1914, stores siphoned off some of the private shopkeeper's most valued customers, those who placed the biggest orders and were regarded as the most creditworthy.[13] He had to fight to hold on to them.

### Catering for the masses: co-ops and multiples

While the department stores were making a bid for the retailer's wealthier customers, the multiples and co-operative stores were capturing his more reliable working-class trade and creaming off the increased spending power of the majority of the population.

Although markedly dissimilar in many respects, these two newcomers shared significant common characteristics. Both concentrated initially on a narrow range of standardised products for which there were steady, consistent levels of demand and accessible sources of supply. Both negotiated discounts with suppliers for bulk purchase or diversified vertically into production to reduce costs. The Co-operative Wholesale Society, founded in 1863, co-ordinated buying for the retail societies and produced its own branded products.[14] Multiples like Freeman, Hardy & Willis, the River Plate Meat Company and Singer's developed out of manufacturers' or suppliers' desires to secure outlets for their products which traditional retailers were unwilling to handle. Others, like Lipton's with their tea plantations, made the transition from retailing into production.[15] Both types of shop sold at fixed prices, took their shops to the customers through extensive branch networks and traded on a strict cash basis to keep overheads low, although the co-ops encountered some difficulty maintaining this policy during trade depressions. Neither consequently reached the very poor sections of society whose irregular earnings or habits obliged them to rely on credit; their customers remained the 'better sort' of working class right through the pre-war years.[16] Neither offered elaborate services or plush amenities in their early years as part of their drive to keep costs to a minimum to allow lower prices or increased dividend. Both were initially heavily concentrated in purveying foodstuffs, especially non-perishables, which they emphasised were pure and unadulterated, the co-ops in particular posing as early health food shops. By 1914 both had made inroads into other markets, especially clothing and household goods.

There, however, the similarities end. The co-ops' organisation and distribution of power were essentially decentralised; the multiples were the brainchilds of single entrepreneurs who often controlled their empires dictatorially from a central office or, later, through the board of a limited liability company. The multiples aimed for rock-bottom prices; the co-ops fixed theirs by reference to local price levels and paid quarterly dividends to members based on their purchases in the stores. Multiples were purely profit-making organisations; the co-op movement, especially through the Co-operative Union founded in 1873, clung precariously to various higher ideals ranging from the creation of a society organised entirely on co-operative lines, through schemes to raise moral or educational standards of members by providing reading rooms, libraries and classes, to the simple uncomplicated desire to improve material well-being by supplying wholesome, unadulterated produce at reasonable prices.[17] For a minority of members, therefore, co-operation was more a way of life than a retailing venture. The co-ops also had a more specific geographical coverage than the multiples. Until the very end of the century they were concentrated in northern textile or industrial towns where manufacturing provided regular employment and a more homogeneous working-class experience out of which such communal self-help was likely to arise. Elsewhere, railway colonies like the Great Eastern's at Stratford (Ilford), naval dockyard towns like Plymouth, Sheerness or Southampton, or the Royal Arsenal also enjoyed the benefits of strong co-ops but more cosmopolitan cities and thinly populated rural areas were so called 'co-operative deserts'. London was largely devoid of them in the 1900s, a situation one contemporary attributed to its lack of a 'social and industrial bond'.[18]

Of the two types of organisation the co-ops had the earlier origins, isolated examples being found in the eighteenth century. After a brief, unsuccessful romance with Owenite Socialism in the 1820s and 1830s, they emerged on a more practical, permanent basis after 1844.[19] The Rochdale Pioneers in their small store in T'owd Lane are generally credited with introducing the practice of giving cash dividends on purchases to members to encourage them to patronise their shop regularly, and although they may have been preceded in this policy by some earlier co-ops, none of them enjoyed their success or campaigned so actively to ensure its adoption by other societies.[20] From Rochdale, over the next two decades co-operative crusaders succeeded in spreading the movement throughout south Lancashire and into Yorkshire. Membership of co-op societies passed the one hundred thousand mark in 1863, and by 1881, when the first accurate figures become available, there were 971 societies, still clustered predominantly in the North, boasting over 547,000 members. By 1914 there were 1,385 societies, some of them now very large and the result of amalgamations, with over three million members. Annual turnover, already an impressive £15.4 million in 1881 had rocketed to £87.9 million. While still primarily concentrating on groceries and provisions, stores also increasingly sold meat, milk, greengrocery, men's and women's clothing, bread and household goods and offered undertaking, insurance and even banking services.[21] Where this was carried out under one roof co-op establishments began to resemble department stores for the working classes, even aping them in their architectural embellishments, the Lancaster society expending £22,000 in 1905 on imposing central premises with a Renaissance façade.[22]

Nothing seemed capable of halting this growth, the high level of dividend making membership very attractive. In the early 1900s nearly one third of all societies paid dividends between 3s and 4s in the pound, the equivalent of up to a 20 per cent price reduction. A few paid significantly more. In national terms the co-ops' share of the retail market has been estimated at only 7 to 9 per cent by 1910 but their impact on certain trades and in towns where they established strong footholds was monumental.[23] In St Helens for example, the co-op in 1900, after only sixteen years of operation, was estimated to have enrolled half the town's families as members.[24] In Bolton it claimed over seventy-five per cent of the town's trade by 1909.[25] Few spared a thought for private traders whose livelihoods seemed threatened by such progress. Those who did regarded his 'sacrifice' as an inevitable step on the road of economic progress. 'In a free industrial community', observed one co-operator, 'there is no such thing as a prescriptive right to a weak economic position.'[26]

The multiples with their price-cutting policy of 'small profits, quick returns' also presented a marked contrast, and threat, to the traditional retailer and his practices. Such chain shops were largely unknown in mid-century.[27] Even by 1875 there were only twenty-nine firms with an estimated 987 branches, most of them accounted for by W. H. Smith's and Menzies' railway news-stalls and the Singer Manufacturing Machine Company's tied outlets for sewing machines. Over the next forty years there was a remarkable expansion in the number of firms with ten or more shops to 433, claiming some 22,755 outlets between them.[28] Footwear manufacturers like Freeman, Hardy & Willis, George Oliver, and Stead & Simpson began to open chain stores from the 1870s. Eastman's, Dewhurst's, the River Plate Meat Company and – the largest of them all by 1914 with over a thousand branches – James Nelson & Sons purveyed frozen meat imports which began to arrive in the country after 1884. Tea, often pre-packed and branded, freed from crippling import duties, dairy products and cold meats were at the heart of the grocery giants' trade. From humble beginnings in Glasgow in 1871 Thomas Lipton's business grew to over 450 shops by 1900.

International Tea Company and Home & Colonial after early teething troubles developed on similar lines. Maypole Dairy Company relied heavily on the working classes' inexplicable yearning for unappetising margarine.[29] Jesse Boot expanded from pharmacy into fancy goods and stationery.[30] W. H. Smith's in the book trade, Hepworth's, Foster Brothers and the Cash Clothing Company in men's wear, Salmon & Gluckstein the tobacconists, Maynard's the confectioners are other examples of market leaders in their respective fields. There were also novel variety stores like Marks & Spencer offering everying at 1$d$ and from 1909 Woolworth's with its blanket prices of 3$d$ and 6$d$.[31] From the 1890s the pace of expansion quickened and although in many trades they had still made only minor inroads, Jefferys concludes that 'By 1914 there was practically no important consumer goods trade in which multiple shop retailers were totally absent'.[32]

### Prophets of doom

While late Victorian and Edwardian manufacturers felt their prosperity and security endangered by new competitors from overseas, independent retailers obviously faced threats from these new species of shops at home. Although, as in industry, the dangers were exaggerated, for these shops appeared at a time of growing consumer demand which cushioned the impact on independent tradesmen, the latter still experienced a deep psychological crisis, a growing anxiety and fear for their future.

They could take no comfort from the outpourings of informed pundits who presented a gloomy diagnosis of their situation and ultimate fate. No one held out much hope for their survival. Economists like Alfred Marshall viewed the process of concentration as the working out of indisputable economic laws.[33] Charles Booth and his meticulous assistants compiling their mammoth social survey of London in the later 1880s and 1890s concluded that the success of large-scale retailing was inevitable, at least in the food trades. 'It is now exceedingly difficult for the man with only one shop to make a living. In a few years' time the trade will probably be confined to large firms and a certain number of very small shops in poor districts where the master is on the same social level as his customers.'[34] To those with a more evolutionary outlook, the process represented a manifestation of Social Darwinism. Articulate tradesmen, calling for a rapid adaptation to the new environment or the implementation of 'conservation measures' designed to protect themselves, suggested that they would otherwise share the dodo's fate.[35] In 1902 the independent grocer received the ultimate accolade, a *Times* editorial, prophesying 'The Passing of the Grocer', crushed between 'the upper and nether millstone', a metaphor that was to remain popular throughout the decade.[36]

Fictional references in the works of socially conscious authors also accepted the inevitable extermination of the private retailer. Not surprisingly H. G. Wells was a prominent expositor of the 'crushing' theory. The helplessness of Mr Polly's little outfitters in Fishbourne High Street, his 'Roöotten, Beëëastly Silly Hole' which consistently failed to pay its way, was symbolic of the plight of all shopkeepers. The rapid changeover in proprietors in the rest of the street further served to emphasise the precariousness of the existence. In an openly didactic passage he quoted an unnamed, esteemed gentleman, a 'gifted, if unpleasant contemporary':

> The secular development of transit and communication has made the organisation of the distributing business upon large and economical lines inevitable: except in the chaotic confusions of newly opened countries, the day when a man might earn an independent living by unskilled or practically unskilled retailing has gone forever.[37]

Robert Tressell, in his *Ragged Trousered Philanthropists*, written between 1906 and 1909, saw the process as part of the monopolistic tendencies of capitalism, 'A Smallman', with his shop sign 'faded as to be almost indecipherable', being inexorably forced out of business by the 'Monopole Stores' over the road with its 'huge gilded letters' and bustling cash trade. Even Tressell appears touched by the fate of the man who, for whatever reasons, gave much-appreciated credit to workers in times of need.[38]

### The consolidation of small-scale retailing

Observers of the retail sector emphasised the large organisations and assumed that the small or medium-sized shops were declining. Tradesmen and skilled retailers, however, attached more significance to the less obvious threat they faced from expanding ranks of semi- and unskilled shopkeepers. Overpopulation, too many shops, worried them more than evolution or potential extinction. They detested these swarms of intruders, as they saw them, who colonised every working-class street and apparently cornered the local markets. They also brought shopkeeping itself into disrepute, denying wealthier brethren the social esteem and respect they felt their capital, skill and position ought to command.

Whether Jefferys was right to suggest that 'there was an increase in the number of shops and that this number certainly increased at a faster rate than the rate of increase in population' is open to dispute.[39] Shaw and Wild suggest that this was in fact not so and that mid-century ratios were only maintained.[40] What is indisputable is that there were a staggering 607,300 retail outlets listed in the

Census of Population in 1911. This represented one retail outlet for every fifty-nine members of the population in England and Wales at this date, a figure only matched by one of the mid-century towns – Nottingham – cited by Alexander. Surveys of food outlets by Medical Officers of Health also reveal the extent of this alleged surfeit of shops. In Blackpool, a town with a residential population of 47,348 in 1901 and 58,371 in 1911, a 1906 list read as follows: 180 bakeries, 169 supervised milk sellers, 129 ice cream dealers, 51 cowsheds (town dairies), 79 fish, chip and tripe shops, 40 fish dealers, 250 provision dealers, 67 fruit shops, 25 frozen meat and 105 butchers' shops, 182 sweetshops, 58 restaurants, 'etc'.[41] These were not just summer traders, catering for the holidaymakers. The textile town of Blackburn exhibited a similar ratio for fried fish and tripe dealers to its population over ten years earlier. Even omitting this trade, ice cream sellers and restaurants there was still approximately one shop for every fifty residents in the town and this calculation takes no account of retailers of non-perishable foodstuffs or consumer goods.

Numbers alone tell us very little about such shops' share of the retail market or the level of competition which existed. Multiples, co-ops and department stores enjoyed a greater market share than their numbers alone would suggest. Conversely, if there was a disproportionate increase in small establishments this does not itself prove that they increased their share of the market or that they took away larger traders' customers. It could merely have encouraged their immiseration. Certainly few small shopkeepers struck it rich. Most, like Robert Roberts's family in their corner shop in Salford, were hard put to maintain a decent standard of living just above that of their working-class customers.[42] Those that prospered still found it difficult to progress beyond a certain point, usually that at which they had to consider greatly increasing their overheads by taking on labour or moving away from their original area into larger premises. Although shopkeeping was viewed as a recipe for rising from lower social classes, it is difficult to find many who actually did so. On the contrary, their vulnerability is suggested by the high turnover of proprietors listed in commercial directories.

A close examination of a working-class quarter of Blackburn reveals much about the changing pattern of retail provision and residents' shopping habits.[43] The area, known as Audley, was little more than a mile to the south-east of the town centre, but uphill and the 'wrong' side of the railway and the Leeds and Liverpool Canal. A mixed residential and industrial area, it was encircled by brick works and, especially to the north along the canal, cotton mills. Its core was tightly packed with banks of terraced houses, schools, pubs and yet more mills. In 1885 its four main, predominantly residential perimeter and access roads were dotted with sixty-nine retailers and craft workshops. Thirty of these were simply listed as 'shopkeepers' while the list of specialist traders confirms the working-class nature of local trade: four cloggers, four boot and shoe makers, three tripe dressers, five butchers, five confectioners, seven unclassified general drapers, two fruiterers, two fishmongers and a scattering of other businesses. There were also several small co-op stores, branches of some of the ten societies in the town – so close, bemoaned one shopkeeper, that 'you can spit upon seven of them from any place in town'.[44] These sometimes shared their premises with craft/retailers. Significantly there were no grocers or bakers. Nine years later, apart from the co-ops, only seven of the original proprietors remained. By 1905 only four of them, or members of their immediate families survived: a draper, clogger, shopkeeper turned confectioner and shopkeeper turned grocer. Only six of the new arrivals in 1894 were still in business.

A change of proprietor usually involved a change of business use. Fifteen shops of 1885 had reverted to private housing by 1894, occupied in the main by members of the working classes, although two were now doctors' practices – an indication of better health as well as wealth in the area. Apart from the seven proprietors trading continuously over the first nine-year period, only three other premises retained their original specialisms and two of these were simply 'shopkeepers'. Clearly such retailers could not count on obtaining anything for 'goodwill' if they sold out. Several more succumbed to the co-ops which increased their number of branches, even extending premises by taking over neighbouring houses. Possibly some of these small proprietors made enough money to move up and out of the area – although, since they were already trading in the busier local streets and would lose custom by moving, it is difficult to visualise where they would have gone. A number must also have died. But the high turnover is still striking.

Family-run neighbourhood shops, possibly handed down through successive generations, are singularly absent from this picture. They were, in fact, a small minority of local shops, tucked away deep inside the inner residential area. Yet commentators and historians have clung to a stereotyped, polarised view of retailing with large concerns and a horde of tiny general shops, or misleadingly titled 'corner' shops. Rather than expanding in number, the unclassified 'shopkeepers', so numerous in the earlier decades of the century, virtually disappeared from these working-class streets, and even from the inner residential zone, after the 1880s. Thirty were listed in 1885, nineteen in 1894, one in 1905. In their place we find a much greater number of small specialists. In 1905 there were seven fried fish shops, unknown twenty years earlier. The area boasted eight newsagents and stationers, two of them doubling as Post Offices, where there had been only one in 1885. There were fourteen grocers as well as a similar number of drapers and an increased number of glass and china dealers, greengrocers, confectioners, baby linen dealers, hairdressers, furniture dealers and even the odd baker. Significantly the only trades to suffer a drop in numbers apart from the general shopkeepers were cloggers, boot and shoe makers and tripe dealers. This was a more prosperous, consumer-orientated society than it had been in the 1880s, capable of supporting a sophisticated local network of small, specialist working-class shops.

It is possible, of course, that some shopkeepers were simply re-classified by the compilers of the directories, perhaps at their own request, without substantially changing their trade. The emergence of the 'grocer' in this district certainly needs to be treated cautiously. Of the fourteen listed in these streets in 1905, ten occupied premises previously run by unclassified shopkeepers. A similar re-christening was apparent in the side streets; all three of the shopkeepers in the largely residential Pendle Street blossomed into grocers in the late 1890s. This change of name usually coincided with a change of proprietor but even the solitary individual who remained in business throughout the twenty-year period changed his title from shopkeeper to grocer. Possibly this change reflected an increase in business or increasing specialisation in these shops so that their proprietors now dealt in grosses or narrowed their stock holdings. From what oral recollections and working-class autobiographies tell us about such shops, however, the opposite was true; they sold in small quantities and dealt in everything they could possibly sell. Either way, the assumption of the 'master grocer' title by such men is significant and did nothing to enhance the status of the long established, more substantial grocer who had cherished his separate identity and title throughout the century.[45] His trade or status, or both, seemed to be seriously in jeopardy.

## The threat from below

Did such small specialist and general shops pose an economic threat to the substantial private tradesmen? Those which supplied products and services which were not, and never had been, provided by larger retailers did so only indirectly by creaming off the increased purchasing power of the working classes. This was true of fried fish shops, hairdressers, confectioners, greengrocers and frozen meat retailers. There is some evidence, however, to suggest that others dealing in provisions, clothing and household utensils did actually reduce the private tradesman's custom or income. This was because conditions operating earlier in the century to the latter's benefit, restricting small shopkeepers' activities or making them dependent upon the larger shopkeeper, no longer obtained.

In early and mid-Victorian towns most shops and houses had been within a few hundred yards of the central marketing area.[46] Only in large cities had there been any real potential for dispersed shopping centres or outlets to develop. The 'shopkeepers' of Blackburn in the 1820s, for example, were situated close to their larger rivals, occupying the same streets in many cases, all close to the town centre.[47] This was still true of slowly growing market or provincial towns like Tonbridge, Canterbury or Kendal well into the twentieth century. Elsewhere, however, with substantial housing development on the outskirts of towns, centrally situated tradesmen were becoming separated from their customers, and not just those from the prosperous suburban middle classes. Those from more humble backgrounds, although, as in Audley's case, barely a mile from the centre, were sufficiently deterred by the distance from walking into it to make their small, frequent purchases. For jewellers, furriers, high-class tailors, ladies' outfitters and booksellers who relied on occasional purchases of expensive goods, this spatial separation and specialisation was unimportant. For the substantial food retailer, especially the grocer, it was not. By providing delivery services he held on to his wealthier customers but these were scarcely viable propositions for the purely working-class trade. The small shopkeeper, moving out of the centre along with the working population, distanced from his rival, now had the inestimable advantage of convenience. As oral recollections confirm, local shopping centres or the neighbourhood corner shop displaced the town centre as the hub of working-class shopping activities.[48]

The expansion of specialist wholesaling firms also contributed to the larger trader's problems, especially in the food business. Although in some trades and rural districts where demand was small and scattered local shops continued to rely well into the present century on the dealers to be found in nearby town centres who doubled as wholesalers and retailers, the growing amount of trade handled by small shops encouraged new wholesalers to emerge to cater specifically for their needs. Some producers of popular proprietary articles even sent their own representatives or travellers into working-class areas in an attempt to gain footholds in the expanding market. Private tradesmen no longer shared, as they had done earlier in the century, even indirectly, in this important business.

Tradesmen took comfort from the high casualty rate among small shopkeepers but unfortunately there was no shortage of recruits to replenish their numbers. Shopkeeping continued to be viewed as a stop-gap, a cushion for the less fortunate members of society; widows, semi-invalids, retired people or those with family problems. But it also had much more positive attractions. It could supplement family income since the breadwinner's wife and children often took responsibility for shop management. It was also conceived of as a passport to independence, social status, even wealth, an escape from the confines of working-class life.[49] Furthermore, entry into retailing was becoming easier. Rising incomes, new savings institutions, even the co-op's dividend system, encouraged the accumulation of the limited capital which it required.[50] Selling pre-packed or ready-to-sell merchandise supplied by commercial travellers required little skill or even capital if such men advanced credit. Manufacturers and suppliers gladly showered the small shopkeeper with posters and placards to promote their wares.

Grocery was the most common trade for unskilled recruits since entry restrictions were minimal, demand was regular and shops had no need to be situated on main thoroughfares; but many other trades could be increasingly 'picked up'. Some, like fish friers, were new but others had previously been the domain of craft/retailers who suffered along with the larger tradesman. Boot and shoe makers were ousted not just by the multiples but also by unskilled general retailers like the Weller family (tobacconists in Margate) who operated a mail order business for shoes in the rear of their premises.[51] Traditional butchers in some areas were challenged by dead meat retailers and, increasingly in the 1900s, by chains of frozen meat salesmen. Confectioners no longer relied on their own home-made sweets but on proprietary brands. Small-scale, labour-intensive baking, requiring little capital or skill, attracted many recruits despite falling prices and demand. Greengrocery demanded little of its entrants.

Retailing, therefore, was opened up by a de-skilling process, a greater availability of capital and easier access to supplies. There were simply many more shops owned by individual proprietors. As Part III of this book illustrates, the pace of change and its consequences for specific retailers varied enormously, both between and within trades, but with the emergence of large-scale organisations and the mushrooming of small shops no one, it seemed at the time, had cause for complacency. It was a more uncertain, insecure world for the tradesman than it had been half a century earlier.

### Rates and other problems

Pressures on the retailer were compounded by several other developments of the late Victorian and Edwardian period.

The expansion of consumer spending which had ushered in retail change had also provided a cushion for the individual shopkeeper. Real wages, however, which had risen dramatically by over forty per cent between 1880 and 1896, stagnated and even fell marginally in some years in the period up to 1914. The total market consequently ceased to grow at the same rate; the pressures of

45

competition increased.

This ominous development was accompanied by a tightening up of the law on trading practices which threatened to make even the most honest, unsuspecting retailer open to prosecution for a variety of trivial offences. Even more dangerous after 1908 was the government's willingness to consider legislation to restrict employers' freedom to hire labour for as long as they wished, the Shops Bill of 1909 proposing that assistants be limited to a maximum of sixty hours per week. This promised to improve further the prospects of the small, family run shop at the expense of the employers of labour, raising costs at a time when they could least afford to meet them.

Important though this shop hours issue was, it was overshadowed by another – rates. Individually and collectively shopkeepers never tired of complaining about the burden of local taxation, its method of assessment and its alleged inequitable treatment of retail premises, especially those in central trading areas. 'The crushing load of the rates, then going up by leaps and bounds, owing to the socialistic tendency of the local authorities, made me feel peculiarly bitter,' wrote one singularly hard-pressed tradesman in his memoirs, 'especially when I saw the troops of able-bodied men slouching about the workhouse recreation grounds.'[52] Local trade associations demanded municipal retrenchment in language reminiscent of the Radicals of the 1830s or Gladstone himself at his peak and the National Chamber of Trade appeared before government enquiries into local taxation calling for drastic remedial action.[53]

Their concern was justified. The percentage of total government expenditure spent by local authorities rose from 45 per cent in 1890 to 55 per cent fifteen years later.[54] Despite central government grants to cover additional costs, especially those incurred by the Education Act of 1902, and the rise in rateable value brought about by urban expansion, there was a massive increase in the rates. These had been rising slowly throughout the nineteenth century but from the late 1890s right through to 1914 with only a temporary plateau around 1908 the pace noticeably quickened. Rates throughout London rose by between thirty and fifty per cent between 1891 and 1906.[55] In Exeter a rate of 2s 4d in the pound in 1887 had been converted to a staggering 6s 2d by 1914.[56] The rates levied per head of the population in Sheffield rose from £1 5s in 1893 to £1 19s seventeen years later.[57] Nationally revenue from rates doubled between 1895 and 1908.[58] The causes of this are various: a less favourable money market for raising cheap loans for development; a residential building boom of the late 1890s which required municipal investment in sewers, roads, lighting, etc.; the expansion of the education service and possibly a rise in poor relief as unemployment increased with the downturn in trade.

The increased expenditure on these services did not provide any obvious immediate return for those who were particularly hard hit by the rise in rates — retailers, centrally-situated workshop proprietors and small landlords. It also coincided with a particularly severe reversal in business fortunes and confidence as consumer spending stagnated, competition increased and, after the collapse of the building boom by 1905, surplus housing stock depressed residential rent levels. Less able to pass on the increase in costs in the form of higher prices or rents, these men bore the incidence of the tax increases, paying a higher percentage of their gross profits in rates than almost any other businessman.[59] It was this issue, more than any other, including the Shop Hours Question, which politicised shopkeepers and galvanised them into action. Depressed trade and rising costs threatened their prosperity and very existence even more than the emergence of new forms of competition. The fight for survival was on.

## Notes to Chapter 3

[1] Mathias, *First Industrial Nation*, pp. 375–82.

[2] G. Crossick, 'The emergence of the lower middle class in Britain: a discussion', in G. Crossick, (ed.), *The Lower Middle Class in Britain*, 1977, pp. 17–21.

[3] Robert Roberts, *The Classic Slum*, Manchester, 1971, Penguin ed., 1973, p. 32; C. Ehrlich, *Social Emulation and Industrial Progress – the Victorian piano*, Belfast, 1975, pp. 4–10; on diet, P. Mathias, *Retailing Revolution*, 1976, pp. 16–28; Oddy and Miller, *The Making of the Modern British Diet*; Barker et al., *Our Changing Fare*.

[4] R. S. Lambert, *The Universal Provider: a study of William Whiteley and the rise of the London department store*, 1938; Harrods Ltd., *A Study of British Achievement, 1849–1949*, 1949.

[5] J. W. Ferry, *A History of the Department Store*, New York, 1960, chapters 6 and 7; A. Briggs, *Friends of the People* (Lewis's), 1956; E. Midwinter, *Old Liverpool*, Newton Abbot, 1971, pp. 149–60; J. H. Porter, 'The development of the provincial department store, 1870–1939', *Business History*, XIII, 1971; H. Pasdermadjan, *The Department Store: its origins, evolution and economics*, 1954.

[6] Ferry, *Department Store*, pp. 221–31; W. Hamish Fraser, *The Coming of the Mass Market, 1850–1914*, 1981, p. 132.

[7] H. V. Lanchester, 'The design and architectural treatment of the shop', *Journal of the Royal Society of Arts*, LXI, 1913, pp. 577–89.

[8] W. H. Simmonds, *The Practical Grocer*, 1906, IV, p. 8.

[9] Quoted in A. Adburgham, *Shops and Shopping*, 1964, p. 236.

[10] A. Adburgham, *Victorian Shopping*, Newton Abbot, 1972, a facsimile of Harrods' mammoth catalogue for 1895.

[11] Interview with Lord Harris of Belmont.

[12] B. S. Yamey, 'The evolution of shopkeeping', *Lloyds Bank Review*, new series, XXXI, 1954, p. 56; F. G. Pennance and B. S. Yamey, 'Competition in the retail grocery trade, 1850–1939', *Economica*, new series, XXII, 1955, p. 308; *The Grocer*, 30 June 1900, p. 1766; 7 Dec. 1907, p. 1343; 12 March 1910, p. 724; 23 Dec. 1911, p. 1735.

[13] Jefferys, *Retail Trading*, pp. 18–21.

[14] P. Redfern, *The Story of the C.W.S.*, Manchester, 1913.

[15]Jefferys, *Retail Trading*, pp. 21–9; Mathias, *Retailing Revolution*, chapter 6.

[16]E. Aves, *Co-operative Industry*, 1907, chapters 5 and 6.

[17]Bonner, *British Co-operation*, pp. 115–36.

[18]*Ibid.*, pp. 98–9; Aves, *Co-operative Industry*, pp. 66–72.

[19]A. E. Musson, 'The ideology of early co-operation in Lancashire and Cheshire', *Transactions of the Lancashire and Cheshire Antiquarian Society*, LXVIII, 1958, pp. 117–38; S. Pollard, 'Nineteenth-century co-operation; from community building to shopkeeping', in A. Briggs and J. Saville (eds.), *Essays in Labour History*, 1960, pp. 74–112; T. Tholfsen, *Working-Class Radicalism in mid-Victorian England*, 1976, pp. 162–4, 253–4.

[20]G. J. Holyoake, *The History of the Rochdale Pioneers*, 1857.

[21]Jefferys, *Retail Trading*, pp. 16–18; Bonner, *British Co-operation*, pp. 97–101.

[22]*Lancaster Co-operative Congress Souvenir*, Manchester, 1916, p. 137.

[23]Jefferys, *Retail Trading*, p. 19.

[24]T. C. Barker and J. C. Harris, *A Merseyside Town in the Industrial Revolution*, Liverpool 1954, pp. 477–9.

[25]F. W. Peoples, *History of the Great and Little Bolton Co-operative Society*, Bolton, 1909, pp. 183, 409.

[26]Aves, *Co-operative Industry*, pp. 50–2, 66.

[27]Alexander, *Retailing*, pp. 103–7.

[28]Jefferys, *Retail Trading*, pp. 21–9 and later chapters.

[29]Mathias, *Retail Revolution*, chapters 6–9; J. A. Rees, *The Grocery Trade: its history and romance*, 1910, pp. 241–53.

[30]S. Chapman, *Jesse Boot of Boots the Chemist*, 1974, chapters 1–4.

[31]Rees, *Marks and Spencer*, chapters 1–4.

[32]Jefferys, *Retail Trading*, p. 27.

[33]A. Marshall, *Elements of Economics*, 1896, I, p. 187.

[34]C. Booth, *Life and Labour of the People of London*, 1896, VII, p. 220.

[35]A Private Trader, 'Shall we survive?', *Tradesman and Shopkeeper*, 20 Dec. 1902, p. 205.

[36]*The Times*, 18–20 August 1902.

[37]H. G. Wells, *The History of Mr Polly*, 1909, Collins ed. 1969, pp. 151–2.

[38]R. Tressell, *The Ragged Trousered Philanthropists*, Panther ed. 1976, p. 324.

[39]Jefferys, *Retail Trading*, p. 15.

[40]Shaw and Wild, 'Retail patterns', p. 280.

[41]*Blackpool Gazette*, 31 August 1906, 3 Sept. 1909. I am grateful to John Walton for these references.

[42]Roberts, *The Classic Slum, A Ragged Schooling*, Manchester, 1976.

[43]I have used Slater's *Directory of Lancashire*, 1885; Kelly's *Directory of Lancashire*, 1905; Barrett's *Directory of Blackburn and District*, 1894.

[44]*Tradesman and Shopkeeper*, 1902.

[45]Roberts, *Ragged Schooling*, p. 7.

[46]Shaw and Wild, 'Retail patterns', p. 288.

[47]Baines, *Lancashire*, I, pp. 514–22.

[48]Confirmed by Elizabeth's Roberts's detailed oral history surveys of Preston, Barrow and Lancaster for this period and Kent Oral History Collection.

[49]T. Vigne and A. Howkins, 'The small shopkeeper in industrial and market towns', in G. Crossick, *The Lower Middle Class*, p. 187.

[50]P. H. J. H. Gosden, *Self-help*, 1973, pp. 207–58.

[51]Interview with Mrs. D. Eady (born 1899).

[52]F. T. Bullen, *Confessions of a Tradesman*, 1908, p. 169.

[53]See Chapters 6 and 7.

[54]U. K. Hicks, *British Public Finances*, 1954, p. 108.
[55]A. Offer, *Property and Politics, 1870–1914*, Cambridge, 1981, p. 283.
[56]R. Newton, *Victorian Exeter, 1837–1914*, Leicester, 1968, pp. 210, 298.
[57]H. Keeble Hawson, *Sheffield: the growth of a city, 1893–1926*, Sheffield, 1968, p. 28.
[58]Offer, *Property and Politics*, p. 226.
[59]*Ibid.*, p. 288.

PART II

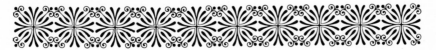

*The fight for survival*
*1890–1914*

# CHAPTER 4

# *'A multiplication of conveniences'*

Private shopkeepers have always regarded themselves as 'the most individual-minded people'.[1] Hard work, dedication, initiative – these are the keys to success for many recruits to the trade and are widely championed by successful businessmen to bolster their own self-image and public esteem. Men like Lipton and Boot appeared to be living proof of the Smilesian doctrine of self-help and 'removable inequalities'. Potted life histories of such men, emphasising their humble origins and the 'dramatic change effected by hard work' sustained this essentially mid-Victorian creed well into the twentieth century.[2] 'Grocers of Today', accorded special praise in *The Grocer*, invariably reiterated well-worn clichés. Christopher Elliot, president of the Newcastle Grocers' Association, attributed his pre-eminence in the trade to 'personal attention to business, to not being afraid of work, facing difficulties when they arose and overcoming them . . . supplying quality not quantity . . . pleasing customers in every respect' and, significantly, to 'refraining from cutting'.[3] Orphaned as a small boy and apprenticed to the trade, E. H. Booth, a successful Preston grocer, published 'a simple record of my life' specifically to encourage 'every poor boy who may be similarly situated to persevere' and follow his example. 'To all such I would say, strive to cultivate a feeling of self-respect and self-reliance; trust *only* in your own individual efforts for I never knew anyone get on who was constantly leaning on others.' His own rise he attributed solely to 'truthfulness, industry and integrity'.[4]

Not surprisingly, therefore, individual traders tried to improve their ability to compete in the harsher economic environment. The most obvious and immediate response would have been price reductions. Open price competition previously common only in the drapery trade was adopted increasingly during the second half of the century. By 1900 the practice of haggling over price lingered on only in market or itinerant trading or in those crafts which catered for individual, specialised tastes. 'Value for Money' as opposed to the distinctive quality of the goods offered was emphasised more. Staple goods or popular brands were offered as loss leaders; tea, soap and bread were sold near to, or in some cases below, cost price by grocers to attract custom. Independent shopkeepers were not slow to realise, however, that price wars were potentially disastrous. Multiples and co-ops were better placed to obtain cheaper, bulk supplies, benefit from economies of scale in distribution and consequently undercut them. Even if successful in retaining trade, price cutting could not fail to reduce profit margins and, unless the shopkeeper actually increased his share of the total market substantially, his gross profit as well. The most likely outcome, warned editors of trade journals and various trade associations' leaders, was failure and ruination.

Wherever possible shopkeepers continued to emphasise forms of differentiation other than price to woo customers who valued quality, service, personal attention, friendly chats, deliveries, distinctive products and credit. In those shops with more affluent clientèle, 'serving' a customer involved far more than the simple interchange of goods and money. It became almost a ritual. On entering such an establishment the customer, especially the female customer, would be welcomed by the proprietor or shopwalker and offered a chair. Domestic servants and children were also treated courteously since it was recognised that they could influence the shopping habits of their employers or parents. If customers went by their own private transport business was often done outside the shop. As one lady recalls, 'I remember driving into Ashford in the dog cart and we stopped outside the fishmonger. He would come out in his striped apron and ask what we wanted. We'd just sit there and he'd go and get it and put it in the cart and we'd go again. That happened at most shops. Practically nobody went into a shop at all. My mother never set foot in a butcher's shop in her life. I didn't until after the war, the last war.'[5]

Since middle-class customers increasingly resided some distance away from the shopping centre, the retailer generally felt obliged to deliver to those who did not possess their own transport. 'You never thought of carrying a heavy load. You expected things to be sent. There was no question of not having somebody to send. They always did have somebody to send.'[6] Errand boys, on foot with a basket or handcart or, from the 1890s, mounted on bicycles, performed this service locally, often working to a predetermined, advertised timetable and route. In 1900, T. D. Smith & Son, family grocers in Lancaster, promised 'Three Dispatches to all parts each day (except Wednesday), 10.30 a.m., 2.30 p.m., and 6.30 p.m.'. In common with other traders they also used vans, rail or carrier services for outlying towns and villages, regularly delivering up to twenty miles away, all goods 'Carriage Paid to our Customer's Door'.[7] Such was the service offered that it was possible to shop without ever leaving the comfort of home, at least for those whose expenditure merited special attention on the part of the retailer. Most provisions could be ordered at the door from representatives who called at pre-arranged times, or through mail order. Even tailors, drapers and hairdressers were willing to travel to attend to valued customers. Lord Harris recalls, 'My mother insisted on the barber coming out here several miles from Faversham and using our brushes, not his.'

The tradesman was also obliged to adopt a subservient, deferential stance, even indulging in sycophantic fawning to attract custom. Newcomers to a neighbourhood were inundated by personal calls offering assurances of unparalleled attention. Correspondence was always couched in the most respectful terms. 'Soliciting a continuance of your esteemed custom which it is always my aim to merit, I am, your obedient servant . . . etc . . .' 'We recognise that in a business of dimensions such as ours there can scarcely fail to be occasionally some slight cause for complaint. Should you ever have any such reason you will be doing us a real kindness by at once informing us of the same.'[8] Even the penny-pinching non-entity of George and Weedon Grossmith's *The Diary of a Nobody* (1892), Mr Charles Pooter, a clerk living in a north London suburb, was accorded such personal attention although his more forthright suppliers objected to his air of superiority and made it clear to him that he did not really deserve it. In larger establishments, where the responsibility for ordering was delegated to the cook, butler or even general servant, the unfortunate tradesman or his representative found himself forced to ingratiate with domestics at the 'tradesman's door', having to resort to flattery, even bribery, to retain custom. Those in the middle classes like W. MacQueen Pope who benefited from such servility and service looked back longingly in old age to those halcyon days:

> The idea of the tradesmen in those days was that they were there to please the customer. A complaint made them tremble, a threat to take your custom elsewhere brought them figuratively to their knees with abject prayer and apologies. They could not do enough. The housewife was their living, their prosperity, their very existence depended on her favour. They actually believed it was their job to please her, and they did their best to do so.
>
> A shopkeeper was selling his goods in competition with many others. He had to please you or you withdrew your trade. He was not your master, you did not cringe and beg for favours. The boot was on the other leg; he did the cringing. On moving to a new district, or when a couple of newly wedded Middle Class young people entered their home, there was a state of siege. Tradesmen of all kinds came to the door, begging their custom. They waylaid them and solicited their favour. They almost came to blows over a potential customer. It was possible to live for a week on the free samples which poured into the house. And civility was the rule. Let a person in a shop be rude – a customer was lost for ever![9]

## Credit

The strict cash policy of the multiples and co-ops allowed, in some cases obliged, shopkeepers to offer another inducement to customers – credit. The dangers of extended or indiscriminate credit were widely recognised but most trade manuals and journals nevertheless openly recommended its adoption. 'A discreetly managed credit system, with its consideration for the customer's convenience, is one of the weapons wherewith the retailer may best defend himself in competition with mammoth stores and more "company shops" which press him so closely in many towns.'[10] Credit, of course, had long been part of the retail scene, but although they could produce no statistical evidence to support their views, most commentators agreed that it was increasing significantly by the late nineteenth century. Certainly those involved in all types of trade at the time emphasise its importance in their recollections. 'You always had to give credit in a little shop. That's what used to keep the general shop going because if you didn't give credit you never got any trade. Unfortunately, of course, you got caught out sometimes, but, there you are, you had to take that risk. Father used to say, ' "They come in my shop for credit and when they get any ready money they go down the high street" '.[11] When Joseph Houghton brought out his father's bakery business at Shorne, near Gravesend in 1900 he paid £225; £113 of this was for 'book debts', money owing to the business by customers. As his son recalls, 'Those days, believe me, you wouldn't do any trade if you didn't allow credit'.[12] This, not cash trading, was the basis of much retailing.[13]

Credit had obvious advantages for wealthy, aspiring customers. It boosted their spending power by postponing the day of reckoning, sometimes for as long as a year. 'Everything was on account. The tailor was the fellow who was renowned for having to wait for his money. By the time you wanted a new suit you'd probably just paid for the old one. It was really like deferred payment today.'[14] It was convenient, removing the daily chore of having to deal personally with every delivery boy who called at the house. Servants could be sent shopping without having to entrust them with money. The possibility of petty street thieving was reduced since there was no need to carry cash when out shopping. The 'book' in which all purchases were painstakingly recorded by shop staff could be a valuable aid to household management. The accumulation of considerable outstanding sums contributed to the aura and importance of what was essentially a very mundane activity – the monthly, quarterly, or even annual settling of accounts. The possession of a 'book' among the middle classes, the amount of credit allowed and the ease with which it was obtained became status symbols in their own right. To be denied credit was one of the worst blows that could be inflicted upon a respectable, and by implication thrifty and independent, successful middle-class family. To be refused was viewed as an insult and slur on the character. Creditworthiness implied financial soundness and moral probity.

The retailer, on the other hand, had to balance the extra custom it was intended to bring against the inconsiderable inconvenience and expense of operating a credit system. Selling on credit, he would have to carry large working capital reserves to avoid having to buy his stock on credit, a practice which entailed the loss of discounts offered by suppliers for cash transactions and which subsequently forced up his own prices or reduced his profit margins. He was obliged to adopt a costly and elaborate method of book-keeping and there was the possibility of persistent, possible disastrous losses from bad debts.[15] Yet credit had advantages too. Customers of a 'conservative turn of mind', less price-conscious and more interested in service and convenience, could be acquired. The trader, therefore, could retain a higher profit margin, even charge interest on accounts, and yet hold on to his share of the market. The close personal acquaintance with customers which usually went with the granting of credit strengthened the customer loyalty and 'goodwill' so vital to the success of many higher-class businesses.

The proliferation of services and the practice of giving credit were also noticeable in shops with working-class custom. Purchases of furniture, clothes and household goods usually involved credit transactions or hire purchase agreements. Tallymen, independent dealers or representatives of retail outlets, secured orders at the customer's door and then called regularly to collect interest and capital repayments.[16] With such durable products the vendor was always in a position to repossess items legally if payments fell behind but such security was obviously not available for those selling perishable products. Credit was generally withheld by tobacconists or newsagents who relied on a passing trade but bread, milk, groceries and meat could all be obtained on credit and were regularly delivered as well. Whether it was pressure of competition, social pressure from within the local community or a combination of both which encouraged this practice is less clear. 'Tick' or the 'slate' was not just a convenient way of settling accounts at the end of the week although for weekly wage earners this aspect was obviously important and assisted budgeting. Nor was it the straightforward means of confirming social status that it was higher up the social ladder. It is true that respectable working-class families in receipt of a regular income were likely to be allowed longer credit than those generally regarded as shiftless, incapacitated or in casual employment, but such families, when in employment, preferred to pay cash. Those raised in such surroundings recall being indoctrinated with that most basic of Victorian virtues, thrift, 'If you couldn't afford a thing, well you jolly well couldn't have it.'[17] Nor would the more affluent working-class families benefit from shopping regularly at the local corner shop. Multiples and co-ops catered specifically for them. Shopkeepers required a tough skin, however, to refuse credit to the poor. The withholding of assistance from such people was in effect condemning them to reliance on the detested poor law or to destitution. 'Damn it all,' grumbled Robert Roberts's father in his little Salford shop after one customer had asked for money for the gas meter, 'We lend 'em food, now we gotter loan 'em the light to eat it by! It's not a shop, this, it's a bloody benevolent society.'[18] The more substantial private tradesman, less troubled by such matters, tended to attribute the frequent failures of such small shopkeepers to their ineptitude, a fitting fate for such undesirable interlopers into retailing, not to the impossible social pressures they faced. He and his account customers clearly adopted a hypocritical view of working-class credit; it discouraged thrift, promoted lax morals, encouraged wasteful habits. Account customers were apparently immune from such scourges.

### 'Open all hours'

In the West End, the Mecca of the affluent shopper, few stores remained open after 6.00 p.m. on weekdays, and Saturday was accepted as a half day by 1894.[19] A similar situation existed in centres of other large cities. Even the purely cash traders could afford to close relatively early, relying on their cheapness to attract daytime custom. All other shopkeepers who relied to any extent on working-class custom felt obliged to keep open for very long hours.

Food retailers kept open till midnight or later on Fridays and Saturdays but the practice was widespread in other sectors too. One draper recalls, 'There was no question of having any specified times. You kept your shop open as long as you could . . . on Saturday we never closed at all.'[20] 'This would be about 1910 when my grandfather was still in the shop,' remembers another provincial grocer's son, 'He'd say to me Saturday evening, "Bertie, run along the road and see if Mr So-and-So is shut yet." I'd go running back to grandfather. "No, he's still open grandfather." "Oh, well, we shall have to keep open a little longer." This might be 10 o'clock. It was like that in those days. There was no 6 o'clock, slam the door and clear off.'[21]

Sunday trading was also on the increase. Effectively unhampered by legal restrictions (the Lord's Day Observance Act of 1677 had been amended in 1871 so that no prosecutions could be brought by individuals unless they had the written agreement of local police and legal authorities to do so),[22] more shops, especially those in the working-class areas of large cities or those likely to benefit from passing trade like confectioners, newsagents and tobacconists, set the pace. The evidence presented by over three hundred trade associations, police chiefs, local authorities and sabbatarian groups convinced two select committees on Sunday trading that the problem, as they saw it, was now reaching epidemic proportions and that 'the more respectable class of traders are powerless to prevent it since it was practised almost entirely by small shopkeepers and street traders'.[23] Only in Hull and Swansea were there attempts to crack down on the practice with any degree of commitment.[24]

Understandably, the small shopkeeper with few overheads, unpaid family assistance and living accommodation on the premises, found it easier to offer this service than the employer of labour. His representatives took a sympathetic view of the working-classes' habit of shopping late or on Sunday mornings, a habit which many not involved in the trade found totally mystifying. Thomas Layman of the Shopkeepers' Defence League explained to the Select Committee on Shop Hours in 1886 that it was a simple matter of necessity: 'the very poor have not the time to come out in the daytime. They are obliged to come out chiefly at night'.[25] Larger traders and their assistants argued that it was the result of bad management of time and money, indicative of a general decline in morals and consideration for others. 'The working classes', bemoaned Kenneth Milligan of the Scottish Shopkeepers' and Assistants' Union in 1893, 'who are in many cases clamouring for an eight hour day for themselves, were the worst offenders, and seemed callous to any interest but their own.'[26] Long hours were not popular, therefore, with most traders. They increased their costs, left them open to accusations of labour exploitation and the desecration of the Sabbath, separated them from their families for inordinate lengths of time especially if they now resided some distance away from their shop, and 'left them with even less leisure time than their assistants'. Until the First World War, however, they had only limited success in restricting trading hours.

### 'Advertise and keep alive'

The tradesman also increasingly depended upon advertising in his fight for survival. Customers had to be made aware of the range of goods stocked, the prices charged and manifold services offered. Recourse to advertising was not, of course, unique to this period, but its scale and methods employed had changed markedly.[27] Not all were affected in the same way. Craft/retailers who controlled the quality and determined the individuality of their products, could still rely to some extent on their products 'selling themselves' or on word of mouth. Tailors, dressmakers, cabinet makers, even specialist bakers, fancy confectioners and grocers with their own brands could all appeal on this basis. For the retailer of prepackaged, branded products, however, the situation was less favourable. Brand name advertising by enterprising producers like Lever, Cadbury, Beecham, Mazawattee and Hudson's and their campaigns to persuade shops to stock their products provided no guarantee that the individual shopkeeper would be a beneficiary of their promotional activities and expanding demand. As one guide for *The Practical Retail Draper* explained in 1912, 'the retail shopkeeper fails in his plans of salesmanship if he does not advertise or take some step to secure for his own personal aggrandisement the benefits this outside advertising is bringing to his door'.[28] Others phrased their advice more poetically:[29]

> WAKE UP MAN!
> Tell us, are you advertising
>     In the same old foolish way
> That your grand-dad did before you
>     And persist 'it doesn't pay'?
> Think the whole world knows your address,
>     'Cause it hasn't changed in years'?
> Wouldn't the bathos of such logic
>     Drive a billy goat to tears?
> 'Just a card' is all you care for
>     Hidden, lonesome and unread
> Like the sign upon a tombstone
>     Telling folks that you are dead.
> Wake up, man, and take a tonic,
>     Bunch your hits and make a drive,
> Run a page, and change your copy,
>     ADVERTISE and keep alive.

To support such general exhortations there were numerous articles and volumes on the 'Art of Publicity', 'The Psychology of Advertising' and organisations offering correspondence courses on 'The Science of Salesmanship' advising the enterprising shopkeeper to adopt a wide range of practical aids.[30]

Evidence suggests that many retailers heeded this advice or at least improvised their own plans of action. Commercial trade directories expanded their coverage, listings and advertising columns. Advertising revenue was certainly instrumental in fostering the growth of the local press. Lengthy price lists, in effect mini-catalogues delineating the shop's entire stock were common in the better class of trade by 1900, printing being subsidised by revenue from manufacturers' advertisements. Thousands of circulars were distributed to promote special offers or entice new custom. In 1888, for example, T. D. Smith, the Lancaster grocer, countered the appeal of the co-op to the town's 'thrifty housewife' distributing 4,350 specially-printed circulars to the 'working-class in town'. A periodically revised 170-page price list was supplied to regular customers in the 1890s. Free samples of certain goods were also offered as incentives to buy at his shop.

The importance of being 'modern' and 'progressive' was emphasised by all proponents of aggressive marketing. The positioning, and above all, the appearance of the premises themselves were of primary importance in this policy. Prominently positioned, attractive shops were considered to advertise themselves so that whenever possible, prime sites were sought and shop frontages redesigned to allow maximum display of goods to act as 'silent salesmen'. An alluring window display was considered 'the best and cheapest advertisement a retailer can have', which, if it was brilliantly lit and unshuttered, could even function after dark.[31] Despite advice heaped upon the retailer, acquiring the art of window dressing appears to have been a painful, and in some cases, an expensive process. Enthusiastic novices simply crammed available space with as much stock as possible. Other displays, 'bordering upon vulgarity' had the undesired effect of attracting 'a gaping crowd of street urchins', repelling respectable customers.[32] As Mr Polly's apprentice friend Mr Parsons discovered to his cost, 'Cosy Comfort at Cut Prices' was still not considered *au fait* in the window of a high-class draper.[33] In a few cases, however, window displays proved *too* successful. West End department stores whose huge Christmas displays attracted large crowds in 1909 were prosecuted by the Metropolitan Police for encouraging an obstruction of the pavement. A. W. Gamage, a leading store owner, protested violently, arguing, perfectly logically, that theatres ought to be similarly penalised for encouraging queues. At the other extreme those with inadequate window space resorted to displaying their goods on the pavement. These also fell foul of the law; North Staffordshire police, for example, prosecuted them for obstructing the right of way.[34]

Numerous other expedients were also common by 1900. Sandwich boards were paraded through the streets on the shoulders of luckless individuals. Attractive delivery carts and vans invariably carried the proprietor's name and address in large letters, a practice which also exempted them from the need to obtain a carriage licence. Motor vans in the Edwardian era, despite their renowned unreliability, were tentatively recommended by pundits for their novelty and consequent publicity value. The telephone, introduced in the 1880s, was also being employed in the higher-class trades although the speed of its adoption would appear to have been slow. As late as 1912, Mr Wadsworth, a Halifax draper whose trade was reputed to have grown by 'leaps and bounds', achieved a certain notoriety by filling one of his valuable display windows with telephone equipment and exhortations to passers-by 'to ring up on any occasion for advice on any purchase'. Arguably his greatest asset was his phone number – 'One Halifax'.[35]

All these measures designed to improve competitive ability and increase turnover had one major drawback; they demanded increased expenditure and investment at a time when some shopkeepers felt they were unable to afford such bold steps. In addition to such outward looking, almost Keynesian, policies recommended by journals like the *Retail Trader*, therefore, there were widespread attempts to economise on general running costs and even instances of 'unfair' or dishonest practices. We shall consider these in the next chapter.

## Notes to Chapter 4

[1]F. Bechhofer et al., 'Small shopkeepers: matters of money and meaning', *Sociological Review*, new series, XXII, 1974, pp. 465–82; T. H. Lewis, (ed.), *Modern Retailing*, 1949, I, pp. 43–5.

[2]*Retail Trader*, 'Businesses that grew', 8 March 1911, p. 15.

[3]*The Grocer*, 17 Feb. 1906, p. 445.

[4]E. H. Booth, *Shadow and Sheen*, 1897, published privately in conjunction with *A Century of Progress, 1847–1947*, 1947, p. 33.

[5]Interview with Mrs J. Wray, vicar's daughter, near Ashford, Kent.

[6]Interview with Miss D. Taylor (born 1892), wholesaler's daughter, Canterbury.

[7]Printed ephemera in owner's hands.

[8]*Ibid*.

[9]W. MacQueen Pope, *Twenty Shillings in the Pound*, 1948, p. 217.

[10]Simmonds, *Practical Grocer*, I, p. 102.

[11]Interview with Mr James Medhurst (born 1900), son of a small shopkeeper and publican.

[12]Interview with Mr Basil Houghton (born 1894), baker's son; figures are drawn from papers in his possession.

[13]N. Griffiths, *Shops Book: Brighton, 1900–1930*, Queenspark, Brighton, 1979, pp. 53–9; W. Hamish Fraser, *The Coming of the Mass Market, 1850–1914*, 1981, pp. 85–93.

[14]Interview with Lord Harris.

[15]On the inconvenience of credit, see Chapter 13.

[16]Penn, *Manchester Fourteen Miles*, pp. 173–5 for a picture of one tallyman; Fraser, *Mass Market*, pp. 87–9.

[17]Interview with Albert Broadribb, (born 1902), London postman's son.

[18]Roberts, *Classic Slum*, pp. 82–3, 105; *Ragged Schooling*, p. 17.

[19]Royal Commission on Labour, P.P. 1893–94, XXXVII, p. 3; South Wales also enjoyed early closing, *ibid.*, P.P. 1893, XII, p. 90.

[20]Interview with Mr R. Rabson, (born 1889), draper's son, Ashford, Kent.

[21]Interview with Mr E. A. Stanger, (born 1900), grocer's son, Tenterden, Kent.

[22]Wigley, *Victorian Sunday*, p. 124.

[23]Select Committee on Sunday Closing, P.P. 1905, VII, pp. 33, 51, 106, 127, 134, 179; Select Committee on Sunday Trading, P.P. 1906, XIII, pp. 334, 321.

[24]Sunday Trading Committee, pp. 34, 329–33.

[25]Select Committee on Shop Hours' Regulation Bill, P.P. 1886, XII, p. 133.

[26]Royal Commission on Labour, P.P. 1893, XXXIV, p. 438.

[27]E. S. Turner, *The Shocking History of Advertising*, 1952, chapter 6; B. B. Elliott, *A History of English Advertising*; Fraser, *Mass Market*, pp. 134–46.

[28]F. W. Burgess, *The Practical Retail Draper*, c.1912, V, p. 143.

[29]*Retail Trader*, 27 Sept. 1910, p. 19.

[30]E. A. Spiers, *The Art of Publicity and its Application to Business*, 1910; W. D. Scott, *The Psychology of Advertising*, 1909; *The Grocer*, May supplement, 1906; *Retail Trader*, 25 Oct. 1910, p. 23.

[31]Simmonds, *Practical Grocer*, I, pp. 197, 207.

[32]*Ibid.*, p. 201.

[33]Wells, *Mr Polly*, p. 39.

[34]*Retail Trader*, 22 Nov. 1910, p. 19; June 1912, p. 339; *The Grocer*, 3 Feb. 1912, p. 336.

[35]Burgess, *Retail Draper*, II, pp. 233–6.

# CHAPTER 5

# Economies and labour problems

Casting around for any economies they could make, shopkeepers found their freedom of action rather restricted. There seemed to be three possible options. First they could cheat, resorting to blatantly dishonest, unscrupulous trading methods. Second, they could improve efficiency by introducing machinery, eliminating waste or implementing bulk buying. Finally they could economise on labour, undoubtedly their greatest single item of expenditure.

## Dishonest trading

Food adulteration, misrepresentation of goods, short measure – such social evils detrimental to the public interest were all unlawful.[1] The first Adulteration of Foods Act had been passed as long ago as 1860 after Thomas Wakley and Dr Arthur Hassall writing in the *Lancet* had exposed the unsavoury, positively harmful practices prevalent in the low-class trade. Further tougher measures in 1872 and 1875 and the formation of the Society of Public Analysts in 1874 greatly increased the scope and effectiveness of the law and by the late 1880s most local authorities had appointed professional inspectors and analysts to enforce it. An Amendment Act of 1879 had extended their powers of inspection to spirits, while the Margarine Act of 1887 endeavoured to stamp out the practice of selling this novel, rather unappetising grease as butter to an unsuspecting public largely unaware of the distinction. The Sale of Food and Drugs Act of 1899 covered all ingredients used in food preparation and consolidated previous legislation while the government continued to extend its powers of regulation to milk (1901) and butter (1902). By the 1900s almost all goods sold in food shops, certainly by grocers, were subject to detailed legal controls.

There were more wide-ranging restraints on business activities affecting all traders. Under the Merchandise Marks Acts of 1887 and 1891 a shopkeeper could be prosecuted for applying false descriptions to any products – attempting to pass off foreign meat as English, describing second-rate china as 'Dresden' and so on. Misrepresentation was further controlled by the Sale of Goods Act, 1893, which made it illegal to sell goods not suitable for the purpose for which they were advertised. The Weights and Measures Acts of 1878 and 1889 required shopkeepers to possess accurate equipment when selling goods by weight or volume and to make it available for inspection when requested to do so by a local authority official. In addition, those selling stamps, watches, liquor, tobacco, patent drugs, fireworks, meths or petroleum, or involved in pawnbroking, were allowed to trade only under licence.[2]

By the 1900s, therefore, many potential abuses or methods of inflating profit margins had been outlawed; hardpressed shopkeepers resorted to such tricks at their peril but they undoubtedly did so. The watering down of beer and milk continued, water was patted into slabs of butter, short weight bread was sold especially on bread rounds, 'bags' of coal or groceries without specific weights were retailed, excessive amounts of soil were left on root vegetables. Generally speaking, however, the scale and nature of such undesirable activity was negligible in comparison with earlier periods.

Shopkeepers had an ambivalent attitude towards such restrictions on their freedom of action. The complexity of shop law, and the fear of unwittingly falling foul of it, undoubtedly won recruits for the local and national trade associations which expanded rapidly in the 1890s and were concerned, like their union counterparts for workers in industry, with monitoring the implementation of legislation, defending members unjustly prosecuted and laying down recognised, legally acceptable definitions of certain practices. Grocers prosecuted under the 1887 Merchandise Marks Act, for example, for selling one pound of tea or sugar inclusive of wrapping paper without specifically stating this, were vigorously defended by the National Federation of Grocers' Associations. Its position was upheld in 1892 when an appeal court overturned the conviction of a Wolverhampton grocer (Harris v. Allwood) on the grounds that 'this was a practice universally understood all over the kingdom and . . . well known to buyers and sellers, and that there was no intention to defraud', a ruling that was upheld in a similar case in 1901. Nevertheless, one outcome of the proceedings was the publication by the National Federation of an acceptable list of paper weights and a warning to all members that 'Tea wrappers should bear the additional words, "This packet is sold as gross weight, including the wrapper" '.[3]

Generally, however, traders gave the government's refereeing rôle a guarded welcome. While expressing collective disquiet about over-zealous interpretation and enforcement of legislation and the lack of compensation for shopkeepers found guilty of selling sub-standard products bought in good faith from a supplier, the retail trade did not object to restrictions on 'unfair' competition which threatened to bring their profession into disrepute or damage the genuine trader's prospects. Indeed, they even pressed for the introduction of more legislation; grocers, found in the ranks of early Victorian food reformers, were still campaigning in 1906 for further controls on butter marketing.[4] Such restrictions did not, they argued, represent a breach of cherished *laissez-faire* or the indefensible interference by the state in the free market, rather they created the conditions under which 'fair' or 'legitimate' competition could flourish. As we shall see, their view of what constituted 'unfair' competition was an elastic one and they were to demand further assistance far beyond that which politicians were willing to consider.

### Economising

Legitimate economies which did not involve labour saving were few. Trivial amounts were saved by eliminating waste and penny-pinching on the 'little things' recommended by journalists in the retail press: re-using string or wrappers, requiring assistants to provide their own uniforms, pens or pencils, returning to suppliers boxes, bottles and packages with deposits upon them. Savings on capital expenditure could be counter-productive given the acknowledged need to have well situated and attractively fitted-out premises. Pavement displays, if employed as a substitute for shop and window modernisation, could be false economies since a boy had to be employed to prevent losses from pilfering. Transferring to cheaper or more lowly rated premises could seriously dislocate the pattern and volume of trade. Attempts to reduce recurrent outgoings also met with little success. Bulk buying of commodities at discount prices was not feasible unless there was a large, quick turnover; many continued to prefer substantial mark-ups on a smaller volume of sales, however, to allow them to offer credit and service. Moves to save on labour, fuel and lighting by instituting voluntary early closing agreements met with limited success while there was little relief promised from the increasing burden of urban rates.

Wages were a major expense for all but the small family shopkeepers yet there was a relative dearth of labour-saving devices and significant problems involved in making use of those that did exist. F. W. Burgess, a leading draper, concluded sadly in 1912 that 'The introduction of machinery and labour-saving devices in the mill found no parallel in the retail shop',[5] but information on the cost, reliability, depreciation and running costs of such machinery as did exist was regularly provided by the retail trades' journals. Much of it, however, could only be utilised in certain trades: the sewing machine in clothing and leather goods; tea mixers, fruit cleaners, grinding mills and coffee roasters in grocery; dough kneading machines in baking. Even then, unless the machines were intensively used for a large proportion of the shop's trade, savings were trivial. The grocer, for example, required a formidable array of specialised equipment before he could consider reducing his labour requirements. Although in the long term such investment may have resulted in greater efficiency and lower costs, the initial effect was to raise them considerably. Furthermore, the installation of machinery brought retail premises under the Factory Acts which laid down minimum requirements for health and safety and restricted the employment of women and children.[6]

The most widely adopted labour-saving devices were those which simplified bookkeeping or lowered delivery costs. In larger establishments the cash railway system where money and bills were transported in enclosed capsules on overhead wires or built-in chutes to a central finance office saved time and eliminated the possibility of assistants' errors or fraud in the handling of money. Smaller shops, especially hygiene-conscious butchers, opted for the simple expedient of a separate cash desk where all transactions were carried out. The cash register was another device with obvious advantages. By 1911 the National Cash Register Company claimed to have sold a million machines and its advertising campaign extolled the virtues of the 'spy on the counter'. 'A feature of our latest models are [sic] that they place each assistant on his own responsibility. Each of their sales are [sic] automatically added into separate totals, each has his own cash drawer which makes him individually responsible for every penny of his employer's money that he handles. The Retailer is therefore able to tell the industry and honesty of every assistant.'[7]

Bicycles were increasingly used from the 1890s to speed up deliveries, while the following decade witnessed the beginning of a popular debate on the respective merits of the motor-driven delivery vans and the tried and trusted horse and cart. Obvious advantages of the new technology were that it provided 'a motive power which does not shy, and, if properly handled, has no inclination to run away, which is not subject to sudden and prolonged attacks at the busiest seasons, does not take cold if left standing after a quick run and – no small consideration – requires no Sunday grooming or attention'.[8] One enthusiast claimed to have effected a sixty-six per cent reduction in his labour costs by buying a motor van but it would seem that high initial outlay and the infamous unreliability of these early vehicles deterred most retailers from making the changeover before 1914. The scarcity of horses during the war was to provide the negative spur to the quicker adoption of motorised delivery vans and bikes.

### Diluting the labour force: women and children

The limitations of such mechanical aids ensured that retailing remained essentially a labour-intensive business. Indeed the proliferation of services and long opening hours implied that it was likely to become even more so in the foreseeable future. The small shopkeeper continued to survive by relying on unpaid family help, his wife running the business for much of the day assisted by the children at peak periods. The private tradesman's family was unlikely to have worked; his higher social position and aspirations, shared by his wife, militated against such a policy. For much of the nineteenth century his employees had been predominantly male and lengthy apprenticeships had been deemed necessary to acquire a thorough knowledge of the trade's productive, processing and retailing aspects. As skilled men shopworkers had commanded good wages and nurtured hopes of running their own shops. Even in the drapery trade where the amount of skill required had been severely reduced by the introduction of mass-produced cloths, a mockery of an apprenticeship system had survived. Faced with increasing competition and a de-skilling of some trades by the turn of the century, however, there was clearly a possibility that this position would no longer apply. Pressures to reduce wages, worsen conditions or introduce cheaper juvenile or female labour into the workforce mounted.

The prospect of retailing becoming commonly regarded as women's work and the inevitable lowering of its social status which this implied was not appealing to independent-minded traditional proprietors and we should not exaggerate the extent to which females infiltrated many trades. Within a shop they had considerable limitations. They were unsuited to rough or heavy manual work involved in unloading or transferring stock in butchery, baking, ironmongery or furnishing. Counter assistants or cash clerks were the only posts they could aspire to in such trades. Wherever a detailed knowledge of specific skills, acquired through either a formal period of apprenticeship or long training remained necessary, as in chemists or high-class grocery, male employment also remained the rule unless, as with dressmaking, the final product was sold exclusively in a female market. If labour costs were of secondary importance, as in jewellery, the shopkeeper's major outlay being on stock, the incentive to hire women was reduced. In tailors and outfitters where men were the main customers, or in trades where customers spent hefty sums on individual items and valued what appeared

67

to be authoritative assurances from assistants, men remained firmly in the majority. Even in shops where assistants were female, the manager and shopwalker were invariably men. Not until the First World War depleted the number of male assistants and created a serious labour shortage, therefore, did many shopkeepers, encouraged by government training schemes, come to accept women as an integral and permanent element in their workforce. The persisting respectability of shopwork continued to attract a good supply of young male recruits, 'smart young juniors, full of smart juniosity . . . the Shoveacious Cult', so despised by the ageing Mr Polly who found himself 'too old at forty' to be a draper's assistant. Nevertheless even before 1914 women had made significant inroads into some trades.

Unfortunately census returns do not provide satisfactory figures for the number of assistants in the retail trade and we have no information on the size or status of businesses which relied on female labour. What is clear is that the number of female 'dealers' increased dramatically between 1881 and 1891 and again in the 1900s, and that women formed an increasing proportion of the retail workforce. Only a small number were actually returned as employers or in business on their own account in 1901 and 1911; the vast majority were assistants. These were employed in trades which retailed pre-packed products, where the work required service but no handling of heavy goods, no processing, manufacturing or repairing. In all the new multiples and department stores, therefore, and in milliners, clothes and household goods dealers, fancy goods shops, tobacconists, newsagents, stationers, china dealers, refreshment rooms, restaurants, confectioners and fruiterers, women comprised a large and increasing percentage of the staff. According to one authority there were close on half a million female assistants by 1914.[9]

Statistics on child and juvenile employment are even more notoriously unreliable than those on women, much of it remaining unrecorded. Although it was not a new practice, the evidence collected in the 1900s suggests that it was increasing, with a majority of working-class school children and leavers spending part of their working life in retailing. By 1911, employment 'in and around' shops accounted for over fifty per cent of children engaged in part-time work while still at school and for 47 per cent of all boys between fourteen and eighteen years of age.[10] Except in small family shops they were rarely to be found serving behind the counter, but they were ideally suited to almost every other variety of shop-related work. Children as young as eight or nine delivered milk, bread and newspapers before school commenced, while a wide range of shops employed them for deliveries and errands at weekends and during the evening when they were also free. Boys were generally out of doors, possibly minding pavement displays or simply acting as door boys for some of the high-class shops and department stores, attractively dressed but superfluous, unskilled personnel. Their primary function, however, was to fetch and carry, to provide the short-distance delivery service in urban areas so vital to the majority of retailers' continued existences. 'Every wire has a boy on the end of it' was literally true.[11] 'They are like postcards, so easy to send and so cheap, that everyone likes to have one handy.'[12] After leaving school their job specifications changed little until they were sacked on reaching adulthood or demanded men's wages.

Tradesmen experienced few problems with recruitment. On the contrary, they were sometimes unable to meet fully the demand for shopwork that existed. While still at school it was possible for a child to earn 3s to 5s a week and on leaving and taking up full-time employment that could easily be raised to 6s or 8s, an attractive prospect for the child and his family and a fortune compared with the pittances offered in comparable unskilled jobs or even apprenticeships. Some aspiring working-class parents actively encouraged their children to enter retailing regarding it as a respectable profession, offering better opportunities for social advancement. To have a boy 'in business' or 'in commerce' was in itself a status symbol. Shopkeepers pandered to this misguided attitude by referring to their young staff as apprentices and some even used this as an excuse to pay lower wages or even charge premiums. There were also no insurmountable barriers to entry for most youngsters. Elementary schools strove to inculcate them with the basic rudiments of reading and writing but often all they needed was a knowledge of the area they lived in where they would be delivering. Shop work also attracted recruits out of simple necessity; it filled an important niche in the juvenile labour market. On leaving school at fourteen, or even earlier if he had passed the labour examination or had achieved the requisite number of attendances during his school life, a boy had few other job opportunities in many parts of the country. He could not yet do man's work; his physique, restrictive factory legislation and trade union policies effectively prevented this. Many apprenticeships recruited at sixteen so even if he intended to follow another trade a few years in a branch of the distributive trades was on the cards.

There was also a veritable plethora of shop girls to choose from. In part this, too, was a reflection of the lack of alternative occupations for women, especially those which did not, like teaching or nursing, require long periods of training. But shopwork was also sought after as a respectable occupation, superior to factory work or general skivvying. In addition it was still possible to obtain board and lodging in establishments in some parts of the country, a factor which no doubt swayed parents who would otherwise have been hesitant about letting their offspring leave home to work. In Wales, even lawyers, clergymen and farmers

69

placed their daughters in the trade.[13] Most shop girls did not view their position as permanent: 'They regard it as respectable and accept a small salary in the hope that it will not be for long. Marriage is their ultimate and not remote hope.'[14] Nevertheless, there were always plenty of recruits to take their places, despite the fact that their pay was rarely more than half that of men, even in the same trade, most of them receiving less than 12s a week, £25–£30 per year, hopelessly inadequate if they had to support themselves.[15] As a workforce they were also more malleable, more willing to accept what should have been unacceptable wages and conditions. Assistant commissioners reporting to the Royal Commission on Labour in 1893 were unanimous in their views; there was 'no sign of any desire' for unionisation. Despite obvious hardships in some establishments, 'of expressed discontent there is very little'. Girls, they concluded, had 'the patience and endurance of martryrs'.[16] Few followed the lead of Margaret Bondfield, assistant secretary of the National Union of Shop Assistants and the first woman delegate to the Trades Union Congress, and in the 1900s there was only a trickle of recruits to the union.

This recruitment of children and females remained almost entirely free of legal restrictions. The Shop Hours Act of 1886 had limited the employment of children and young persons 'in and around' a shop to seventy-four hours per week but this proved no real obstacle and the act was only patchily enforced. The 1902 Inter-Departmental Committee on the Employment of School Children deliberately refrained from recommending action which would have disrupted commercial life and concurred with retailers' views that 'moderate work' of a few hours a day, even while still at school, 'was not injurious but positively beneficial', strengthening the body, acclimatising the child to the world of work. Although the ensuing Employment of Children Act of 1903 prohibited all street trading for the under-elevens, it expressly permitted the door-to-door deliveries of newspapers, milk or other items bought from a shop.[17] Isolated bye-laws infringed on specific tradesmen – the employment of lather boys in barbers' shops, 'the worst form of shopwork', was forbidden in London for example – but otherwise shopkeepers were relatively unaffected by the arm of the law.[18]

Despite widespread publicity given to the degrading conditions under which some female shop assistants worked, there were no restrictions on their employment either. A proposal to include a clause limiting their hours of work in the bill of 1886 failed, as did all later attempts to assist them in this sphere. The only success was an Act of 1899 which obliged shopkeepers to provide seats, one for every three females employed, but few local authorities appointed inspectors to enforce it. Indeed, by 1904 only eight of the 449 inspectors responsible for the enforcement of all shop legislation had no other public duties.[19]

70

In view of the government's willingness ever since 1833 to provide effective legal protection for women and children in employment, this consistent refusal to act appears paradoxical. Given the considerable pressure from the 1890s for an expansion of job opportunities for women, however, such protective legislation which actually threatened to reduce them would have been totally unacceptable to feminist pressure groups like the Society for Promoting the Employment of Women. Shopkeepers also pointed out that limiting the weekly or daily hours of female employment to less than the normal shop opening hours would mean either that male assistants would be more heavily worked at certain times of the day or, more likely, that women would be dismissed and replaced by unskilled male labour. Furthermore, feminist groups objected to the principle behind earlier regulatory legislation, namely, that women were either too immature or subject to their husband's control to be considered 'free agents' capable of negotiating their own contracts.[20] The question of female labour, therefore, became inextricably bound up with the wider campaign to improve the conditions for all shop assistants, irrespective of sex or age, and the National Union of Shop Assistants prided itself on being the 'first union to work for the regulation of hours by legislation applying equally to its men and women members'.[21]

### The shop hours question

The absence of legal controls did not imply public approval of the shopkeepers' treatment of their assistants. Far from it. From the 1880s there was mounting criticism of the conditions under which some assistants were forced to work which culminated in a campaign to abolish the living-in system where board and lodging were part of the payments made and to introduce a maximum working week for all employees.

The hapless shopkeepers, by providing work for an army of juveniles, were cast as arch-villains aiding Britain's declining industrial position in the world and her miserable military performance in the Boer War. These concerns prompted reformers of various hues in the Edwardian period to pay more attention to the period of adolescence to ensure that future generations would be better fitted for work and the defence of the country. It appeared that in 'the most important epoch of their lives' which should have been an 'apprenticeship to civilisation' youngsters were being exploited for 'present commercial utility' in an environment prejudicial to growth'.[22] Retailing was a 'blind alley' occupation, holding out little prospect of permanent employment for the vast majority of young people engaged in it.[23] They acquired no skills of use later in life. On the contrary, shopwork, easily obtained, was also lightly discarded, boys drifting aimlessly

71

between jobs with no thought for the long term. Young shopworkers were effectively casual labourers involved in 'remunerative loafing', their employment 'seldom a desirable one'. At best they drifted into 'the dreary morass of unskilled labour' or the armed forces, at worst they became unemployable, a burden rather than an asset for the country. 'The tale of a boy's life is a series of unrelated incidents', declared Spencer Gibb, 'it needs to be unified by progressive organisation in the interests no less of national character than national economy.'[24] Shopwork was clearly one of these unrelated incidents.

The outcry about the degrading conditions under which some female shop assistants worked was even more persistent and emotive, receiving widespread publicity. The small National Union of Shop Assistants, often supported by large store owners like Debenham or Derry, West End employers who were in a position to provide better wages and conditions, regularly campaigned for the introduction of universally enforced minimum standards. Doctors emphasised that the long hours which shop girls worked and the nature of their work contributed, amongst other things, towards 'varicose veins, neuralgia, anaemia, lung troubles, consumption, muscular weakness, nervous prostration, intestinal disorders, pregnancy complications and unhealthy offspring'.[25]

There were horrific reports of the exploitation of young men and women in certain establishments, many of them it seemed in the cheaper drapers' shops of the larger cities. Numerous rules compensated for the lack of natural work discipline imposed in factories by the pace of machinery. There were fines for lateness, mistakes on bills, general negligence, unkempt appearance, lack of civility or humility in dealing with customers, failure to effect a sale and a host of other trivial offences. Where it was employed, for it was not as widespread outside the clothing trade as contemporary crities suggested, the living-in system gave the tradesman unparalleled and unjustified control over his employees' personal lives and allowed him to pay pittances as wages. Unhampered by any legal restrictions, hours of work were also exceptionally long in almost all trades, ninety per week if worst reports are to be believed, while meal breaks were shortened, even dispensed with entirely.[26]

The shop assistants' unions could do little to prevent these abuses. The diversity of shop work, its geographical spread, high staff turnover, lack of time or freedom, all this and the presence of large numbers of young women and youths in their ranks, militated against assistants' attempts at unionisation. The National Union of Shop Assistants, formed in 1891, could claim to represent only a small percentage of the workforce and offered little industrial resistance. Although membership increased significantly in 1911 when the union became an approved society for administering the National Insurance Act, only an estimated thirteen per cent of all distributive workers were unionised by 1914.[27] These included co-operative employees who formed their own Amalgamated Union of Co-operative Employees in 1891 and who were the only workers with any economic muscle. The co-ops' strong market position and obvious interest in furthering the material and moral welfare of the working classes meant that they enjoyed significantly shorter hours and better conditions.[28] Retailers elsewhere, however, were given a comparatively free hand in determining working conditions and only the government seemed capable of ending possible abuses which this involved. Just as factory owners in the 1830s and 1840s had found themselves embroiled in a widespread emotional campaign over factory reform, so now did the shopkeepers become the unenviable focus for criticism from diverse pressure groups fighting to obtain for the assistants what they seemed incapable of achieving for themselves, supporting them in their lobbying of the government for legal intervention. Whether conditions were indeed as horrific as some accounts suggested is immaterial; the issue achieved national prominence. Assistants enjoyed the support of the medical profession, politicians like Sir John Lubbock, C. F. G. Masterman, Sir Charles Dilke and successive Home Secretaries in the Liberal administrations, Herbert Gladstone and Winston Churchill. Sabbatarians supported them in their efforts to end Sunday work, humanitarians in their battles against living-in and long hours. Even many shopkeepers openly called for remedial action. Yet all this failed to achieve more than a meagre half-day a week off and recognised meal breaks, established by the lightweight Shops Act of 1911. Before we can fully appreciate 'the amazing reluctance of even a progressive reforming government to act on a matter of such great concern to so many citizens'[29] we need to be aware of the activities of the army of trade associations which feature so prominently in the debate. These were symptoms of the third and final response of the private shopkeeper to the pressures of business, collective as opposed to individual action, either to provide mutual support or more commonly to restrict 'excessive' or unfair competition.

### Notes to Chapter 5

[1] J. Burnett, *Plenty and Want*, 1966, chapter 10; for specific trades see Perren, *Meat Trade*, pp. 5–68, 84–91, 107–13, 133–40; Rees, *Grocery Trade*, pp. 179–92.

[2] Simmonds, *Practical Grocer*, IV, chapters 13, 14; *The Bakers' Times*, 1910–11.

[3] Simmonds, *Practical Grocer*, IV, p. 248.

[4] *The Grocer*, 14, July 1906, supplement, p. 3; Anon., *Past and Present in an Old Firm*, 1907, p. 11.

[5] Burgess, *Retail Draper*, V. p. 146.

[6] Simmonds, *Practical Grocer*, I, pp. 81–2.

[7] *Retail Trader*, Oct. 1911, p. 124.

[8]Simmonds, *Practical Grocer*, I, p. 129.

[9]L. Holcombe, *Victorian Ladies at Work*, Newton Abbot, 1973, chapter 5 and appendix 3, pp. 205–9 is the best introduction to this subject.

[10]R. Bray, *Boy Labour and Apprenticeship*, 1912, pp. 122–3.

[11]Canon Scott Holland, quoted in Bray, *Boy Labour*, p. 124.

[12]Mrs H. Bosanquet, *The Standard of Life*, 1898, p. 178.

[13]Royal Commission on Labour, P.P. 1893–4, XXXVII, p. 236.

[14]*Ibid.*, p. 314.

[15]Estimates vary but all agree that women received no more than fifty to sixty per cent of men's wages. Assistants were understandably reticent about providing information to outsiders.

[16]M. Bondfield, *A Life's Work*, 1948, pp. 24–73; Royal Commission on Labour, P.P. 1893–4, XXXVII, pp. 1–4; Holcombe, *Victorian Ladies*, pp. 119–29; E. Cadbury, *Women's Work and Wages*, 1906, pp. 117, 258.

[17]Interdepartmental Committee on the Employment of School Children, P.P. 1902, XXV, p. 21; Employment of Children Act, P.P. 1903, I, pp. 811ff.

[18]Employment of School Children Committee, p. 274.

[19]P.P. 1904, LXXXVII, pp. 987–99; on the Act see M. H. Irwin, 'The Shop Seats Bill Movement', *Fortnightly Review*, LXXII, 1899, pp. 123–31.

[20]Royal Commission on Labour, p. 313; Select Committee on the Shop Hours' Bill, P.P. 1892, XVII, pp. 327–35.

[21]Bondfield, *Life's Work*, p. 59. A not altogether accurate claim.

[22]Reformers' literature is replete with such phrases. These are culled from A. Freeman, *Boy Life and Labour*, 1914, pp. 96, 206; E. J. Urwick (ed.), *Studies in Life in our Cities*, 1904, p. 305.

[23]A. Greenwood, 'Blind-Alley labour', *Economic Journal*, XXII, 1912, pp. 309–14; *The Times*, 13 Feb., 1912.

[24]S. J. Gibb, 'Boy labour: some studies in detail', in J. H. Whitehouse (ed.), *Problems of Boy Life*, 1912, p. 78.

[25]Royal Commission on Labour, p. 318.

[26]The flavour of this literature can be savoured from W. Anderson, *The Counter Exposed*, 1896; W. Paine, *Shop Slavery and Emancipation*, 1912; M. Bondfield, 'Conditions under which shop assistants work', *Economic Journal*, IX, 1899, pp. 277–86; Fabian Society, *Shop Life and Reform*, 1897; J. Hallesworth and R. T. Davies, *The Working Life of Shop Assistants*, Manchester, 1910; P. C. Hoffman, *They Also Serve: the story of the shop worker*, 1949; *Daily Chronicle*, 'Life in the shop', Feb.–March, 1898; Holcombe, *Victorian Ladies*, pp. 108–17; C. F. G. Masterman, *The Condition of England*, 1909, pp. 127–33.

[27]H. A. Clegg, A. Fox, A. F. Thompson, *A History of British Trade Unionism since 1889*, I, *1889–1910*, Oxford, 1964, p. 468.

[28]Bonner, *British Co-operation*, pp. 128–30.

[29]W. Whitaker, *Victorian and Edwardian Shopworkers*, Newton Abbot, 1973, pp. 172, 163.

# CHAPTER 6

# 'Unity is strength'

## Trade associations

Despite price competition in lower-class drapers and the existence of food adulteration and unsavoury practices elsewhere to increase profit margins or raise turnover, informal agreements to live-and-let-live and abide by acceptable codes of conduct on pricing and competitive behaviour had prevailed for much of the nineteenth century. From the 1880s there were moves to formalise such agreements to provide mutual self-help and restrict unwanted competition. 'Co-operation in one form or another is a necessity in the face of modern competition', insisted one respectable trade journalist, 'for to any man of common sense the value of combination is self evident.'[1] Clearly, despite their public utterances to the contrary, shopkeepers were far from individualists or ardent supporters of the operation of free market forces.

By 1900 most urban areas contained traders' organisations parading under a variety of possible banners: Chambers of Trade, Chambers of Commerce, or simply trade associations. Some recruited from among all local traders, regardless of specialisms; others restricted membership to those in certain occupations. The former's catchment area could vary considerably, encompassing an entire town or simply particular quarters of it, sometimes with interests which clashed with those of retailers elsewhere. In cities like Manchester and London, separate organisations for the city centres and suburbs were evident but even within provincial towns clearly distinguished, often hostile associations could be found. In Blackpool, for example, the Blackpool Traders' Association for centrally situated retailers competed with the South Shore Traders' Association for a larger share of council spending on transport, lighting, paving and general improvements in their areas.[2] The existence of a Master Bakers' Protection Society in London could not prevent the emergence of numerous suburban societies between whom no love was lost in the battle for customers, each defending its own members from intruders from outside.[3]

Organisations which demanded trade qualifications for entry frequently affiliated to a district or national association which then claimed to represent the entire trade on issues of general concern. Grocers, drapers, meat traders, bakers, jewellers, booksellers, chemists, pawnbrokers, dairymen, fruiterers, tobacconists, confectioners, hairdressers, various wholesalers, costermongers, auctioneers, publicans, small shopkeepers and many more were all organised on regional or national lines by 1914. In addition, from 1896 there was the National Chamber of Trade, the retailer's equivalent to the Trades Union Congress or Employers' Federation, the 'Traders' Parliament', claiming by 1910 to represent over a hundred thousand trading establishments, a thousand of them as individual members, the rest through some three hundred affiliated federations and associations. Like the T.U.C. it was essentially an advisory and policy co-ordinating body, boasting a Parliamentary Committee through which it sought allies among M.P.s from the major parties, lobbied government on topics of concern and monitored legislation which, although admirably intended to benefit the public, sometimes gave the trader 'something less than justice'.[4] These wide-ranging associations were supplemented by a number of specific pressure groups set up to remedy certain grievances. Two were particularly active: the Early Closing Association, a national body formed in 1842 to cordinate the activities of local groups which had pressed for shorter hours throughout the nineteenth century, and the Traders' Defence Associations which fought a sporadic, occasionally dazzling, but ultimately unsuccessful war against the co-operative movement.

Although many national federations were formed at about the same time as the unskilled workers' New Unions between 1889 and 1891, they were far from the retail trade's equivalent. Members, and certainly the leaders, were men of capital and skill, employers of labour in the main, descendants of the mid-century shopocrats or skilled retailers like butchers and saddlers. The exceptions to this were those trades dominated by small shopkeepers like greengrocery, confectionery and bakery but their level of organisation and the degree of protection they afforded were generally inferior. The bakers' comparative failure to organise effectively on a national basis in the pre-war decades, their numerous rival associations and internal bickerings, and the fall in membership during particularly depressing years like 1910, symbolises the problems facing such small men. Arguably those most in need of association were those least likely to be involved. Their main initiative was the National Federation of Shopkeepers' and Small Traders' Protection Associations in 1905, but this was primarily a defensive body jolted into life by larger retailers' attempts to obtain legal restrictions on trade, especially opening hours, which were seen as detrimental to the small man's interests.[5]

The proportion of tradesmen actively participating in such organisations remains unclear but, bearing in mind the scattered, diverse nature of retailing and the potential problems it faced, the figures claimed by their spokesmen are far from unimpressive and the level of organisation compared favourably with that of unionised workers in many industries at this time. Employers were certainly far better organised than their assistants. The National Federation of Grocers' Associations claimed over fourteen thousand members by 1910, 'some of them very large tradesmen' and two thousand of them in London alone affiliated through their own Metropolitan Grocers' and Provision Dealers' and Oilmen's Associations. A large percentage of the estimated fifty thousand not involved in the National Federation appear to have been small, general shopkeepers for whom such men had little time or sympathy; indeed, they sought to put them out to business. The National Federation of Meat Traders' Associations, primarily a northern-based organisation, could substantiate the allegiance of nearly 150 associations and over a thousand individual members. The National Federation of Master Bakers' Associations' total of five thousand was more modest, reflecting the difficulties involved when organising small traders beyond local level. Among the regional organisations, the Manchester Retail Traders' Association comprised 1,078 'of the principal shops' in the city centre, all of them with rateable values in excess of £40 per annum. The Newcastle-upon-Tyne Incorporated Trade Protection Society boasted between twelve and thirteen hundred shops 'of all classes' including small businessmen, although the context in which its leaders emphasised this latter point must shed considerable doubt upon its veracity.[6]

### Good comradeship and good business

Although the restriction of competition occupied a conspicuous place among their aims it is important to stress that these associations also fulfilled more innocuous, even praiseworthy functions.

At local level they cemented existing networks of personal relations, organising excursions, concerts, social gatherings, sporting events, providing premises for convivial gatherings. They were intended, in short, to foster 'good comradeship' and 'fraternal feeling', out of which, no doubt, more reciprocally beneficial deals would arise.[7] Related to this were philanthropic activities intended to promote public acceptance and approval, and friendly or benevolent society activities, gradually organised on a national basis by the federations, to provide aid to distressed members or their dependants. There were insurance services to mitigate the worst effects of business failure, theft, accidents or ill health, group rates being negotiated with commercial insurance companies on favourable terms. Frequent news sheets or hefty journals served to disseminate information and advice on significant developments affecting the trade or locality which might affect members' businesses: changes in shop law, the appearance of new products, technological innovations, details on the pros and cons of motorised delivery vehicles. Some local associations managed to arrange joint bulk buying of certain commodities to obtain discounts from suppliers, or, as among Southport drapers, to form a parcels delivery company. Mutual self-help was also evident in the retention of solicitors' services to advise members who crossed swords with the growing army of police and officials appointed to enforce trade law. National federations were formed before the really damaging consequences of increased competition had been felt, a fact which suggests that one of their initial aims was to prevent or monitor government activities and trade developments considered harmful to profitable trading. Rather than desperate responses to immediate crises, therefore, associations represented a practical response to an increasingly complex business world, and one that was being progressively brought under state regulation and inspection in ways which were not always popular with tradesmen.

There were also commendable local efforts to promote trade by advertising the attractions of a particular town's shopping centre. Some associations nurtured more ambitious schemes to attract new industry and employment to their areas as a means of increasing trade on a more permanent basis. The Irish Industrial Development Associations, local bodies of leading manufacturers, clergy, public officials and traders, specifically designed to act in this way, were regularly held up as admirable examples to follow but imitators in the rest of the United Kingdom were slow to appear.[8] Ealing tradesmen, however, were ambitious enough to launch an 'All British Shopping Week' in 1910 cashing in on manufacturers' concern over foreign imports, gaining their financial and personal approval. For the November spectacle, 'The main thoroughfares of the borough were gaily decorated in honour of the event. During the week there was a street pageant – in which the flags and samples of the produce of various British dominions were borne by Boy Scouts – a torchlight procession and military tattoo in aid of the King Edward Memorial Hospital Fund, and a patriotic concert'. Emotional and patriotic appeals clearly featured more than the quality of British goods in their advertising. Four hundred shopkeepers participated in a similar event the following March and at least twenty representatives from other provincial associations attended the inaugural meeting of the 'All British Shopping Movement' the same year. This enjoyed a brief spell of popularity, vigorously championed by the Union Jack Industries League under its chairman Viscount Hill and by the retail press which proffered advice on how to mount an event, but its success would appear to have been short-lived.[9]

## Retailers' watchdogs

Less ambitious, at least in the early stages, but ultimately far more significant, were traders' joint efforts to remove common grievances, to create a more satisfactory environment for the pursuit of profit. These centred on two related campaigns: criticism of the tax system and surveillance of legislation, local and national, to ensure that it did not seriously threaten their interests.

Associations were among the more persistent proponents of local government retrenchment. In Joseph Chamberlain's home city of Birmingham, for example, tradesmen circulated a questionnaire to ascertain candidates' views on the issue in local elections of 1912. 'Will you', it concluded, 'if elected, consider yourself a guardian of the public purse and keep rates as low as possible, consistent with efficiency and true economy?'[10] Blessed with mixed success tradesmen's representatives proposed fundamental overhauls of the country's fiscal and administrative systems to ease the burden of taxation. Their case was presented most forcibly and succinctly by the spokesman for the National Chamber of Trade appearing before the Departmental Committee on Local Taxation in 1912. He made, in the words of one of the committee members, a series of 'courageous proposals'. Compound householders whose landlords paid the rates should, he argued, receive separate notification of the rates payable on their property because, effectively paying the rates as part of their rent, 'They do not realise that they are paying rates at all' and 'vote for anything . . . the man who will promise them the most luxury gets their support'. Central government ought to take over a large share of the cost of providing 'national services' at present provided by the local authorities out of their rates: one hundred per cent of expenditure on lunatic asylums, main roads and bridges and seventy-five per cent of that on police, poor relief and education. Full control of how this money was spent was to remain with the local authorities where shopkeepers possessed significant personal influence. To finance this transfer of responsibility, the income tax threshold should be halved from £160 to £80 to tax the working man 'who ought to pay towards the upkeep of the country in which he lives' since it was 'human nature to prize that for which you pay'.[11] Other traders placed more faith in Lloyd George's attempt to reform local taxation by introducing land taxes but that such proposals for more central government responsibility should come from 'individualist' shopkeepers, traditional champions of weak central control, is significant and we shall return to its implications in due course (Chapter 7).

Traders' organisations also monitored the activities of local and national government, vigorously opposing any measures likely to affect their members. Locally this could embrace almost anything: municipal housing and improvement schemes, street trading and market regulations, even trivial items like Godalming council's imposition of a ten miles per hour speed limit on motor vehicles in the town which traders claimed would deter motorists from visiting their shops.[12] National bodies expressed concern over some aspects of proposed shop legislation, National Insurance plans, the take-over of telephones by the Post Office and the possible introduction of a cash-on-delivery service which threatened to expand mail order business.[13] They gave evidence before official enquiries into the bankruptcy laws hoping to obtain simpler and cheaper means of pursuing bad debtors. They demanded a reduction of allegedly extortionate railway freight charges. They called for changes in trade union law to require strikers to pay compensation to tradesmen who lost business as a result of industrial action.[14] Meat traders opposed restrictions on private slaughterhouses and pressed for clarification on compensation procedures for confiscated, diseased meat. Bakers' associations tried to rouse their members to oppose the Bread Acts. In these and other spheres it is difficult to criticise the activities of the trade associations but their energies were also expended in other quarters less conducive to the advancement of their customers' interests.

## The evils of competition

Much energy was expended in reducing 'unfair' competition, restricting the operation of the free market. Here again, their tactics resembled those of the trade unions with attempts to control entry into certain trades and to maintain a 'fair return' on their business by implementing common pricing policies. Despite a preference for collective action they were not averse to appealing to the state for assistance on some issues although unlike their counterparts in Germany they did not take the final step of seeking separate political representation at national level to achieve their ends for, as we shall see, their position did not merit it and the major political parties showed themselves willing to consider their grievances.[15]

Artificial restrictions on entry into retailing were difficult to enforce, but several trades sought to professionalise their callings by instituting recognised periods of training and paper qualifications, capitalising on the national concern about de-skilling in the British economy before 1914. Grocers emphasised the dangers to public health of unqualified grocers purveying unwholesome, adulterated foodstuffs, chemists played on the dire consequences of quack medicines. Extensive trade manuals like W. H. Simmonds' *The Practical Grocer* (1906), emphasising the 'Science of the Grocery and Provision Trades' and J. Aubrey Rees' *The Grocery Trade: Its History and Romance* (1910) were products of this drive to enforce minimum standards for entry. Their efforts, and those of the National Federation, led to the establishment of the Institute of Certified Grocers in 1909 which published practical guides, ran technical classes and set approved examinations. This did not, of course, prevent unqualified shopkeepers setting themselves up as grocers but it at least allowed those in the honourable sector of the trade to display proof of their expertise.[16] Chemists were rather more successful but few other trades thought it expedient or feasible to pursue such a policy; they preferred other methods.

Fears of debilitating price wars led to growing support for those who called for the end of 'senseless price cutting, a great evil in itself' and extolled the benefits to be enjoyed from 'the mutual arrangement of price and the agreement to cease selling at practically cost price'.[17] The belief in price-inelastic demand, a fixed market which could not expand sufficiently by price reductions to maintain gross profits, ran through this line of argument which also stressed that shopkeepers deserved, as a right, a 'living profit', regardless of the market value of their services, a concept which had parallels with labour demands for a 'living wage' or 'fair day's pay'. To maintain this 'fair remuneration' shopkeepers from the mid-1890s increasingly turned to widespread collective action to ensure 'protected prices' or resale price maintenance where manufacturers were persuaded to stipulate retail prices for their products which could not be varied.[18]

Local efforts to reach price agreements by grocers' associations, drapers, bakers and ironmongers enjoyed mixed success. Without entry restrictions or effective sanctions on recalcitrant traders, it often needed just one 'cutter' or blackleg to set up a high-price area for the agreement to collapse. Retailers appreciated that they required the backing of suppliers in their fight. Chemists were well placed to achieve this. With significant barriers to entry, the possibility of substituting their own concoctions for the products of manufacturers who refused to operate sanctions against price cutters and an ill-informed, less price-conscious public who equated expense with efficaciousness, they were the first to institute national agreements on pricing in 1896 through their Proprietary Articles Trades Association (P.A.T.A.), convincing suppliers to withhold supplies to retailers who sold below agreed prices. Within ten years the association boasted a membership of two hundred manufacturers and three and a half thousand retailers and published its own newspaper, the *Anti-Cutting Record*.[19]

The chemists, however, were not just 'defenders of their own interests' but, through their active campaigning, were 'propagandists of an idea'. William Glyn Jones, the driving force behind their operations, sought support for a general price fixing organisation encompassing all retailers rather than those in specific trades, the equivalent in some respects to working-class attempts at general unionism after 1889. His higher ambition remained unfulfilled but several other trade associations and their suppliers were persuaded to adopt similar tactics. Booksellers eliminated price competition with the net book agreement of 1899 which soon encompassed a substantial section of the trade.[20] Leading manufacturers and larger retailers established the Saddlery and Harness Makers' Proprietary Articles Trade Association in 1906 which fixed prices for a variety of leather goods.[21] Although discussed at the inaugural meeting of the National Federation in 1891 it was not until 1900 that grocers formed their own Proprietary Articles Committee which hoped to negotiate a minimum fifteen per cent return on sales.[22] By 1914 some degree of resale price maintenance, however limited, had spread to household products, ironmongery, agricultural implements, stationery (including Christmas cards), tobacco and smokers' requisites, photographic materials and even some bread and confectionery.[23]

The movement's success, however, was to be consolidated between the wars and we should beware of exaggerating its achievements before 1914. Manufacturers were only won over to the cause if the trade associations could claim to represent the majority of the relevant shopkeepers and could guarantee, therefore, that they had muscle to enforce sanctions. Sometimes even their most ardent supporters despaired of them achieving this. The ex-grocer W. H. Lever, a keen proponent of price fixing for his soaps and active in the formation of the National Federation in 1891, refused a request in 1906 for further price increases arguing that 'Cutters who are not members of your associations throughout the country would not follow the advance and we should have no means of forcing them to do so because those declining to follow would be too numerous for us to deal with'. Cadbury's reply to a similar request four years earlier had been substantially the same.[24] Even those schemes which were successful among private tradesmen failed to force the co-operatives to raise their prices sufficiently to take account of the dividend they paid which traders argued was the equivalent to a price cut. The Co-operative Wholesale Society simply increased the production of its own branded products to counteract any boycott by manufacturers.[25] Nevertheless, retailers were gaining valuable allies in their war against price cutters, even Jesse Boot coming to accept the P.A.T.A.'s policies after initial opposition,[26] while there were probably numerous local initiatives which enjoyed partial success in mitigating the worst effects of price competition without catching the public eye.

Complaining bitterly about real or potential competitors also remained a popular pursuit for all tradesmen. Hawkers, street markets, manufacturers who sold direct to the public, mail order businesses and tallymen were all subjected to verbal abuses. Even the clergy were not immune; their innocuous fund-raising bazaars and clubs through which church members subscribed for bulk purchasing caused them to be portrayed as deceitful traitors, perpetrating a stab in the shopkeeper's back. 'If religious trading was not checked', declared one particularly vindictive grocer in Darwen, 'traders would have to consider the question of places of worship being assessed along with places of business.' Church clubs, despite their charitable intentions, were 'one of the biggest injustices to grocers that could be imagined'.[27] Their full fury, however, was reserved for 'a communistic and anti-Christian movement which seeks not only to deceive the working classes but also the extinction of the private trader'.[28] This was the Co-operative movement.

### The anti-co-op movement

Ever since the successful formation of the Rochdale co-op in 1844 private tradesmen had expressed disgust, anger and indignation at the movement's activities.[29] The development of middle-class co-ops like the Army and Navy Stores had sparked an attempt to obtain legal restrictions on the movement but it was with the massive expansion of working-class stores in the 1880s that permanent resistance groups materialised dedicated to circumscribing their freedom of action or eliminating them entirely. Scottish traders were in the vanguard of this attack, forming the Traders' Defence League in 1886 and publishing their own newspaper, the *Scots Commercial Record*. Despite legal setbacks like the one suffered by Scottish butchers who attempted to deny their co-operative competitors access to fresh meat markets, and the retaliatory measures instituted by the Co-operative Vigilance Committee which exposed the less savoury practices of the private trader, the league was to remain vocal and active throughout the pre-war period, giving succour to its English counterparts through the energetic and crusading leadership of Robert Walker and John Macphie.[30]

Tradesmen in northern towns where co-operation thrived were banding into local organisations by the 1890s. Spearheaded by the grocers, they claimed wider support from other traders but the challenge they presented was frequently feeble.[31] Stagnating business and *The Times*'s 'Passing of the Grocer' scare of

[1] ' "BOS AMERICANUS;" OR YANKEE BEEF AND BRITISH
BUTCHER': Punch's view (1 March 1877) of the likely impact on the British farmers
and butchers of cheap North American beef imports which increased dramatically from
the mid-1870s. In reality the consequences were not so dramatic.

84

[2] 'HERCULES AND THE WAGGONER. Hercules, "Put your shoulder to the wheel, my lad! and try CO-OPERATION yourselves!"' – Old Fable': Punch's advice (25 January 1879) to private retailers complaining about 'unfair' co-op competition anticipated their later policy of pooling resources (see p. 83–90).

THE WORKER FOR "DIVI." AND THE SATISFACTORY RESULTS.

[3] 'THE TRUTH ABOUT "DIVI"': a cartoon of September 1902 from The Tradesman and Shopkeeper, a specifically anti-co-op newspaper. No doubt the characters from St Helens and Hull (see p. 88) were meant to be recognised; note the glasses. The original was large enough to be displayed in shop windows.

Presented as a Supplement with
**THE TRADESMAN AND SHOPKEEPER.**

# CO=OPS. AND "DIVI."

## A DIALECT SONG

Words by E. C. MATTHEWS.

Music by DENHAM HARRISON.

[4] Where and by whom this strange song was to be performed remains a mystery; at tradesmen's socials perhaps. The dialect spelling is, to say the least, original and unique but presumably is meant to be understood by potential customers of the co-op.

86

# CO-OPS. AND "DIVI."

## A dialect song

[1] Now, I'd heer'd missus talkin' about some great big shops
Weer they sould welly ev'rything; they called 'em all Co-ops.
An t'missus said they're gradely places, 'cos the more you spend
You're better off, yer get it back, i' brass called "dividend".
I thowt it strange, but said "Owd wench, tha's bound to have thee way".
She joined t'Co-ops, and used their shops for butter, sugar, tay;
But, by gum, but I've greeted since, it wor a cruel day
When first I heerd about Co-ops and "Divis".

[Spoken] I'm nobbut a labourin' chap; but t'way ma missus 'splained things to me, I wor to be like a partner in t'concern; and' I began to think in a year or two I'd be a Pierpoint Morgan or a Rothschild. And when I passed the shops I'd been dealin' at for years I fair turned my nose up at 'em, an' said "You're nobbut a lot of daylighters, a robbin' workin' foak, takin' their money, an' givin' nowt back."

[Chorus] It wor "divi", you kneaw we were wantin',
Ev'ry man now must say t'will be nice,
To get all the "divi", no matter now if he
Be charged a bit more in the price;
So we started Co-oping and ended in popping,
Of "Divi" we get such a lot.
If Co-operation is good for the nation,
I says that it's all "Divi" Rot.

[2] We varry soon began to find a pound seemed summat short,
At least, it didn't seem to last exactly as it ought;
But missus said, "It's all right, Ben, for at the quarter's end
You'll want to fetch a great big sack to hould your dividend;
An' off we'll go to Blackpool, have a pleasant holiday
When our Co-op. Society gives us brass on Divi day."
Oh yes, We've been to Blackpool. Why, I couna pay my way,
Since first I heerd about Co-ops an' Divis.

[Chorus] It wor "divi", etc.

[3] Now, I've a little lad o' six, just started goin' school,
But fairly good at figures, he says: "Dad, you're a fool,
It's only simple 'rithmetic, yo' see, Dad, less you're blind,
the Stores is nowt but robbin' you, why, even I can find
You pays far more than t'private shops for ev'rying yo' get,
Aye, twenty-five per cent. at least on that, Dad, yo' may bet,
then gets half back in "Divi"; aye, you'll die a rich mon yet,
*In t'poorhouse.* Lave your Co-ops and your Divis.

[Chorus] It wor "divi", etc.

1902 breathed new life into them. In this year St Helens, cruelly yet justifiably described by the *Wheatsheaf* as a 'blot surrounded by a smell and situated between Manchester and Liverpool',[32] achieved notoriety for its hard-pressed Traders' Defence Association's vigorous boycott of the town's thriving co-op and its example inspired imitators elsewhere to be more determined. The co-op in the town was a late developer, being successfully formed only in 1883 but by the turn of the century its members encompassed over half of the town's population and it had ambitious plans for a large central store.[33] Traders' fears were understandable and they embarked upon a public campaign of persistent emotional vilification of the co-op and the foundation of its success, the 'divi'. This involved an attempted embargo on supplies of manufactured goods to the co-op, the financing of specifically anti-co-op candidates in local elections, and a boycott on the employment in their own shops of any one who shopped at the co-op or was related, however distantly, to someone who did. When these made little headway they imitated their rival, forming the St Helens and District United Traders' Profit Sharing Association to pay dividend to their own customers.[34]

The pitched battle in St Helens fuelled an impressive national resistance movement. Within months Traders' Defence Associations existed in Hull, Wigan, Leeds, Barrow, Newcastle, Plymouth, Ilford (Stratford) and Blackburn and over the next few years they were to appear, sometimes only briefly, in all the co-operative strongholds. The St Helens group issued a guide book, 'How to fight the Co-op: A guide and commentary based on the St Helens Experience' and the *Tradesman and Shopkeeper*, a London-based newspaper with a reputed circulation of over ten thousand, emerged to supply news of the struggle throughout the country, publicise manufacturers who had agreed to withhold goods from the co-op, and advise on legal and practical matters. Trade journals like the *Grocer*, despite reservations about the tactics adopted, gave the movement qualified support.

While it lasted, the movement aroused considerable interest and emotions but by 1906 it was one the wane. Traders discovered that their action actually lost them custom, presenting the co-ops with an ideal opportunity to advertise themselves to a wider audience. Sympathetic manufacturers found that their goods were dispensable to a movement which had the capacity to produce its own substitutes, and they withdrew. The *Tradesman and Shopkeeper* ceased publication after losing a libel action brought against it by the Plymouth Co-operative Society in March 1906. Adverse criticism of the co-op persisted, however, while Robert Walker's Traders' Defence League, based now at the Corn Exchange, Manchester, the headquarters of the Lancashire grocers, survived.[35]

## The public image

Tradesmen's propaganda against large competitors like the co-op was replete with assertions about preserving, not restricting, 'pure' competition which was invariably equated with the preservation of individual proprietorship and seen as vital for the future success and prosperity of Britain. 'It is individual enterprise which has made our country the great nation it is, commercially and otherwise', declared John Cottam, secretary of the St Helens Traders' Defence Association, 'every invention and every extension of trade and commerce, every improvement of machinery and method of transport are due to individual enterprise.'[36] Just as cartels and corporations were inflicting untold damage on British industry, so too were monopolistic multiples and socialistic co-ops contrary to the customer's long-term interest, 'social evils' in the same way as food adulteration and misrepresentation of goods were. Those who rallied to the 'growing ranks of individualism', therefore, claimed that they did so out of a sense of public duty, rather than narrow self-interest. Subtly, their individualism eventually came to mean support for more government restrictions on business activity, support for and even control of the individual rather than non-intervention.

Multiples, far from being the products of successful individuals' enterprise and consequently deserving of praise, were accused of destroying the incentive to work by denying shopworkers the opportunity of 'getting on' and of establishing themselves as independent businessmen in their own right. The prospect of remaining a wage-earner for life, they argued, discouraged thrift among employees, encouraging them to waste their income and time on frivolous, unproductive acquisitions and pursuits. The low margins on which multiples operated could only be conducive to illegal, corrupt practices by managers to preserve gross profits. Furthermore, although price-cutters in the short term, in the long run, as effective monopolists once they had squeezed the private trader out of business, multiples would raise not lower prices.[37]

Similar charges were levelled at the co-op. Instead of raising the standard of living of its members by giving good value for money, encouraging thrift by paying dividend, and promoting responsibility and initiative through its democratic organisation and educational programmes, it was transformed by its opponents into a monster of unparalleled corruption, deceit and extortion. It defrauded and misled customers because its dividend represented only a fraction of its total profits, most of which, it was alleged, were embezzled by managers or siphoned off by societies to finance subversive 'socialistic' ventures. Co-ops, thundered the *Tradesman and Shopkeeper*, were 'leading people to become thriftless by training them to depend on others instead of becoming self dependent'. They were 'rendering the future of municipal government difficult, if not impossible, by destroying the rateable value of shop property and retail trade premises. If Co-operative Societies swept the board of small traders as is their avowed intention, hundreds of happy working business couples who are not only the backbone of Church and State, but a splendid example of real thrift and industry to the younger generation would be squeezed out of existence by a cast iron mechanical monster which owns neither soul nor conscience.'[38]

### Ideology and politics

Despite the strong emotions which these new large competitors aroused, tradesmen seemed remarkably reluctant to seek the sort of state aid which was being demanded by their continental counterparts faced with similar but apparently less serious threats to their livelihood.[39] An attempt to revise the law which exempted co-ops from paying income tax on the amount that they distributed to members as dividend was the only significant political move of note and this proved unsuccessful, a government enquiry in 1905 dismissing the traders' case out of hand.[40] Political successes in other areas also seem to have been limited; there was a further clamping down on street trading by children, controls on dishonest trading practices, the blocking of Post Office plans to introduce cash-on-delivery in 1904 and a Shops Act of the same year allowing, but not obliging, local authorities to enforce half-day or early closing.

This apparent disregard for the political option has been attributed to the intense individualism of the British retailers, but this was not really the case.[41] It was, in part, another manifestation of a more widely held preference in Britain for solving economic problems by economic methods and the implementation of voluntary, collective restraints on unfavourable practices. This was exhibited for much of the same period by the British trade union movement, despite its likewarm support for the Labour Party after 1900. Unlike most continental countries Britain had, therefore, no tradition of government control and involvement in the economy on which to build. There was also, despite appearances to the contrary, no disastrous crisis facing the private trader. The threats posed by the new multiples, co-ops and department stores were real enough but increasing consumer spending cushioned the private trader until at least the late 1890s and, significantly, when there was a downturn in trade between 1910 and 1914 it was the food multiples, especially the meat retailers, who had relied on this new purchasing power, which seemed to suffer the biggest setbacks. When retailers did consider that the state could be of assistance they did not hesitate to enlist its aid, relying on M.P.s with trade backgrounds to present their case – W. H. Lever, Hudson Kearley, A. H. Scott, A. Richardson, T. B. Silcock and Thomas Lough.[42] They could also count on the support of unwitting allies like Sir John Lubbock whose adherence to the shop assistants' cause led him to fight for shorter opening hours against the express desire of the Liberty and Property Defence League of which he was a member.[43] Trade associations occasionally grumbled that there were too few retailers in Parliament but they had little need or realistic hope of more.[44]

As we have seen, tradesmen's 'individualism' was little more than a front, capable of being discarded when circumstances dictated. It had not deterred them from demanding strong government 'moral' intervention or supporting specific municipal undertakings for most of the nineteenth century and it did not prevent them from organising to provide mutual self-help and to restrict competition. Interestingly, they also showed no sympathy for those 'happy business couples' in their small shops or street traders and costermongers who might more correctly be regarded as exemplary individualists, working exceptionally long hours, striving against the odds to maintain a decent living, offering a valuable service to the public. These hardworking, self-employed businessmen were subjected to persistent abuse from larger, employing private traders who feared them more than the new competition from multiples and co-ops. The small shopkeeper, they claimed, encouraged the working classes to be thriftless, even 'debauched with credit', by providing tick, while his late opening and Sunday trading led to their mismanagement of time and the breaking of God's day of rest. The service he offered was also poor. By selling in small quantities he overcharged his customers. Lacking adequate knowledge of trade and short of satisfactory, hygienic storage space, he was likely to purvey adulterated, damaged or substandard products. Small shopkeepers contributed nothing to the community at large or the all important public interest; they were in short 'social evils'.

Here, where their interests and social status were more clearly threatened, substantial tradesmen were not slow to demand unprecedented state interference with individual freedom, calling for compulsory early and Sunday closing to rob the small man of his most valuable competitive weapon – long opening hours – disguising their real intentions, however, as a disinterested crusade for the improvement of shop assistants' hours of work. Deprive the family shopkeeper of the opportunity for exploiting his relatives by restricting the hours he could open and the 'Shop Question', as it was known, was immediately solved. No matter that this represented an unprecedented infringement of the self-employed man's freedom to work when he wished. There were, announced one leading Yorkshire tradesman, too many such small shops, and 'a good many more than are really doing any good at all, and it [early closing] would really be a benefit to them even if it made some of them extinct because they are only doing harm to other traders and they do no good to themselves'.[45]

In this field tradesmen were well ahead of contemporary views of the state's legitimate powers to control individuals' activities while their concern over the other issue which dominated their thoughts, the burden of local taxation, also pushed them towards demanding more central government expenditure and power, an apparently anomalous situation for self-confessed proponents of cheap government and *laissez-faire*. It is to these important political considerations that we now turn.

### Notes to Chapter 6

[1] Simmonds, *Practical Grocer*, IV, p. 272; see also Burgess, *Retail Draper*, IV, pp. 90–7.

[2] *Blackpool Gazette*, 18 March 1910.

[3] *The Bakers' Times*, 1887, *passim*.

[4] *Retail Trader*, July 1911, p. 4.

[5] *The Shopkeeper*, Sept. 1908–June 1909.

[6] Deputations received at the Home Office since the Introduction of the 1910 Bill. P.P. 1911, pp. 109, 224, 171, 164; Departmental Committee appointed to inquire into Combinations in the Meat Trade, P.P. 1909, XV, p. 211; H. W. Macrosty, *The Trust Movement in British Industry*, 1907, p. 255.

[7] Burgess, *Retail Draper*, IV, p. 89.

[8] L. M. Cullen, *An Economic History of Ireland since 1660*, 1972, p. 164; *Retail Trader*, 1 Feb. 1911, p. 20.

[9] *Retail Trader*, 22 Nov. 1910, p. 15; 8 March, 1911, p. 15; 15 July 1912, pp. 361–2.

[10] *Ibid.*, October 1912, p. 434.

[11] Departmental Committee on Local Taxation, P.P. 1912–13, XXXVIII, pp. 402–11.

[12] *Retail Trader*, July 1912, p. 379.

[13] *The Grocer*, 1911, 1912, *passim; Retail Trader*, Jan. 1913, p. 12; July 1911, p. 4; Nov. 1911, p. 137.

[14] Departmental Committee on the Bankruptcy Law and its Administration, P.P. 1908, XXXIV, p. 49ff; *Retail Trader*, Jan. 1913, pp. 5, 12; Sept. 1911, p. 167.

[15] R. Gellately, *The Politics of Economic Despair: shopkeepers and German politics, 1890–1914*, 1974.

[16] Ress, *Grocery Trade*, pp. 344–7.

[17] Burgess, *Retail Draper*, IV, p. 90.

[18] B. S. Yamey, 'The origins of resale price maintenance: a study of three branches of the retail trade', *Economic Journal*, LXII, 1951, pp. 522–45; for later expansion, H. Levy, *Retail Trade Associations*, 1942.

[19] Macrosty, *Trust Movement*, pp. 249–54; Yamey, 'Origins', pp. 530–1.

[20] M. Plant, *The English Book Trade*, 1939; Levy, *Trade Associations*, chapter 2; Macrosty, *Trust Movement*, pp. 251–2.

[21] *Saddlery and Harness*, 1905–6, *passim*; Macrosty, *Trust Movement*, p. 255.

[22] *The Grocer*, from 1901 the annual July supplements on the National Federation's A.G.M.

contains reports on the P.A.T.A.; Macrosty, *Trust Movement*, pp. 256–64.

[23] Levy, *Trade Associations, passim*; Jefferys, *Retail Trading*, p. 54.

[24] *The Grocer*, 8 Sept. 1906; Macrosty, *Trust Movement*, pp. 260–1.

[25] Macrosty, *Trust Movement*, pp. 253, 263.

[26] Chapman, *Jesse Boot*, p. 115.

[27] *The Grocer*. 13 Jan. 1912, p. 86.

[28] *Tradesman and Shopkeeper*, 6 Sept. 1902, p. 26.

[29] See for example, *The Co-operator*, LXIII, 1 May 1855; *Co-operative News*, 17 Feb. 1872. I am grateful to Neil Angus for these references.

[30] Bonner, *British Co-operation*, pp. 112–13; *Tradesman and Shopkeeper*, 23 August 1902, p. 11.

[31] Peoples, *Bolton Co-op*, pp. 183–4, 207, 311.

[32] *Wheatsheaf*, Sept. 1902, p. 43.

[33] Barker and Harris, *Merseyside Town*, pp. 477–9; *Liverpool Daily Dispatch*, 23 July 1902.

[34] *St Helens Newspaper and Advertiser*, 18 July 1902; 23 March 1906; *Tradesman and Shopkeeper*, 16 August 1902.

[35] *Tradesman and Shopkeeper*, 1902–6; *Retail Trader*, August 1912, p. 389; August 1911, p. 62.

[36] *Tradesman and Shopkeeper*, 16 August, 1902, p. 3.

[37] *The Grocer*, 14 Jan. 1911, p. 85; 13 Jan. 1912, p. 139; 17 Feb. 1912, p. 151.

[38] *Tradesman and Shopkeeper*, 16 August 1902, pp. 3–4.

[39] Gellately, *Politics of Despair*, chapters 4 and 5.

[40] Departmental Committee on Income Tax, P.P. 1905, XLIV, pp. 430–52, 301–11.

[41] Crossick, 'Lower middle class', p. 17; 'La petite bourgeoisie britannique au XIX$^e$ siècle', *Le Mouvement Social*, CVIII, 1979, pp. 44–5.

[42] *The Grocer*, 7 July 1906, p. 13; 13 Jan. 1906, p. 110; *Dod's Parliamentary Companion*, 1909.

[43] N. Soldon, 'Laissez-faire as dogma: the Liberty and Property Defence League, 1882–1914', in K. D. Browne (ed.), *Essays in Anti-Labour History*, 1974, p. 228.

[44] *The Grocer*, 22 Jan. 1911, p. 222.

[45] Select Committee on Shops (Early Closing) Bill, P.P. 1895, XII, p. 701.

# CHAPTER 7

# Political demands: shorter hours and lower rates

### The long struggle for early closing

Long hours had always been endemic to retailing, especially in the working-class trade, but they were never popular with those shopkeepers who employed assistants. Attempts to reduce opening hours can be traced as far back as 1825 but they were local and uncoordinated in the main, enjoying patchy success.[1] Momentum was gained in the 1880s. Thomas Sutherst's Shop Hours' League, founded in 1881, drawing support from employers and assistants alike, and the Early Closing Association dating from 1842 led the way joined in the 1890s by the emerging trade associations, the National Union of Shop Assistants after 1891, various humanitarian and religious groups and politicians like Sir John Lubbock, a tireless campaigner for improved working conditions. Although voluntary agreements achieved some success especially in the large city centres where high-class establishments closed as 'early' as 7 p.m. some nights in the week and negotiated a 'half-day' 4 p.m. one day a week, most reformers put their faith in a legal solution.[2] The Early Closing Association abandoned its voluntaryist approach in 1889 leaving only a small rump of ineffective non-interventionists who ceded to form the Voluntary Early Closing Association in 1892. Tradesmen's spokesmen giving evidence before the four official enquiries into shop opening hours appointed by the government between 1886 and 1901 spoke virtually with one voice. In 1901, 290 trade associations gave their unqualified support to proposals for legally enforceable, compulsory early closing, only those representing pawnbrokers and off-licences opposing, most of their trade being carried out in the evenings.[3] (Significantly, their associations had been among the first recruits to the strictly individualist Liberty and Property Defence League when it was formed in 1882.[4]) There were also few dissenting voices heard before the two enquiries into Sunday trading in 1905 and 1906;

only a few small shopkeepers, mainly food retailers, objected but even some of these sought relief from their self-enforced slavery.

Faced with such pressure and a mounting public outcry about the plight of over-worked shop assistants whose case the employers claimed to be presenting, it is somewhat surprising to find that the government did so little. The 1904 Early Closing of Shops Act was far from satisfactory as far as the trade was concerned. This empowered a local authority to make legally enforceable orders if so requested by over two-thirds of shopkeepers in any trade within its area of jurisdiction. Blurred distinctions between trades, the distrust and opposition of small shopkeepers and the complexities of the procedure laid down in the Act probably account for the miserable adoption of its provisions. By 1909 fewer than fifteen thousand shops had been covered.[5] There was no shortage of private members' bills proposing tougher legislation but they all failed. Why should this be so?

Those directly threatened by the possibility of early closing and the complete abolition of Sunday trading mobilised themselves for defence: the Shopkeepers' and Small Traders' Protection Association, the Travelling Auctioneers' League, the Bethnal Green Costermongers' Union and the Whitechapel and Spitalfields Male and Female Costermongers' and Street Sellers' Union.[6] Several wholesaling firms also threw their weight in behind the small family businesses.[7] But such organisations were really unnecessary; neither Conservative nor Liberal administrations had any intention of introducing legislation which threatened to put small shopkeepers out of business. Early closing promised to do just this, discriminating against the self-employed and family-run businesses by outlawing their main competitive weapon, to the advantage of the larger employers of labour. There was no evidence that was even remotely convincing to suggest that the small shopkeepers desired early closing; just the opposite. Yet it was equally unsatisfactory to exclude such shops from any legislative controls because this would have unfairly penalised the substantial tradesmen. The unfortunate shop assistants for whose benefit such restrictions were being considered, at least by disinterested politicians, were the victims of a conflict of interest between different types of retailers. What prevented an easy solution to their plight was not the opposition of the majority of the organised, allegedly individualist, *laissez-faire* tradesmen but the ideological scruples and electoral considerations of the major political parties. Similar obstacles, in the form of Jewish shopkeepers and customary market stall holders, foiled moves to effect a complete ban on all Sunday trading.[8]

A new interpretation of Liberalism and the responsibilities of the state, less shackled by purist notions about the inviolability of individual freedom, seemed

95

to offer a ray of hope. In 1908 miners were ensured a maximum eight-hour day by law, the first major state limitation on the freedom of adult males to negotiate their own conditions of employment. In the same year Sir Charles Dilke presented a private member's bill supported by the National Union of Shop Assistants and their parliamentary representative, James Seddon, Labour M.P. for the Newton division of Lancashire, which proposed that a similar formula be adopted for the retail trade. A direct, statutory maximum working week of just sixty hours for shop assistants would replace the indirect solution offered by contentious early closing proposals. For the first time the government expressed its willingness to consider this option. Herbert Gladstone, the Home Secretary commented, 'Personally I have long ceased to be terrified at the old argument that we ought to do nothing which might by any chance interfere with the free discretion, as it is called, of adult people to wear themselves to death by working at their employment'.[9] Recognising that a shortage of parliamentary time would prevent Dilke's bill becoming law during that session, Gladstone promised to give the matter government backing and to introduce a similar bill the following year.

### The Shops Act of 1911

Envisaging a major outcry from those shopkeepers who employed assistants, Dilke had also included provisions for the compulsory closing of all shops in the first draft of his bill. Whether he realistically expected to be able retain this is very doubtful in view of the earlier controversies which such proposals had aroused, but the net result was that trade associations had warily given him their lukewarm support. Gladstone's subsequent proposals betrayed a basic misunderstanding of the issue and were less satisfactory. Trusting in union members to report infringements of the law, placing greater faith in the conscientiousness and powers of local authority inspectors, insisting that shopkeepers were very law-abiding and would not employ assistants for more than sixty hours even though their premises might be open for much longer and delighted to have found such an apparently easy way around the perennial problem of what to do with the small shopkeeper, he omitted all clauses referring to compulsory early closing from his bill. If shopkeepers really felt strongly about it, he argued, they now had the incentive to utilise the voluntary machinery established under the previously ineffective 1904 Shops Act, if, that is, such employers of labour were in fact in the majority as they claimed, forced to remain open by the obstinate anti-social behaviour of a minority of small men. Without such successful local action, however, the small shopkeeper could remain open as long as he liked while the employer of labour's ability to meet his challenge was seriously weakened by the new proposals concerning his assistants.

Private traders were horrified at this turn of events. The solution now proposed would have precisely the opposite effect to that which they so fervently desired, benefiting the small shopkeeper at their expense instead of forcing him to abandon his practice of long opening hours. Yet they could scarcely oppose the bill outright because it promised to achieve precisely what they had claimed to be their disinterested humanitarian aim for so long, the easing of assistants' hours of labour. When Winston Churchill took over as Home Secretary in February 1910, Gladstone emphasised that the bill was 'of quite first rate importance' but by this time he was aware of the problems and warned that it was 'undoubtedly a difficult one and will necessitate a great deal of trouble'.[10] The luckless Churchill was to liken his efforts to secure a reasonable compromise to 'feeling my way along between Scylla and Charybdis every inch'.[11] The episode was to prove one of his less glorious or publicised failures. When the bill was eventually passed most of the main clauses, in Churchill's words, had been 'relegated to the category of waste paper'.[12] Only minor provisions dealing with assistants' meal breaks and half holidays remained. The bill's emasculation reflects the considerable strength and influence which organised tradesmen possessed and their deputations to the Home Office in 1910 bring home how completely they jettisoned their publicly avowed ideological principles when their own self-interest was endangered, when the small shopkeeper and street trader appeared to be about to gain an 'unfair' advantage.

They first tried to convince Churchill of the urgent need to re-introduce early closing proposals along with a few more 'slight amendments' relating to flexibility over the sixty-hours clause and overtime allowances which would have made the act unworkable. 'Close as much as you like so long as you close all the shops together and then there will be equality ... These small rooms would become great channels for distribution if they enjoyed the privileged position you are giving them under the Bill', argued Thomas Lough, M.P., representing the grocers. 'Every shop must close under the Bill' was a point of view repeatedly put to the Home Secretary.[13] Allowing exemptions from a ban on Sunday trading, also part of the bill, was similarly deemed 'unfair'; the government had considered allowing Jews and customary street markets to trade on the Sabbath as well as dealers in milk, confectionery, medicines and other goods considered indispensable in the public interest. Neither Churchill nor his progressive colleague, Masterman, felt themselves able to contemplate such 'unprecedented legislative interference' in the affairs of the self-employed. Churchill would only agree to consider ways of improving the machinery for obtaining voluntary early

97

closing.[14]

Failure on this front forced tradesmen to consider even more extreme tactics, arguing that 'members of a family should be treated as assistants' and subject, therefore, to the same legal controls as other employees. All shopkeepers with assistants supported this line, even small employers who continued to oppose compulsory weekday restrictions on opening because of their reliance on working-class custom – bakers, hairdressers, fruiterers and dairymen in particular. 'You are penalizing the man who employs labour and contributes far more to the upkeep of the country by paying wages', explained one aggrieved retailer, 'A man could work a vast business round the corner or next door with three or four sons or daughters ... and he could oppose the man who is employing labour'. If 'family' members were excluded from the provisions as was proposed then the law would simply become unworkable; 'I am afraid', one grocer remarked wryly, 'there will be extraordinary extensions of the family circle if the Bill becomes law.' Another conjured up the prospect of a massive population explosion as hordes of small shopkeepers turned to procreation in an attempt to boost their free labour supply: 'This is not a Bill for the propagation of large families', he declared righteously, but then added, 'if it were, it would be all right.'[15]

The Home Secretary's initial response to such arguments was far from favourable. 'In practice', he maintained, 'there is a great difference between the kind of relation which prevails between an employer and his servant and the kind of relation which obtains between a father and a son or a husband and wife.' Continued representation on the point, however, persuaded him to shift his stance. It was necessary he decided to 'stop trading on relations as if they were pack animals'. He proposed to redefine 'family' as husband, wife and one other member, all others were to be classed as assistants except in shops below a certain rateable value which were to be exempted entirely from this provision since they were 'more in a state of stagnation than a state of competition ... and it is really not worth worrying about them'. Fortunately, the dropping of the sixty-hour week for assistants also made this dangerous precedent for state interference in family affairs, championed by the tradesmen, unnecessary. It was not written into the bill at any stage but Churchill clearly gave it serious consideration in a desperate attempt to placate the hostile trading community.[16]

The tradesmen's greatest success, however, was the undermining of official confidence in the bill. They simply pointed out the inequities it would create, the inconvenience it would cause for the general public, the impossibility of enforcing it without an army of inspectors, the impracticality of drawing up voluntary local closing orders. Consequently, realising that the bill as it stood would be talked out by the tradesmen's parliamentary allies, Churchill succumbed, dropping all the major clauses which had aroused such opposition. 'This poor little Act', as *The Shop Assistant* dejectedly called it, was scarcely a triumph for the government or the unfortunate shop workers who bemoaned their 'political impotency' and the fact that they 'were about the only class of industrial workers passed over' by a reforming government.[17] It represented rather a successful counter-attack by employing tradesmen, very few of whom objected to its final form even though it failed to give them the early closing they desired. The National Federation, declared *The Grocer*, 'is deserving of great credit for the strenuous and successful efforts it has made to secure the withdrawal' of the most 'objectionable features' of the bill, notably the hated sixty-hours clause. The National Chamber of Trade pointedly congratulated the despondent Churchill and his staff on 'the patience and genius' which they had exhibited in their forlorn efforts to solve the problems of conflicting interests.[18]

Tradesmen did not have to wait long to realise their ambitions. Unlike most government controls, war-time restrictions on opening hours, introduced to save fuel, were not swept away in the post-war stampede to dismantle the state's newly acquired regulatory powers. Indeed, the Shops Act of 1920 was specifically passed to retain them and renewed annually until the small shopkeepers' organisation finally dropped all opposition to early closing having found that trade had not suffered adversely. The government placed it permanently on the statute book in 1928.[19] Further restrictions on Sunday trading were also imposed in the inter-war years. In a comparatively short time retailers had effected, with government assistance, a massive reduction – the speed and magnitude of which has not been matched anywhere else in the economy – in their hours of work.

### Speculations

The havoc wreaked on Churchill's Shops Bill is illuminating and suggestive. It demonstrates beyond all doubt that, with the exception of the small family businessmen, shopkeepers were far from committed to free competition and had no qualms about calling upon the state to restrict the freedom of the individual, even the self-employed, when it suited their interests. Even more fascinating is their success in emasculating the bill in the face of apparently overwhelming odds. The shop assistants' case for a sixty-hour week had the backing of a Liberal government whose record in protecting sweated workers was exemplary, politicians on both sides of the House, doctors, clergymen, the popular press, the general public and the king. So determined was Churchill to appear as their saviour that he retained responsibility for the bill even after his move to the Admiralty. Why were the blatantly self-interested tradesmen allowed to humiliate the government in this way?

The search for an answer leads us into uncharted historical territory and only a tentative hypothesis can be suggested here. Probable clues can be found in Churchill's correspondence. In September 1910, before the deputations had started, he wrote cautiously but optimistically to Asquith of the need to 'walk warily so as not to offend or frighten our numerous supporters among the small shopkeepers. I hope, however, to make friends with some of these through their organisations and trade societies during the passage of the Shop Hours Bill in the Autumn and I am inclined to think that . . . it will be possible to conciliate them'.[20] Who precisely he had in mind is not clear. The tradesmen who opposed his measure were indeed numerous and in layman's language might well have been considered 'small' since there was, and is, a tendency to label all those below department stores' proprietors and controllers of multiples in this way, but they were far removed from the corner shopkeepers who generally approved of the bill but had no political clout. Again, a letter from Thomas Wiles, Liberal M.P. for Islington, a few months later, warned Churchill that, as it stood, with its clauses giving favourable exemptions for Jews and street traders and its potential benefits for the small shopkeeper, the bill was political dynamite. 'At a meeting of the London Liberal members held today, I was desired to convey to you the following resolution which was carried unanimously, "that it is expedient that clause 4 dealing with Sunday closing be omitted from the Shops Bill". I may say that *the feeling among our constituents is very strong* against the special facilities which are being proposed for Jewish traders' (my italics).[21]

It is feasible to suggest that the Liberals put great emphasis on retaining the political allegiance of their traditional supporters. Drafting a measure which seemed to show that their real sympathy lay not with the shopkeeper but with his unionised assistants was a major tactical blunder on the part of well-meaning M.P.s who failed to grasp the complexities of the retail trade or the true motive behind the tradesmen's crusade for early closing. Could it be that, despite the predominantly working-class electorate, politicians endeavoured primarily to act in the interests of the *petite bourgeoisie*: the shopkeepers, small businessmen and property owners? The Liberal government's record in social reform does not seem to imply this; its fiscal policy does. Throughout the nineteenth century the question of taxation had lurked behind almost every political act. It continued to do so, but, despite their efforts, the Liberals failed to solve the pressing problem of inflated local rates and this contributed significantly to the undermining of their political power, locally and nationally. Shopkeepers and other long standing

Liberal supporters were to find a new home in the transformed Conservative party.

## *Tightening the municipal purse-strings*

The rates issue dominated Edwardian local politics and those candidates who promised relief for the ratepayer rather than prestigious or productive municipal improvements or welfare schemes enjoyed most electoral success. What was true of Ashton-under-Lyne held for the rest of the country; 'In municipal politics the rates issue was dominant and elections were a sort of Dutch auction to see which party could run the town more cheaply'.[22] In Leeds alleged municipal extravagance and waste were the key issues in 1907.[23] The London Municipal Society, with its emphasis on the virtues of economy and the dangers of 'Progressive-Socialist wastrels', masterminded a political breakthrough on the London County Council in 1907, turning a Liberal majority of 82–35 in 1904 into a Conservative one of 79–37.[24] An 'Economy Party' swept to power in Cardiff in 1903.[25] Sheffield's leading personalities preached a similar gospel. Herbert Hughes, mayor in 1905, argued that 'the greatest need of Sheffield at that time was rest from heavy expenditure'; his successor in 1911, Albert Hobson, followed in his footsteps with his down-to-earth slogan, 'Tighten Your Belts'.[26] Parsimony and petty-mindedness characterised the policies of Edwardian town halls, the flavour of the popular attitude to local finance being encapsulated in a Birmingham resident's letter to the press; 'One must cut one's coat according to the cloth at one's disposal. My grandfather did not spend five-twelfths of his income for my benefit and I for one strongly object to paying 8s 4d in the pound rates for the benefit of posterity.'[27]

Increasing municipal miserliness was accompanied by a significant change in the social composition of local councils. Gentlemen and large businessmen, who had occupied the most important posts, retired or were ousted by a swarm of professionals, small capitalists and property owners and, above all, shopkeepers. Already a sizeable minority of councils in the nineteenth century, this last group now consolidated its hold over local government; in comparison, the much vaunted and publicised working-class and Labour presence was derisory. In Blackpool throughout the 1900s shopkeepers never held less than 45 per cent of the seats, twice the level of the previous decade. In Macclesfield they comprised 33 per cent of the councillors in 1890, 50 per cent in 1898 and over 50 per cent every subsequent year up to 1914 by which time they were filling the mayoral office too. A similar situation obtained in Oldham, Blackburn and Accrington and no doubt in most English towns.[28] Symbolically, the leader of Cardiff's

'Economy' party after 1903 was a draper; shopkeepers everywhere continued to champion their traditional 'Radical' policy of retrenchment.

This concern over local rates did not imply a parochial outlook on politics. Generally frustrated in their quest the protesters demanded remedial action from Westminster. This, the Liberals, in power after 1906, ignored at their peril, threatening as it did to increase their political opponents' chances of success. After decades of Liberal ascendancy, the Conservative party was making huge gains in local elections by stealing their rallying cry of cheap government. A trickle of seats in the 1880s had turned into a flood tide by 1908, the high-water mark of the ratepayers' rebellion and a critical year in the parliamentary Liberals' strategy.[29] This swing against the Liberals at local level cannot simply be dismissed as an inevitable recurring feature of politics, the rejection of the party in power nationally whatever its political complexion.[30] It was a steady trend which persisted even after the Liberals had been returned to power twice in 1910, the electoral turnout remained high and contests were fiercely fought. Local politics reflected voters' real and material concern over the burning issue of rates. This was no fickle protest vote.

### The Liberals' dilemma

After 1908 the Liberal government stepped up its efforts to pacify these discontented property owners and small businessmen, but it did so with mixed success. The Liberals' dilemma was plainly evident. For the politicians, if not the rank and file, the prospect of increasing central government's responsibility and tax-raising capacity to ease local pressures was alien to all that 'Liberalism' seemed to represent. The Conservative and Labour parties' solutions generally involved further increasing central government's grants-in-aid, the policy recommended by the National Chamber of Trade by 1912. The Liberals, however, decided to attack the problem by overhauling the taxation system, replacing rates with a tax on land values.[31] Their solution would hit the large property owners and rentier class while relieving the hard-pressed shopkeepers and domestic ratepayers; Lloyd George made this perfectly clear in a number of speeches between 1909 and 1913, including the famous Limehouse speech, where he made direct appeals to the trading community.[32] It was not, of course, a new policy; similar ideas were components of the early Victorian Radical philosophy.

Until such time as the land tax could be introduced, the Liberals and Lloyd George in particular, tried to ensure that the burden of taxation was lifted off the shoulders of the middle-class ratepayer and shopkeeper. Within the so-called

102

New Liberalism of the Edwardian era was much that was 'old', which any nineteenth-century Radical or Gladstone himself would have approved of, and the budget of 1909 'pushed further, and a little quicker, the implications of Peel–Gladstone finance'.[33] The 'People's Budget' was very much a middle-class person's budget in line with previous Liberal fiscal policy. It soaked the rich with higher death duties and surtax, and raised the tax on less desirable working-class pleasures of beer and tobacco. Nothing was done to increase the burden on the middling ranks of society.[34] Pressure, too, was taken off the local poor rates with the centrally financed Old Age Pensions in 1908 and the National Insurance schemes of 1911, the latter largely paid for by large employers and the workers themselves. By 1913 the Liberals were even reluctantly resorting to more grants-in-aid as a stop-gap measure.

It has been suggested that Lloyd George's land tax plans, if implemented, would have destroyed his career and the Liberals' political stock in the country. This seems unlikely. It would seem rather that it was the failure of these plans which disillusioned the party's traditional supporters. Despite Lloyd George's and Churchill's efforts, the property-owning middle class, small businessmen and above all the shopkeepers continued to drift into the Conservative ranks where they have remained ever since. With both political parties attuned to their needs, however, and with a strong foothold in local government it is not surprising that the shopkeepers did not consider creating a new political group to present their case. The force behind nineteenth-century Gladstonian Liberalism, shopkeepers have become an important element of the twentieth-century Conservative party which has inherited the Radicals' crusade for cheap government. Indeed, in recent years there is even evidence to suggest that their influence on party policy is increasing still further, while on the economic front (see the Aftermath) they have met the challenge of new competitors with remarkable success.

### Notes to Chapter 7

[1] Whitaker, *Shopworkers*, chapters 2 and 3; Alexander, *Retailing*, pp. 191–2.

[2] For a struggle in one town see Mass Observation, *Browns and Chester*, 1947, pp. 117–19.

[3] Select Committee of the House of Lords on the Early Closing of Shops P.P. 1901, VI, p. 6.

[4] Soldon, 'Liberty and Property Defence League', p. 213.

[5] Return of closing orders made by local authorities under the Shop Hours Act, 1904, P.P. 1909, LXXIX, p. 831.

[6] Deputations received at the Home Office since the introduction of the 1910 Shops Bill, P.P. LXXXIX, pp. 109–39, 254–61; *The Shopkeeper*, 1908–9.

[7] Deputations at the Home Office, pp. 118–19.

[8] *Ibid.*, 119–34; Select Committee on Sunday Closing, 1905, pp. 13, 194–6; Joint Committee on Sunday Trading, 1906, pp. 309–16.

[9]*Parliamentary Debates*, 4th series, 1 May 1908, CLXXXVII, p. 1544.

[10]Letter to Churchill, 19 Feb. 1910, in R. S. Churchill (ed.), *Winston S. Churchill, II, The Young Statesman Companion*, 1966, p. 1140.

[11]Deputations at the Home Office, p. 298.

[12]*Parliamentary Debates*, 5th series, 8 Dec. 1911, XXXII, p. 1776.

[13]Deputations at the Home Office, pp. 87, 110, 165.

[14]*Ibid.*, pp. 88, 288–92.

[15]*Ibid.*, pp. 88, 103, 110, 125, 193, 230, 234, 276.

[16]*Ibid.*, pp. 167, 88, 293.

[17]*The Shop Assistant*, 6 Jan. 1912, p. 8; 20 April 1912, p. 265.

[18]*The Grocer*, 9 Dec. 1911, p. 1581; 13 Jan. 1912, p. 143.

[19]Departmental Committee on the Shops (Early Closing) Act, P.P. 1927, XII, p. 886; Whitaker, *Shopworkers*, pp. 166–8; Holcombe, *Victorian Ladies*, p. 132.

[20]Churchill, *Young Companion*, II, p. 1201.

[21]*Ibid.*, p. 1260.

[22]A. Hall, 'Social control and the working-class challenge in Ashton-under-Lyne, 1886–1914', University of Lancaster unpublished M.A. dissertation, 1975, p. 28.

[23]*The Times*, 2 Nov. 1907.

[24]K. Young, *Local Politics and the Rise of Party*, Leicester, 1975, pp. 93–97, 223.

[25]M. Daunton, *Coal Metropolis: Cardiff, 1870–1914*, Leicester, 1977, p. 207.

[26]Keeble Hawson, *Sheffield*, pp. 325–6.

[27]A. Briggs, *History of Birmingham*, II, 1952, p. 131.

[28]D. A. Porter, 'The changing composition and influence of elites in Macclesfield, 1890–1930'; G. N. Trodd, 'The local elite of Blackburn and the response of the working class to its social control, 1880–1900'; W. H. H. Wale, 'Politics and society in Accrington, 1878–1914'; D. J. Ganley, 'The social and political composition of Oldham town council, 1888–1939'; all these are University of Lancaster unpublished M.A. dissertations, 1974–6.

[29]C. Cook, 'Labour and the downfall of the Liberal Party, 1906–14', in A. Sked and C. Cook (eds.), *Crisis and Controversy*, pp. 38–65.

[30]A view put forward by M. Pugh, *The Making of Modern British Politics, 1867–1939*, Oxford, 1982, pp. 147–8.

[31]Offer, *Property and Politics*, pp. 164–5.

[32]*Ibid.*, p. 390.

[33]Matthew, 'Mid-Victorian budgets', p. 642.

[34]See B. K. Murray, *The People's Budget 1909–10: Lloyd George and Liberal Politics*, Oxford, 1981.

[5] A small corner shop grocer in Lancaster, *c.* 1927, his sign just readable above the door. Clearly a converted house and a representative of the 'dishonourable' branch of the trade so despised and, at one time, feared by wealthier high street proprietors.

[6] A rather larger family-run shop in Tower Hamlets, Dover, 1910 with the proprietor's eldest son in the doorway. A family of twelve, the Medhursts were primarily publicans; father ran the shop during the day, taking over responsibility for the pub from his wife in the evening. One of his sons recalls, 'Father used to say, "They come in my shop for credit and when they get any money they go down the high street"'.

[*7, upper*] S. H. Juckes, ironmonger, Shrewsbury, 1888. This was clearly a business of some standing: Juckes later became Borough Rate Collector. His range of stock is impressive, with a clear rural flavour – note the sickles.

[*8, lower*] J. R. Sedgwick, second-hand dealer, Dover, *c.* 1905. He is about to be evicted as his lease ends, the property to be demolished, and the walls are covered with defiant slogans. Price was negotiable: 'No reasonable offer refused'.

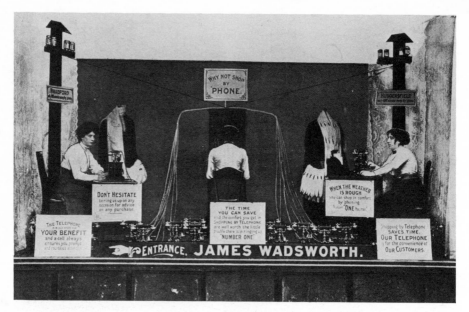

[*9, upper*] This 'exceptionally attractive and forceful' window display by a Halifax draper was highly praised by F. W. Burgess in *The Practical Retail Draper* (*c.* 1912). Wadsworth's trade was reputed to have grown 'by leaps and bounds'.

[*10, lower*] Paraffin was an important domestic fuel. This rural trader's magnificent vehicle was pictured at Hawkhurst, Kent. Note the 5-gallon measure and funnel at the rear and the interesting sideline – Pratt's Motor Spirit.

[*11*] The proud proprietor and his wife at the door of their shop in Shrewsbury, 1888. In addition to selling magazines and periodicals H. E. Studley offered engraving, copperplate and lithographic printing, bookbinding, ruling by machine, and his own patent ledgers, account books and cloth labels.

[12] A novel use for a branded product, Lifebuoy soap. The wearer was probably a collector for the Thames lightermen's union. He could, however, have been a variant of the sandwich-board street walker.

110

[*13, upper*] The flourishing baker's shop of E. Davies and Co. of Shrewsbury also dealt in butter, eggs, provisions and corn. There was clearly an important delivery trade although above the door the conditions of sale stipulate 'All goods sold at the lowest price for cash only'.

[*14, lower*] The new ovens at Marston Brothers' bakery in Ludlow, *c*. 1912. The proprietors advertised themselves as corn and flour dealers, corn and seed merchants, water millers (1895) and wool and manure merchants (1922). Many smaller country millers-cum-bakers suffered in the 1890s as foreign grain and port-based refiners undermined the more profitable side of their business.

[*15, upper*] The County Music Salon, Market Street, Lancaster, opened *c.* 1880 by
John Morland, 'professor of music'. Pianos were increasingly common in working-class
homes by the 1880s as real wages and expectations rose although they were still
expensive. Morland & Ayrton sold nearly new 'specials' from 11 gns to £25 and
craftsmen-built models at 220 gns. The shop's manager later opened his own piano-
tuning establishment.

[*16, lower*] Rather a down-market draper's shop in Shrewsbury probably run by the
wife of its proprietor who probably also operated the Perseverance Implement Depot
further down the street, an ironmongery and agricultural machinery warehouse.

[17] The geographical range of these testimonials is impressive, but they make nonsense of some grocers' claims to produce teas ideally suited to the local water supply. Smith also advertised himself as provision merchant, wholesale and family grocer, coffee roaster, tallow chandler, bacon curer and patent medicine vendor, operating branches in several smaller nearby towns.

113

114

←—[18 and 19] Illustrations from *The Practical Grocer* (1906), 'A smart well stocked interior' and 'A prize window'. Note the chair for customers, modern lighting, decorative plants, range of teas and preponderance of tinned, bottled and packeted foodstuffs.

[20, *upper*] the premises of Robert Marks, Ramsgate, *c*. 1895 described in detail in chapter 9. The display was typical of 'an ordinary day' according to his son Charles who is just visible in the doorway. The small passageway to the left of the shop led to the slaughterhouse.

[21, *lower*] A fine Christmas display by H. G. Surman of Whitstable. Working-class families patronised such butchers for scraps and oddments late on Saturday night.

115

[22] Mrs Bennett and her son Richard outside the family greengrocers in Henry Street, Chatham, c. 1895. Richard, assisted mainly by his young sister Ellen, who describes the shop in detail in chapter 10, was to take over management of the shop before his fourteenth birthday after his mother's death and his father's effective retirement.

[23] The Everndens' saddlers shop in Cranbrook, Kent, c. 1900, with Charles Evernden's grandfather and uncle in the doorway. See chapter 11.

117

[*24, upper*] The village shop at Northbourne, near Deal, *c.* 1909 just before it acquired a post office licence. Despite his shop sign Thomas Bishop was listed in local directories as grocer and tea dealer, indicative of the very broad-based nature of his trade, similar in many respects to the small 'corner' shops in working-class urban areas.

[*25, lower*] A flourishing department store in miniature, Hutchings of Lydd in Romney Marsh, 1910. Note the range of delivery vehicles, the all-male staff, the varieties of uniforms, the impressive window displays and interior lighting and the size of the boot and shoe 'warehouse'. The proprietor was also an insurance agent and tax collector.

# PART III

# *Edwardian shopkeepers at work*

# CHAPTER 8

# 'The passing of the grocer'?

Victorian commentators drew heavily on the draper trade for evidence of retail changes; Edwardians turned to grocery. Substantial independent grocers were seen as the most threatened species, endangered by all the evils of co-operative trading, rapidly expanding multiple giants like Liptons, the Maypole, International Tea Company and Home & Colonial, and small domestic shops selling proprietary goods.[1] Grocery was popularly portrayed as a 'penny in the slot trade' and its practitioners 'salesmen and nothing more'. Leading members of the trade deplored this, bemoaning that 'a respect for and right estimation of the trade and its dignity' was becoming increasingly difficult to find.[2] Entry into their trade, they argued, had been made ridiculously, and dangerously, easy. 'We want', declared *The Grocer* in 1906, partly in jest but not without an element of sincerity, 'an Undesirable Interlopers' Exclusion Act for the grocery and provision trade.'[3] The 'Passing of the Grocer' scare in 1902, initiated by *The Times*, epitomised the current informed view of the 'process of attrition' which was seen to be 'proceeding at such a rate that in many districts he will soon have disappeared'.[4] Booth's London survey arrived at a similar conclusion.[5]

Estimates of various retail organisations' shares of the grocery market do not confirm this view of a rapid and total collapse of the independent grocers, but they do indicate that their share was dropping significantly from a base already well below that found in other trades. Co-ops and multiples took around thirty per cent of the national market by 1914, and this figure was probably exceeded in urban areas of Scotland and the North of England where they were heavily concentrated.[6] It must be remembered, too, that even though the remaining seventy per cent represented a growing volume of trade, this had to be shared with the multitude of small family shops, 'hardly, even the best of them, to be called grocers'.[7] There was, therefore, cause for concern.

The grocers' national organisations and journals, however, refuted suggestions that they were a race doomed to extinction, unwilling or unable to adapt to the new environment. *The Grocer* responded indignantly to *The Times*'s 'journalistic holiday' in 1902. 'The bankruptcy figures quoted are not alarming . . . They also represent, we may be sure, the elimination of the unfit . . . the untrained adventurer or group of tinkers who think they can master its mysteries in a week. A really capable man', the editorial went on to maintain, experienced no difficulties while the grocers' lead in the fight against 'company shops and communistic co-operators' signified evidence of 'vigorous muscular exertion of outraged vitality'.[8] The regular reports of social functions which the journal carried and the potted biographies of eminent 'Grocers of Today' also seem to give the lie to accusations of a failing demoralised profession. Local associations had lively, yet respectable, convivial gatherings and 'soirées' with dancing and singing and – obviously a novel attraction at Preston for the New Year celebrations of 1902 – 'the game of ping-pong' which 'proved a pleasing diversion for those who did not dance'. Maidstone grocers were not so penurious or overburdened with long hours that they were deprived of time for cricket. While those in Manchester vied for trophies amongst themselves at their monthly bowling club, grocers in Blackburn, Preston, Southport and Darwen found time to compete against each other on a league basis. The week-long annual conference of the National Federation of Grocers' Associations, hosted by local groups in turn, was also a grand social occasion. Business was coupled with more pleasurable pursuits: outings to stately homes and beauty spots, uplifting and educational visits to local factories laid on by manufacturers with an eye to increasing their number of outlets, garden parties and, of course, formal balls and mayoral receptions.[9] These were no penny-pinching meetings attended by small frightened shopkeepers. They were gatherings of men holding positions of power and influence in their own localities – councillors, aldermen, mayors, J.P.s – who, by uniting sought to increase their social acquaintances with equals, further the cause of their trade and influence national, as opposed to merely local, politics by lobbying and nurturing allies in Parliament. Far more than the rough and ready practical butcher or the overworked master baker, the established grocer was still a man of wealth and prestige.

Beneath this comfortable and reassuring public image, however, grocers were worried about their ability to survive, at least, not without adopting what some regarded as 'radical' innovations: elaborate window displays, the stocking of some of the numerous proprietary articles, the adoption of tight accounting procedures and possible cash discount policies. Consequently they also strove to discredit and hamper those competitors regarded by some as threats to their prosperity and status. Grocers had no affection for the cash multiples, 'this evil class of shop' which exerted a 'maleficent influence' in the trade, but virulent, openly expressed hostility only began to develop during the immediate pre-war years when real incomes stagnated and sometimes fell marginally.[10] Grocers gave solid support, even leadership, to the anti-co-op cause and their National Federation was the only pure trade association to appear with the Traders' Defence League before the Departmental Committee on Income Tax in 1905 to present the case for the taxation of co-op dividend. Individual members of the trade frequently participated in public debates on 'co-operatism', unsuccessfully and in person at the Oxford Reform Club in 1912, for example, but with more success in some periodicals' and newspapers' popular letter competitions which debated the subject.[11]

Alongside praiseworthy calls for the reduction of fraud and deception — 'unfair competition' of the worst kind — the National Federation supported grocers' attempts to reduce more innocent forms of competition between themselves: agreements to phase out the giving of expensive Christmas boxes to customers, efforts to re-institute radius agreements limiting the number of shops in an area, and, of course, campaigns to reduce, even eliminate, price competition, either nationally through the federation's own Proprietary Articles Committee from 1901 or through various local association's initiatives. Had the public been acquainted with these activities the trade's respectable and honest image would have been seriously tarnished. Customers would not have appreciated the president of the Birkenhead Grocers' Association's enthusiasm for its successful arrangement to raise sugar prices in 1911 which, he assured members, had 'saved the trade hundreds of pounds — money which would otherwise, without reason or thanks, have been given to the public'.[12] In the campaign to obtain legislation to reduce opening hours, waverers, like Henry Cushen the federation's treasurer in the 1890s who favoured a voluntary agreement, were soon overwhelmed by supporters of a legal solution, the organisation calling loudly in 1901 for compulsory early closing. 'If we have a Shops Bill at all it should be a Shops Closing Bill', Councillor A. Goodrich, J.P., representing the Metropolitan Grocers' Association, defiantly told Churchill in 1910. 'Every shop must close . . . There must be no distinction between small shops and large, with assistants and without assistants.'[13]

Despite such 'unfair competition', however, the private grocer was still, as *The Grocer* asserted, able to hold his own in the pre-war years although he was gradually to lose ground over the ensuing decades. Where they emerged, co-ops and multiples undoubtedly deprived him of valuable, regular working-class cash customers and meant that he failed to benefit fully from their increased purchasing power, but multiples with their limited range of products and minimal service, and co-ops with their obvious working-class image, did not endear themselves to the more affluent and expanding middle ranks of society who valued quality and personal service above price. By offering distinctive merchandise, immediate unfailing individual attention, regular deliveries, advice on food preparation, unostentatious access to wines and spirits and, above all, longish credit, the private grocer was able to court these people and build up elusive, but valuable 'goodwill' and loyalty. He flourished most healthily in the growing suburbs of the larger cities and in the high streets of those smaller provincial towns away from the Northern and Midland heavy industrial centres. His premises would be characterised, according to Simmonds, by 'an utter absence of anything vulgar or common'. His assistants possessed all the correct virtues, 'good looking young fellows whose speech and manner bespeak intelligence and education . . . "Quality" is brick and stone, "personality" his cement binding all together'.[14] 'Cutting' was allowed on special lines or to clear slow moving stock, but it was clearly not the rule in such establishments.

Even the fashionable Edwardian grocer was forced to adapt to changing market conditions, however. A judicious blend of old and new, mixed with solid application to business and knowledge of the circumstances and needs of customers was recommended as a 'very fair recipe for success' by trade journals. Consequently, his shop premises, style of business and the range of commodities he stocked were all rather different from the mid-century grocers'. Interior fittings and above all the window area had been transformed and modernised to give more effective display. No longer was he a specialist dealer; he had become, in Rees's words, 'the people's indispensable furnisher of conveniences, necessaries and delicacies whose name is legion indeed'.[15] This conversion was not, it is true, a sudden dramatic one. Even before 1850 there had been indications that the previously distinct trades of cheesemonger, chandler, provision dealer and Italian warehouseman were being consolidated under the umbrella title of 'grocer' but by the 1900s the grocer was inundated with a multitude of pre-processed, branded and packaged goods almost unknown half a century earlier.[16] Tea, for example, once the backbone of the high-class grocer's trade, was already being packeted and branded for retail distribution by Horniman & Cassell in the 1850s. Following the abolition of duties and intensive brand advertising it was to become the staple drink of all sections of society. By 1900, although some grocers persisted in blending their own teas and were encouraged to do so by anxious wholesalers playing on the 'battle with the multiples' in their advertisements, even the grocer and tea dealer who considered himself 'master of his trade' and 'would almost have thought himself insulted if advised to buy blended teas as late as the last quarter of the nineteenth century' sold such teas and packeted ones in addition to his own.[17]

What was true of tea held good for other areas of the trade. By 1900 there were over 360 different types of biscuit on the market baked by nationally known firms like Carr, Huntley & Palmer, Peek Frean, Macfarlane Laing and McVitie. There were jams from Keiller, Hartley, and Crosse & Blackwell, pickles from Lazenby's, W. H. Lever's 'Sunlight Soap' and Hudson's, Bovril which promised '100% profit' on its sales, Van den Bergh's margarine, Cadbury's cocoa essence . . . the list, if not endless, is exceptionally long. Such goods, almost entirely absent in mid-century, were to be found in all grocers' shops, large or small, alongside more traditional loose products.

The speed and extent of the transition in the trade, however, varied regionally and between different classes of shops. Many fashionable shops which still bore the hallmarks of the old style of trade remained before 1914 and, what is rarely appreciated, some of these developed into their own multiple chains. T. D. Smith, the family grocer in Lancaster operated ten such shops. The Ludlow-based business of Gaius Smith and Co. had branches in various border towns by 1909: Clun, Craven Arms, Bishops Castle, Much Wenlock, and Church Stretton. By 1922 he also had bases in Presteigne and Tenbury Wells. W. E. Coatman and Sons of Croydon also ran ten shops, with the solitary exception of a Tonbridge branch all of them in Surrey and four in Croydon itself. These were not, in any way, scaled-down replicas of giants like Maypole and Lipton which offered a restricted range of products and employed sales techniques which contrasted sharply with those depicted below: no credit, no delivery, stark premises, rock-bottom prices. They clearly posed no real threat to such high-class establishments. All of the Coatman's branches were licensed to deal in beer, wines and spirits and catered for the cosmopolitan and expensive tastes of the wealthier class of customer. To all intents and purposes the managers of their shops, unlike those in the large, centrally-run multiples, fulfilled many of the roles of individual proprietors. Although decisions concerning the purchase of major items of equipment and some accounts were dealt with from Croydon and he was restricted in drawing money from the bank on the firm's behalf, Mr Headey, the manager of the Tonbridge branch, which is described in detail in the following interview, had full control over hiring, paying and dismissing staff, ordering and pricing stock and supervising the day-to-day affairs of the business.

The art and mysteries of the trade, its traditional practices, skilled basis and high profit margins which so many grocers sought to preserve were to be found primarily in shops like this. The staff, with the exception of the cashier-cum-bookkeeper, were all skilled men. Their pay and conditions were good and, since

124

all were local, none slept on the premises except the manager himself who enjoyed spacious family accommodation above the shop. They conformed to the ideal laid out by Simmonds in *The Practical Retail Grocer*: uniformed, trained, well versed in shop management, polite but effective salesmen and culinary advisers. Although adept at handling customers these grocers were far from being 'mere salesmen'. They possessed a thorough knowledge of the stock they dealt in. Blending tea (still a major profit spinner), grinding and roasting coffee, cleaning, sorting and stoning dried fruits, bottling beers, maturing cheeses, ripening bananas, smoking bacon and patting butter – a job in which even high-class grocers it seems could not resist some underhand practices – all these were still carried on in the premises.

Concessions to progress had not been allowed to vulgarise the business or erode profit margins. The stock was not confined to luxury goods, although these, including fresh foreign fruits in season, were still prominent. It now included a wide range of household necessities and a provisions trade in cheese and preserved meats. The window display was given special prominence and modern lighting. Proprietary goods were obviously stocked and even some special offers were promoted. Innovation, however, had its limits. Price cutting was restricted to special purchases and did not involve a narrowing of profit margins. Direct competition with other traders was restricted by unwritten agreements with travellers to distribute goods and discounts unevenly, a practice rarely documented or considered by outside observers of retail competition. Indeed, judging by the efforts made by manufacturers and suppliers to obtain orders from the shopkeeper, it seems that they, rather than the retailer, bore the brunt of mounting competition. The willingness of some of them to consider price-fixing agreements was understandable.

The description which follows gives a clear picture of shop routine and some of the problems involved in it. Opening hours, although not so long as shops relying heavily on working-class trade, were still long, and Saturday evening, which witnessed a distinct shift in the pattern of trade and class of customer, was still important. The shop assistants' union's growing objections to early closing as a way of reducing hours of labour were well founded since much work here was done after the doors had been closed to customers. Credit loomed large especially for the institutional and wealthy customers who also received privileged treatment when they finally deigned to pay. Deliveries required a substantial fleet of vehicles and a squad of horses which in turn created their own difficulties and expenses: a full-time horseman to care for them, early morning and Sunday work, unwanted vermin, and not inconsiderable waste products. The ingenuity with which this last problem was tackled and the way food waste in the shop was minimised is worthy of note since we have a rare glimpse of a primitive barter economy surviving. The dilemma of what to do with large Saturday takings over the weekend was also overcome by a novel, if rather unsatisfactory expedient.

Of all the traders examined here, Mr Headey undoubtedly enjoyed the most comfortable lifestyle. There were many perks of the job, manufacturers' free samples and seasonal gifts being gratefully received. The family 'lived well', supplementing their diet with 'oddments' from the shop's richly varied stock. Significantly, too, the only references in these chapters to regular days off or annual holidays are to be found here, the manager possibly being better off in this respect than those individual proprietors who were dedicated to, and therefore more tied to, their shops. In common with other traders, however, the family led a relatively quiet, ordered private life, mixing sparingly and then only with relations or others from a trade background, not, it appears, with customers who were usually of a different social class anyway but who, if approached, might subsequently have expected, or been expected by others, to receive preferential treatment.

Harry Headey, the manager's son, was still only a boy of seven when war was declared but, because as he commented, 'I wasn't a kiddie to go out a lot. I was always in the shop and the chaps used to make a fuss of me', he was in a position to observe in detail how the business was run. His vivid memories of life in and around this superior establishment provide a splendid complement to Robert Roberts's equally rich collections of growing up at this same period in a corner shop in a poor working-class quarter of Salford.[18] Together they provide a forceful reminder of the huge range of shopkeepers who could, and did, trade under the sign 'grocer'. The two were indeed worlds apart.

------

### 66 A fashionable grocer

This shop was considered to be the most high-class grocer's in town. Tonbridge, more so then than it is now, was more or less cut in half by the Medway, both socially and business-like. When you got down the bottom end of town you got the Home and Colonial, International, Pearks and all the 'company shops' as they used to be called. They used to have all the cheap and cheerful stuff down there, dried peas and lentils, and they used to fill their damn' windows with *that*! The north end in those days was a *very* different class; the best classes of business were all this side of the river.

We used to open at eight o'clock in the mornings and most nights we shut about seven o'clock—seven thirty, but Friday it was about eight, and Saturday nights we used to shut at ten o'clock. Christmas Eve would be the latest, about eleven o'clock. When they shut the door, that was when the real work started. Every day there was a different job when the shop was shut filling the fixtures. One night would be tea perhaps and another flour and so on, and all this was packed on the counter in bags or cups by hand after the shop had shut. Butter pats had to be all washed, the butter blocks scrubbed, the shop swept out and provision counter scrubbed, tops and shelves too. They were all marble in those days. Then the bacon was put back, muslin hung down over it. There was probably the best part of another hour before they went home but nobody worried about it. It was an accepted part of the job and when the shop was shut the old man usually used to bring up three or four bottles of beer out of the cellar, lumps of cheese and that sort of thing.

Our main customers were connected with Tonbridge School in a big way, both the school and the masters. Dad, being the manager, always went for the best orders in the pony and trap and he used to wear top hat and morning coat. He'd go round to the big houses and districts surrounding and sometimes he was in some of these places more or less all day. I know of one big house where he went round with the housekeeper. They used to start in the kitchen or the butler's pantry and they generally finished up with the gardner or the coachman. He'd take his pencil out from over his ear and he'd tap all these drums they'd got on the shelves – rice, tapioca, semolina. 'That one's down a bit.' Seven pounds of that. 'Yes, that one's down. Better have fourteen of that.' That was how it was done. It wasn't a case of saying well, I'll have a pound to try it. The same with all the rest, the old gardener or coachman. They used to sell gallons of Bluebell and Brasso for cleaning harnesses. He'd say, 'How's the Bluebell this week?' 'Oh, I've only two tins up there. Better have a dozen.' He wasn't spending his own money anyway.

In most cases it was the housekeeper who did the buying but it was nearly always the lady who paid the accounts. What went on in the kitchens and servants' hall didn't worry her. If the cook wanted something, well, let the cook have it. Although you went for the orders, when they paid the accounts they had the carriage out and came round to all the tradesmen at once – butcher, baker, grocer – and made a day of it. That was all you really saw of the lady when she came to pay up. If she was a very good client she was generally invited into the office and out would come the sherry or port or whisky as the case may be. Quite a ceremony it was paying the accounts. Some of them were pretty long winded, mind you, but then that type of trade always was and the very fact that they were long winded meant that they always had to pay the best prices. You didn't lose in

127

the long run. Some of the better ones paid by cheque but the majority of them would be in gold and when I was quite a child I used to go into the office at night and play with a bowl of sovereigns.

At that time grocery was a very different thing from today's supermarket. Every grocer was apprenticed for seven years and every assistant that was taken on was put through a rigorous test. All the stuff was packed on the premises, nothing, or practically nothing, came in packeted, so if a man applied for a job my father used to give him a pound of tea to wrap, a pound of sugar and a cup to turn. These paper cups were folded out of blue graph paper and were used for practically everything in the trade – dried fruit, candied peel, sugar – practically everything except biscuits and flour which were kept in bags. They were comparatively simple to turn but the skill was to turn several hundred uniform because empty they had to fit into each other in a continual chain so that the chap weighing could pull one out and fill it. If a man passed that he was taken on. If he couldn't, then he wasn't a grocer.

I'd like to stress the point that all shops of any size or standing at all had their own brands of tea for which they were famous in the district. Everybody blended it. My father had wrappers printed, worded to the effect that this tea is specially selected and scientifically blended to meet the requirements of the water of the district. In other words, if you took it twenty miles away it may have had no flavour at all. You'd got as many as eight or nine chests of tea, all from different parts, with which you blended your tea and people used to come from miles around for a quarter of your 1s 6d tea or whatever. They couldn't get it anywhere else. Of course, that's where you made the money. You knew what the tea cost and you could fiddle about with it and sell a pound for three or four bob, probably half of which was profit, but the customers had what they liked because your tea was an individual tea. We used also to roast all our own coffee.

All our own bacon was smoked in this establishment. It came in green, mostly Harris's Wiltshire or Denny's Irish, and the sides were hung in the smoke chamber, oak sawdust and old rags were piled inside on the floor and set light to. Why they particularly had to have oak I don't know but that was all they ever used. Deal sawdust for the shop floor, oak sawdust to smoke the bacon. This smoked – and did it smoke! There would be trouble today with the clean air. It went on for about four days, perhaps a bit longer, after which the smoke chamber was opened up and the bacon lifted up on hooks and put in the cellar where it was left till it was cut up. There were times when some of the better customers in the district would bring my father a Scotch salmon to smoke, which my father did, usually getting a bit for his troubles.

We used to clean all our fruit. There used to be sacks of Greek currants and it was nothing to find quite a lot of stones and all sorts of offal in these when they came in, so they went through this currant cleaning machine. Of course, it was turned by hand, there were no power-driven things in the shop in those days. When customers bought raisins the assistants always asked if they would like them stoned. If so, the assistant would run upstairs to the raisin stoning machine in the warehouse and put them through it bringing them all back ready to put in a pudding or cake. These, of course, were stoned after they were weighed. There again, nothing was wasted. These stones were sent to a farmer. He used to put them in cider to help ferment it and give it its own peculiar taste. In due course he would bring us two or four gallons. Knock your head off!

My father would go to the dairy show at the Agricultural Hall, Islington and he used to buy cheeses. These were duly delivered and were kept in the cellar on slate slabs for years in some cases, at any rate for twelve months. He had what they called a cheese iron which was very similar to a corkscrew which he pushed into the cheese, gave a turn and pulled out a wedge of cheese which he tasted. If he thought that the cheese was ready for sale he'd mark it and it would be brought up in the shop. If he didn't think it was mature enough it would stop where it was.

In those days we only had oranges roughly from November up to about April, the Spanish orange season; then people forgot about oranges until the next November. We used to have them twenty a shilling and I have known small ones forty a shilling! My father went up to the City, not Covent Garden, he used to go to the City to the importers, Travers & Sons, to buy these oranges. They were duly delivered to the goods station in a truck and it was one of the highlights of the year when the van brought them up from the station. Barrels of grapes, Spanish grapes, used to come in cork dust and a window display was made of all these things and of course everybody bought. The same thing applied to other fruits, they were all seasonal. There were Canary bananas only at certain times of the year. They used to come in green and we had a banana ripening room where we used to hang them. It was a wooden panelled room, matchboarded, and there were hooks in the ceiling, big hooks because some of these bunches weighed the best part of a hundredweight. Around the walls were gas pipes with every so far a fish-tail burner, that is, a burner with a slit in the top and made like a fan. They were about every foot or so. You used to light these gases and shut the door and there was a little peephole which you could slide a bit back and have a look. If they were ripening a bit too fast you turned some of the gases out, but there was no thermostat or anything of that sort so it was a skilled job. My old man used to say anybody can cook them, in other words the inside of them would still be as hard as a brick, you could snap them like a carrot. You had to regulate your heat so that you ripened them from the inside out if you understand what I mean.

Bananas weren't really a luxury so much as far as the price was concerned but they were for the simple reason that you could only get them at specified times. Trade would be much more healthy then because they didn't get any more bananas for months so when they saw them about, they bought.

We always used to grind our own pepper. People would buy peppercorns. 'Would you like them ground, madam?' 'Yes please.' Upstairs to the pepper grinding mill. Ground pepper. Hearthstones we got by the truckload for cleaning hearths and doorsteps and silversand which was used where they would use Vim or that kind of thing today. There were no tins or packets of detergents; soda was all wrapped, salt was all wrapped. Salt blocks came in at the station and we had a horse and van which would perhaps take all day to clear a truck full. The blocks were about two feet long and about nine inches square at one end tapering to about seven inches at the narrow end. As a boy one of my jobs was to saw these into penny and twopenny pieces, and they were then usually wrapped in newspaper. The salt dust which accumulated was saved and sold to the baker to use in the bread. The very roughest of it, in other words that which was on the floor, was swept up and sold to the bigger houses for gardens, mainly to use on the asparagus beds. Nothing was ever lost or wasted.

We also sold wines, spirits and beers. All the beer and some of the wine, namely port and sherry, was also bottled on the premises. There was a very amusing incident when an old-colonel-type man brought a bottle of whisky back which he said had been watered. So, my father tasted it and he said yes, it had been watered. So the old colonel said 'Well, what do you mean by selling me whisky which has been watered?' and so on. 'Well,' my father said, 'I didn't water it. If I had I should have known how to do it properly. Your butler apparently watered it and didn't know how to do it. If you want it to be undetected except for being weaker you must use boiled water, not tap water.' I daresay the butler or somebody got the push.

Of course, although all this kind of thing meant work, all of it was done at a much steadier pace than these days and my father would maintain that a good provision hand paid his own wages. You see, my father boasted that he could knock four pounds of water into a hundredweight of butter when it was patted up into quarter and half pounds. The butter pats were dipped into a bucket of water. Well, butter wasn't cheap so the man paid his own wages!

In those days nobody poached each other's trade. A baker was a baker, a grocer was a grocer. Bread, for example, you wouldn't think of selling in a grocer's shop. The only time we ever had any cake too was Christmas when we used to sell Huntley & Palmer's, Peek Frean's and those people's, but in the year we didn't do anything with that kind of stuff. We sold biscuits of course. They were in tins and were all weighed out for the customer as required. As the shop kept open till about ten o'clock on Saturday night and there were no night safes at banks my father used to put the day's takings in a biscuit tin for safe keeping. Along the front of the counters there were biscuit tins three or four high and the old man used to pull one out, put the doings in and put it back again. By the time Monday morning came he would be chasing all over the place knocking each tin to see which one had got the money! Of course, he wasn't worried with pound notes, it was all gold sovereigns.

It sounds rather peculiar in these days of high prices, but being a very high-class establishment, one of the main problems was getting rid of the poorer cuts of bacon. Saturday nights, after tea, my father would put trestles in front of the shop stacked up with perhaps twenty or even as many as fifty cheap forehocks or bacon flanks, the belly part of the side. That wasn't a cut that we could sell to our regular customers so it was brought out on Saturday night for the common herd! Pick them out where you like. They came in every Saturday night from the villages round about, places like Hadlow, and they used to push old push chairs and that kind of thing to carry their shopping in. You saw these faces more or less week after week and you'd generally got something for them. Broken biscuits were another thing. You never sold a broken biscuit except when you had a tin of them which sold for a few coppers a pound. As a matter of fact, schoolkids used to come in very often for a ha'porth and they'd get a tidy handful. In the summer, too, fresh butter would soon go rank and people came up to buy this. They bought it as rank butter and used to use it for making cakes and things like that.

My father used to lay on special lines. Say spring cleaning time, he'd have carbolic soap, yellow soap, dishcloths, floorcloths, mops from travellers who used to come round. They'd talk it over and he would take an order for so many gross – they generally talked in grosses not dozens. Well, that man would give his assurance, and you could rely on it, that he wouldn't sell that commodity to anywhere else within striking distance of you. When the stuff duly arrived you had a special display and low prices and there was no fear of another shop doing the same because that traveller wouldn't break his faith. Another thing dad went in for was special displays of jam. At the end of the season before the new fruit arrived, all the jam factories and manufacturers cleared their warehouses of last season's stock and they did it at a very reasonable reduced price. Dad used to get hold of their representative and tell him he wanted a special jam week. In due course he would have a window full of cheap jams. Nobody else had got them so it wasn't a case of competing directly with the bloke down the street because although he might have a special line in something it wouldn't be what you'd got. If any customer came in the shop for something, well, that was the salesman's

131

chance. Every other blimmin' customer had the stuff!

As long as I live I will never accept this supermarket idea of people going round and buying on impulse. They might to a certain extent but my father always adopted the attitude that a good assistant *sold* the customer stuff. The lady would come in: 'Good morning. I have just the thing for you this morning – fresh arrival of what-have-you.' Perhaps she'd only come in for a few items but when she went out you'd got an order book as long as your arm. Very often they would come in and say, 'I'd like your advice. I'm giving a dinner party on Friday. What would you suggest?' That left the door wide open! We'd got glass tongues in similar looking things to the Pyrex dishes you see today, jars of prawns and capers, stuffed olives and I don't know what. By the time the old man had done with them he'd sold them quids' worth of stuff. I'm sure that came out far better than this 'grab what you see' sort of thing.

There was also what you *never* see today in a shop, a grocer's shop or any other, and that was chairs. You always offered the lady a chair and if she'd got a dog you gave the dog a biscuit. Then you started the treatment! You sold the stuff *you* wanted to get rid of, what you were making the best halfpenny out of. The old man might say to the men, 'We've got this to sell. There's a penny a tin for every one you sell.' These blokes would push the stuff and they'd sell it. Mind you, you were responsible for the stuff you sold, both the quality of it and the weight and the country of origin. If they asked for a Greek sultana and you gave them an Australian you were asking for trouble. You couldn't give them any nationality because they would know where it came from in those days. If the shop was busy, too, everybody was called in to help. The old man would call upstairs to the warehouseman, 'George! Get down here in the shop. We're busy.' He'd put a white apron on and serve, it wasn't a case of 'that ain't my job'.

If a man was a real grocer he knew everything from A to Z. He wasn't classed as a grocer unless he did. When the men had been trained they knew everything there was to know about the trade and could tell any customer whatever they wanted to know. In the case of stuff to be cooked they could tell them how to cook it. They could tell them what sauces to use with various things and, of course, where you had a shop like we did with a licence, they could advise on wines to go with a meal. The staff, if they were on the grocery counter, had a white apron with a grey alpaca jacket. If they were on the provision counter they had a white apron, a grocer's apron. That was the recognised sort of uniform.

We had a staff of about twelve. They were all men. A girl or woman in the shop was unheard of. It just didn't go at all except that we did have one girl in the office, Miss Owen, but that was the only female there was and I don't think that after she went she was replaced by another woman. The old man had never worked with girls and he didn't reckon much of it when we went to Reading in 1917 to manage a big shop there. That'd got a staff of twenty-two and about twenty of them were girls. He hadn't been there long and there was a hell of a row. A woman had come in wanting some arrowroot, ground arrowroot for a baby. Well, this girl, instead of admitting she didn't know what it was, or making sure what it was, she thought she knew and gave this woman powdered borax. She went home and gave this poor little devil a dose of powered borax! It was a wonder it never killed it. She came back and there was a hell of a to-do. The old man went off the deep end and this girl started howling. They had to provide a special rest room in those days for girls and she went off up there howling and about two minutes later all the rest of them had gone up to comfort her. There he was left with a damn' great shop and nobody in it. So he sacked the lot. He went round then and got a more cosmopolitan collection of old joshers than you'd ever find. There was a fellow with a club foot. He used to bomp-bomp, bomp-bomp up and down the shop and another bloke he got had got out of the army on the grounds of his religion. A more mixed motley crew you'd never find but he never had another girl. He said it was no business having them in a grocer's shop.

Of course the governor wasn't treated like the governor is today. Everybody spoke to everybody else and they were all friendly. Chaps worked for dad all the time I can remember. The only trouble I do remember was the old man giving one of the blokes the sack for pinching. This chap's fiancée came up and, cor blimey, what she wasn't going to do him! Put a curse on him and his whole family for ever more. All over a few bottles of beer she said. The old man didn't know anything about the beer. He gave him the sack for pinching fruit! But he never prosecuted, it wasn't worth the publicity. He'd just give them the push and that was it because in those days you couldn't get a job anywhere without a reference so it would be no good a chap like that going for a job locally. As soon as they applied for a reference the old man would have said, 'Dismissed for dishonesty' and that would have been the end of it.

The shop didn't shut during the day. The staff had a dinner hour but some used to go twelve to one, some one to two so they never shut. There were no accepted breaks though as such. If the shop was busy, well, they didn't get one and that was that. If my father had got special lines on he had them from Wednesday to Wednesday and he used to dress the window that afternoon, generally one of the chaps fetching and carrying. The provision window, though, had to be changed every day, all the sides of bacon, about ten, bladders of lard and all the rest of the stuff. Incidentally, I think it's pretty safe to say that we were the first shop in Tonbridge to be lit with electric light. We were definitely the first in the north end of town. We had three big arc lamps out at the front which used to light the blimmin' street up, drowning the poor old town's gas lights.

It's quite a job to convince people these days, but travellers used to come into the district and stop perhaps a week, several days at any rate. It wasn't a case of getting back in the car and home that night. They used to hire a cab and trot round their customers. There were no parking problems of course so the old cab would pull up out the front and in the back of it, and on top, he'd have all his cases of samples. The old cabbie brought them in and displayed them all out in the shop, and, especially when the bloke came round about Easter time with all the samples of crackers and things for the following Christmas, you'd have boxes all over the place. You'd get a card — 'So-and-so's representative hopes to call on you on Thursday 13th at approximately two o'clock', and he'd stick to it, more or less within a very short space of time. If he wasn't on his toes then it was pretty obvious that the firm wasn't either. My father was very funny like that. 'If a man can't come for the order on time', he said, 'how the devil do you expect to get the goods on time?' That was his attitude. You knew these reps. They were a distinct type. The ordinary more or less common or garden rep, he just had a grey suit and bowler hat and in winter an overcoat which mostly supported a fur collar according to his status. If he was a head salesman he would have a thick collar. Some of the old high-class merchants, they used to have morning coats and top hat. It all depended on the type of trade they were in.

In dad's position, we were very fortunate. He had a lot of stuff given him by these various travellers to try so that he could personally recommend it. And it wasn't confined to the manager. The provision hands would say if they hadn't got a sample how could they recommend it? So they'd have a sample too. The same thing applied to grocery, biscuits in particular. If they brought out a new assortment or a new variety of biscuits there was a miniature tin, exactly like a biscuit tin only smaller, which was to be left for the staff. I suppose they'd be three or four pounds. Dad used to hand them round and the staff had some. All the travellers on most of their visits gave you something, and the stuff that was given away by these different firms was really remarkable. I know I had a watch when I was at school I was very proud of. It had 'Reckitt's Blue' written right across the face. We got blotters, one every year I believe came from Crawford's the biscuit people. It was leather, no plastic stuff in those days. Of course, you had diaries of all descriptions and then at Christmas they really went to town. You'd get cases of wines and spirits, York hams all 'with compliments'. A lot of that died out with the First War. That was just the chance to drop all these things.

Weights and measures inspectors: they were very frequent. They used to take packets of things off the shelves and weigh them because there was an ideal chance, if you wanted, to fiddle the weights when you weighed everything yourself. It wasn't like a branded product which came in from the factory. If that was wrong that's their worry, not yours. Then there was the sanitary inspector who used to go round the stables. He was more concerned with flies and things like that in the summer. If you had mice or rats you wouldn't half be in trouble. You had to be very careful because the stuff wasn't tinned or packeted but there were always four or five cats on the staff so we got none of that trouble. Another thing my father had – I don't know if it was peculiar to himself or not – was a hedgehog. He said if you'd got a hedgehog in the stables you'd never get rats. I most certainly never saw any. If, as was generally the case with hedgehogs, they got trod on, he used to get round some of his farmer friends and it wasn't long before he got another one.

Our stables, cart sheds, beer bottling cellars, the salt store where we used to store blocks of salt, hearthstone, silversand, the banana ripening room and the coffee roaster were all on the opposite side of the road to the shop. Only the more genteel parts of the job, the pepper grinder and things like that, were in the warehouse behind the shop.

We had horses right up until Dad left here in 1917, five horses. They were very rarely all out at once because you wouldn't be able to work one every day – *they'd* have to have some days off even if you didn't! They were generally sent down from our head place at Croydon. There were two brothers and the father, Mr Coatman, and one or other used to come down every week or so as to look round things in general and he'd say whether we needed another horse or not. Dad was very fond of his horses. Perhaps old Mr Bromley, the stableman, had got his relations coming for Sunday tea. He'd say, 'I was wondering, governor, if you'd be able to feed the horses Sunday night?' My father was a pretty easy-going man and on Sunday he wouldn't go anywhere if it was a case of not feeding the horses.

Horses were a lot of work. They had to be fed at six o'clock in the morning and they were allowed about an hour to have their breakfast. Then they used to groom them and clean them up. By that time it was time to harness them in the carts for the day's work. In the winter there was the added job of taking them to the blacksmith to get them 'roughed' as they called it. They used to put in nails, spikey nails, in the shoes which gripped the icy roads. They wouldn't dig into a concrete road – not unless the horse was about fifty ton like! – but you were dealing with gravel roads so the consequence was that the spikes dug in. My father used to have horse-shoes made with two holes threaded, however, and you could buy from the blacksmiths nuts which were the same kind of things as the nails only a bit more elaborate. If you'd got a frosty day, or it was frosty coming home in the evening, you just stopped the horse, took the nuts out of your pocket and screwed them in these already threaded holes. The problem was keeping the muck out of the holes! You'd find there was God knows what banged in over the days, and all you'd got was a cart lamp which was paraffin with a wick or a candle, so if it happened to be dark it would take God knows how long clearing the blessed hole out.

The oat shucks which came as packing in big barrels of lard for the shop – bladders of lard – were used in the stable to help with the bedding and a farmer used to send a chap in with a load of hay, waggon piled right up high, just low enough to go under the archway into our yard. He used to load back with manure from our dung pits. I don't know if there was any money transacted or not, but I should imagine it was more of a swap than anything since dung was a valuable commodity especially for hop farmers. The same farmer used to have the raisin stones to make his cider.

We had two or three handcarts that went round the town and three vans. These were polished and had yellow wheels with black lining on the spokes and the name on the side done with gold letters in gold leaf. One in particular went round all the outlying districts and used to take all day, getting home perhaps eight or nine o'clock at night. Two of the vans would be covered. They had ash hoops which you tied a sheet over like a covered waggon. The other was more of a waggonette type but instead of having seats in it, it was open. If it rained you got jolly wet and that's all there was to it although you had a sheet to throw over the groceries. In many cases on the rounds you had empties to pick up too. Beer bottles, jam jars, things like that. Jam jars were mostly returnable then, especially the big ones, the seven-pound jars. If a customer didn't send them back he was jolly soon told that these jars were on loan! Buying the jam didn't buy the jars.

Father was paid commission on the profits he made. He had £2 a week and his house plus his bonus or commission which he got quarterly. I don't know exactly how much it was but it was always satisfactory because I know my mother had a new dress or a new hat and I probably had a new coat when he got it. A full-blown counter assistant, he'd be getting about 25s a week, the head provision man had £2 and, as I said before, father said he paid his own wages. The shopmen didn't have a guaranteed holiday but I think Dad gave them several days off. Tonbridge cricket week was the festival of the year round here and he'd always let them have a day down the cricket or perhaps let them go after dinner. There was never any case of stopping pay. The same thing applied to trade exhibitions. I don't mean national exhibitions because that wasn't so simple because of the transport problems, but a biggish firm would hire a room, such as the Market Room at the Rose and Crown, and they would have a display perhaps for a couple of days, a week, perhaps even longer. They'd invite all the local shopkeepers and there would be free drinks, sherry, sandwiches and what have you. With a bit of luck they took a sizeable order. Dad often used to say to the chaps, 'D you want to do down and look for a couple of hours?' It kept them interested in the job and they knew what was then.

Part of Dad's agreement was a week's holiday every year and right up to the First War we went away every year. An aunt had to stay at our place to look after the house because Dad couldn't leave the place unattended because it was licensed and it could never be left empty. The aunt didn't have to do anything with the shop but she was on the premises to meet the requirements of the law. We'd go to Margate, Eastbourne or Hastings where they used to go to the house where they had had their honeymoon. Most Christmases we went to my grandmother's at Thornton Heath and Dad used to hurry up and rush around to get the shop shut in time to catch the train from the station to East Croydon at half past ten or so. We didn't get to Gran's house until about one in the morning.

We lived well. Very well. A very good plain living. One of my father's favourite sayings was that he'd sooner pay a butcher's bill than a doctor's bill. We could have as much meat as we wanted and, of course, we had quite a lot of bacon, tongue and that sort of stuff from the shop. Dad was on the premises so he had his dinner at midday not like a working chap out all day. They might have had to cook at night, but to us, to have a late meal you had to be in high society in those days. We had tea which was bread, butter, jam, cake and so on and then supper which was when the bread and cheese and onions came out. Dad used to bring up all the oddments of cheese off the block after the shop was shut because people would never have dreamed of buying those and sometimes we'd have Welsh rarebit for supper. And we had a general girl, a local girl who used to go home in the evening. She had her meals with us too but after she'd done the washing up at tea time she went home in the region of six o'clock.

The tradesmen in those days would probably be rated as 'middle class', just a notch lower than doctors, dentists and lawyers. They were the professional class and we weren't in quite the same social standing as them or the vet — the vet, of course, was a very important person. We didn't mix with them, only from the business angle, but my father was a bell ringer, master of the bells, so he was automatically invited to all the vicarage garden parties and receptions at high-class weddings. We were on the 'ground floor' so to speak. There were the 'favoured few' which we were fortunate enough to be on the fringe of. We weren't in it but a lot of it rubbed off on us.

My father was always a Conservative. The whole family was. Trade in those days demanded a lot of tact and nearly all the moneyed people in the area were Conservative, so therefore, it paid you to run with them. You might not necessarily always have agreed but if you gave any inclination whatever, or if you were likely to vote for the other side, well, that was one customer gone for a burton. You knew which side your bread was buttered. But I don't think he did it just to get custom, I think those were his ideas in general anyway.

Other than bell-ringing practices I don't think father went out much unless it was anything to do with the shop. He was certainly never a man to go pub crawling, there was no need to, he'd got it on the premises! He never associated with people, not in that sense. Mother, too, used to have one or two friends to Sunday tea but there was none of this coming in for a cup of tea sort of business in the middle of the morning. Mother used to say you never want to have neighbours in your house. You could be neighbourly to them but keep them outside. So it was a formal invitation to tea on Sunday and they turned up in their best bib and tucker. All the best china was on the table and the best silver. About nine o'clock they gracefully said goodbye and in about a fortnight's time you had a return invitation. If you didn't, they didn't get another one. As far as I was concerned it was Sunday School in the morning, Sunday School in the afternoon, so taking that out of it there wasn't much left. Sundays were more or less taken care of. My Dad would sometimes go over to the walled garden we had at the back of the stables on Sunday. He used to go over and potter about and Mum used to go picking raspberries. They were contented with that sort of existence. They didn't consider themselves hard done by. That's how life went on. Whether it was better then than it is now is a matter of opinion but it was certainly far more peaceful.

### Notes to Chapter 8

[1] The model of retail change outlined in Chapter 2 is especially relevant to the grocery trade.
[2] Rees, *Grocery Trade*, p. 348.
[3] *The Grocer*, 17 Feb. 1906, p. 445.
[4] *The Times*, 18 August 1902.
[5] Booth, *Life and Labour*, VII, p. 220.
[6] Jefferys, *Retail Trading*, p. 163.
[7] Simmonds, *Practical Grocer*, I, p. 28.
[8] *The Grocer*, 23 August 1902, p. 425.
[9] *The Grocer*, 11 Jan. 1902, p. 91; 16 August 1902, p. 378; 28 July 1906, p. 242; for annual conference reports see the supplement to the journal published each July.
[10] *The Grocer*, 30 April 1892, p. 904; 13 Jan. 1912, p. 139; Jefferys, *Retail Trading*, p. 139 for the multiples' expansion.
[11] Departmental Committee on Income Tax, pp. 403–9; *The Grocer*, 17 Feb. 1912, p. 472; 20 April 1912, p. 1129.
[12] *The Grocer*, 20 April 1912, p. 1112; Macrosty, *Trust Movement*, pp. 256–64.
[13] Deputations at the Home Office, p. 115.

[14]Simmonds, *Practical Grocer*, I, p. 32.
[15]Rees, *Grocery Trade*, p. 291.
[16]Blackman, 'Grocery trade'; Alexander, *Retailing*, pp. 110–21.
[17]Simmonds, *Practical Grocer*, IV, p. 44.
[18]Roberts, *Classic Slum; Ragged Schooling.*

# CHAPTER 9

# *Butchers*

Men who bought on the hoof, killing and dressing their own meat, had dominated the Victorian butchery trade. Apart from this we know surprisingly little about their activities. Many had city market stalls, but in smaller towns where markets were irregular and even in cities like Liverpool, they operated from fixed shop premises too.[1] Market stalls were probably used to complement their shop trade, to clear cheap cuts, oddments and offal which they could not sell to wealthy customers who, if they followed the advice of contemporary recipe books, ate large quantities of prime quality meat. Fixed premises were, of course, necessary for the slaughtering. Some butchers must have possessed considerable capital since they feature in the lists of parliamentary electors after 1832 as £10 householders and as councillors in new municipal corporations like Leeds where a £30 rateable value or £1,000 capital holding was a qualification for standing.[2] Their links with the domestic agricultural interest is illustrated by their tendency to vote Tory but from the little we know of their local activities they were just as committed to cheap government and low rates as other more Liberal tradesmen.

Development after 1850 reflected the unevenness evident in other trades. London steadily increased its reliance on domestic 'dead meat' and European supplies, the latter accounting for over eighty per cent of consumption there as early as 1877.[3] Private slaughterhouses, under attack from the third quarter of the century as health risks, died out rapidly here as wholesalers and carcase butchers emerged so that it is not surprising to find Charles Booth commenting in the 1890s that 'Butchers in the strict sense of the word, i.e. men who also kill their own meat, are a rapidly decreasing class'.[4] The arrival, from the 1870s of live North American cattle which, like European stock, had to be slaughtered at the port of entry within ten days to prevent possible spread of disease, also meant that similar developments were evident in other large cities by the 1880s, especially in Liverpool and Manchester.[5] By 1897 Salford domestic livestock market supplied a small and decreasing percentage of the animals slaughtered in Manchester corporation's abattoirs, most of them being imported beasts, and the retail butchers relied heavily on wholesale butchers there, only a hundred of them retaining licences for their own slaughterhouses in the city area.[6] Transport improvements, new sources of supply and the emergence of middlemen, therefore, gradually robbed city butchers of their processing roles, transforming them into meat salesmen, but they did not throw up new retailing organisations to challenge their independence. Such developments, it must be emphasised, were not universal or permanent. Many small towns, even cities like Birmingham, were slow to provide public abattoirs.[7] Live foreign imports were also actually dwindling by the Edwardian period as overseas supplies dried up or were excluded from Britain by stringent import controls and health regulations. By 1913 only the Irish cattle trade flourished. By then, however, a more serious threat, the foreign dead meat trade, chilled and frozen meat, had emerged.

Despite experiments with salted and tinned meats, the latter mainly from South America and Australia, as early as 1847, dead foreign imports remained insignificant. Only salted and cured pork made any inroads into the British market and this was sold primarily in provisions shops, not through fresh meat dealers.[8] Chilled beef, transported at 29–30°F and therefore in a soft state ready for immediate consumption, began to arrive from the U.S.A. after 1874 and, from the end of the century, from South America too.[9] Although its texture, appearance and cuts distinguished it from British beef to those who knew how to judge cuts of meat, nevertheless it was generally of good quality and consequently able to infiltrate 'a high class retail trade'. Butchers supplemented their supplies of domestic home-killed meat with it especially at times of the year when domestic prices were high, consequently becoming dependent upon large-scale importers like the Morris Beef Company which dominated the North American livestock and chilled beef trade. A sudden shortfall in supply brought home to many Lancashire butchers just how reliant on such giants they were.[10]

Chilled beef, therefore, contributed to the decline of the slaughterer/butcher; but the retailers' willingness to handle it dissuaded importers from setting up their own shops. This was not the case with frozen meat. First successfully shipped to Britain in 1884, lamb from Australia and, in even greater quantities, beef from the Argentine, only really began to make noticeable inroads into the domestic market by the late 1890s when livestock imports stagnated and adequate quayside cold storage facilities had been constructed.[11] Since the Australian firms involved were relatively small, their exports seasonal and irregular, and their prime product, the deceptively labelled 'Canterbury Lamb', more widely

141

accepted by independent butchers, this aspect of the trade did not significantly disrupt the retail scene except to increase the scope for misrepresentation and fraud.[12] The British butcher, however, was less eager to accept the less palatable South American product and the handful of large firms who dominated its importation were forced to expand vertically into retailing to obtain outlets. There was a rapid and consistent increase in the number of their shops and stalls from the 1890s to 1910, the pace of expansion pushed along by these multi-national companies' huge resources. By 1912 James Nelson & Sons Ltd, controlled 1,500 shops, Eastmans Ltd, 1,400, the London Central Meat Company over 500, and W. & R. Fletcher and the River Plate Fresh Meat Company over 400 each.[13] As even their most enthusiastic supporters admitted, the 'style and fittings' of such premises were 'generally capable of much improvement'. They were often little more than rudimentary stalls in side streets, dealing strictly in cash, their main purpose being to clear as much meat as possible at the lowest acceptable price before it deteriorated. With over forty per cent of meat consumed in Britain coming from abroad by this date, and according to the National Federation of Meat Traders' Association's estimates, some eighty per cent of imported meat being sold through shops which dealt with nothing else, the private domestic butchers, especially those serving the working classes in large conurbations or close to the main ports of entry, began to feel uneasy about their future. 'In many districts, especially in textile Lancashire.' protested Mr Heap, the National Federation's president, 'these foreign meat shops have very seriously injured the vendor of the home produced article.'[14]

British butchers also faced threats from developments close to home. Many provincial towns followed London's earlier lead, wholesalers and carcase butchers increasing in number, diminishing retailers' slaughtering roles. North of the border Scottish co-operative stores emerged as serious competitors with the Scottish Co-operative Wholesale Society organising bulk buying at discount prices on the open market.[15] Between 1890 and 1914 restrictive legislation dealing with the domestic meat trade was further 'considerably extended', providing for confiscation without compensation for the retailer of diseased meat, prosecution for fraudulent misrepresentation, and regulation, even the closure, of private slaughterhouses as public health nuisances. Most worrying was the Public Health Amendment Act of 1890 which obliged all local authorities to provide licensing inspectors for slaughterhouses and encouraged them to provide municipally owned and run abattoirs paid for out of the rates.[16]

Butchers' reaction to these threats was predictable. In Scotland they were to the forefront of the anti-co-op movement fighting an unsuccessful legal case in 1897 in an attempt to deprive the Scottish Co-operative Wholesale Society of access to meat supplies.[17] In England local societies became affiliated to the National Federation of Meat Traders' Associations founded in 1888. This persistently campaigned for better trading conditions and railed against existing or proposed counterproductive legislation. It established a Defence Fund in 1899 to fight 'unjust' meat seizures by inspectors, lobbied the government to introduce compensation for confiscated meat or to make wholesalers or suppliers liable to pay damages, complained about alleged collusion among meat importers in 1908, highlighted the inadequate training given to inspectors, fought railway companies over their apparent discrimination in favour of bulk importers, supported Lord Avebury's forlorn attempts to achieve compulsory Sunday closing and protested vigorously against the Liberal government's proposals on shop assistants' hours in 1910.[18]

Yet the threats to the independent traditional butcher can be exaggerated. Jefferys goes so far as to describe pre-1914 developments affecting the trade as 'adjustments' rather than a major reorientation, pointing out that even in the 1930s 'as much as one third' of the home-killed meat trade involved butchers who slaughtered their own animals. Perren, the leading authority in this field, agrees that before 1914 'The small butcher, purchasing and slaughtering for himself, remained the norm in the home-killed meat trade'.[19] How can we square this with contemporary concern over the trade and the apparent flood of imports?

First we need to appreciate the extent of the foreign meat trade and its overall impact. It is rarely appreciated that, although over forty per cent of meat consumed in the U.K. came from abroad by 1914, sixty per cent of the imports was actually pig meat, much of which, as cured bacon or hams, was sold as 'provisions' through grocers' shops and by specialised pork butchers. This aspect of the trade scarcely threatened the fresh meat dealer.[20] A few cities took the major slice of the imports; London's Smithfield market handled eighty per cent foreign meat, Manchester's market over sixty-six per cent. Concentration in these city areas and in the textile towns where extensive female employment pushed families into relying more on such convenient, easily cooked foods rather than on stews, meant that home meat supplies elsewhere were adequate and continued to monopolise trade. Country districts, smaller provincial towns, even substantial centres like Dundee, Newcastle and Norwich, saw little or no Argentinian beef.[21] Multiple frozen meat stalls also relied heavily on newly-generated working-class demand. 'The middle classes . . . despotically ruled by convention and prejudice' shunned them, as too did more affluent, status-conscious members of the working classes, one young lad recalling that he 'got a jacketing for going in such places' when on family shopping errands.[22] Differentiation in quality and adaptation to

143

such families' specific requirements, cutting to order, extensive credit and the stocking of a broad range of products enabled the traditional butcher to thrive and to ride out the lean years more successfully than his cut-price competitors whose share of the meat market actually fell in the less propitious years.[23] He could also share in the working-class market by practising price discrimination, charging the less price-conscious middle-class customer over the odds for his prime cuts so that he could sell left-overs, 'block ornaments' or pieces for stews, puddings and pies for a few pence. This was undoubtedly a major contribution to the working classes' standard of living and appreciated as such by many who recall the practice yet it has been overlooked by official enquiries and statistics.[24]

The persistence of private slaughterhouses is more problematical. An estimated thirteen thousand still operated as late as 1937; public abattoirs accounted for only twenty-five per cent of the home-killed trade.[25] Only in this year, however, did central government legislation really push ahead with the campaign to force local authorities to provide more centralised facilities.[26] Possibly, too, the skilled butcher's own conservatism and hankering after independence and job satisfaction were important, deterring him from switching to more convenient slaughtering methods.

The following recollection illustrates some of these traditional butchers' shop practices. Born in 1888, the elder son of 'just an ordinary butcher' in Ramsgate, Charles Marks recalls his father's business until it was sold in 1902. As in other trades, the importance of the delivery trade stands out as do the long hours, the credit web, the dependence on late Saturday shopping for the working classes, the slackness of Monday – washing and cold meat day – the continued reliance on male and juvenile labour, and the importance of an impressive window display. Meat was bought on the hoof from local markets and driven home along the public highway, a far from straightforward task but apparently preferable to replying on the temperamental railway companies who never relished this rather messy 'passenger' traffic. The reformers' case for abolishing private slaughterhouses on health grounds is understandable when it is borne in mind that the gruesome butchering described here took place directly behind the shop which was situated in a busy commercial and residential quarter of town. Country butchers were possibly even less concerned about the nuisance they caused, one rural dweller recalling that in his childhood 'The slaughterhouse stank. You've got no idea! You could smell it a mile off and they used to have to pay a man extra to clean out the cesspool where all the blood and rubbish went down'.[27]

The picture of the butchers' assistants resembles that portrayed for London by Booth. Although working long and irregular hours, they do not appear to have

144

been poorly treated, receiving meat allowances to supplement wages. It is also easy to see why the Meat Traders' Federation fought so desperately to prevent the sixty-hour clause in Churchill's Shops Bill going through; it would have wrecked the trade of butchers like Mr Marks. The rough practical handling of the butcher's son, too, is a sobering reminder that legislation to regulate the labour of juvenile employees – full or part-time – did not encompass family members. It was not just the small corner shopkeeper who exploited his family for labour. Charlie Marks's experiences were the antithesis of the stereotyped picture of a comfortable tradesman's son, and they reflect the butcher's rough, rugged outlook on life, his belief in acquiring skills on the job and his scant regard for book learning and social graces.

---

### 66 *A town butcher's son*

Times were very, very different then. We used to do all our own killing. All live stuff. In those days it used to be alternate Mondays for fat stock at Sandwich and Canterbury while Ashford market was regularly every week on a Tuesday and Friday. From Sandwich the bullocks used to be driven by road, by a drover, and then distributed to each slaughterhouse but the smaller animals, pigs and sheep, were brought home either by van or by rail. From Canterbury it all came by rail, bullocks and all, which meant that you had to go up to the railway and drive them home yourself. There was an occasion I had to go up and get some and there was a butcher that had just got one so he asked my father if he could run it down with ours because it's very difficult to drive a single bullock through the streets. I'd have been about twelve or thirteen then, and I'd got to deliver this bullock to this other butcher on my way home with ours. At the top of the High Street, when I got opposite the telephone exchange which was a big house laid back in a garden, a dog ran straight across in front of these bullocks. They went for it and he ran into this telephone exchange! They went on in after him and one went right in the doorway and chased this dog downstairs into the basement. Pulled the bannisters down. They had a hell of a job to get this bullock out back from the basement into the road again. They had to get some chaps to come and take the window out.

When I was going to school I remember my father would say 'Oi! I want you to go to Minster [a village some miles away] and get a couple of calves. I'm waiting to kill them so home as quick as you can get.' Well, that was that. If it was winter time it was dark before I got started and sometimes I used to be frozen, ever so cold. My father'd be there waiting. 'Where the bloody hell have you been to? Come on, I've been waiting on you. Three chaps standing up there scratching their bloody selves waiting for you.' My mother used to say, 'Bob! Can't you see? Look at the poor little kid, he's frozen.' It didn't make no difference. Very often, I'd perhaps go to Sandwich or even to Northbourne [near Deal], when I came out of school to get a calf, maybe two or three pigs. If I didn't do it they'd have to send, and pay, a man so I'd got to do it. That was the idea in those days you see. If it was winter time, coming along the Sandwich road, along the flats, the wind used to come off the sea bitter cold. And I'd only got just a candle light, two lamps, one for each side of the cart. Used to scare the bloody life out of me sometimes but that's what I had to do. It was very hard in a way but it made a man of me.

Every butcher's shop had its own slaughterhouse. You'd have to keep the place tidy because there used to be a public health inspector come up about once in twelve months but you never knew when he was coming. If you lost your licence you'd be buggered up in those days because there was no public abattoir. Out the back of the slaughterhouse we had what we called pounds or lairs and I reckon we did four bullocks a week, twelve to fourteen sheep and lambs and half a dozen pigs. Quite a good trade in those days. There was no gas up the slaughterhouse, only candlelight, and if they were working late the slaughtermen, like the coalmen, used to have a bracket round their head with a candle stuck in the front. If I was up there I used to hold the candle for one of them. The foreman up there, the governor, was my uncle. I would say, 'Can you see?' 'Can you?' 'Yes.' 'Well, that's all right, I can bloody well see if you can.' That's what I used to get. Oh dear, oh dear, we didn't get on at all well.

They often worked very late. Might be short of some things, sheep, mutton or even beef, and there was no real reliance on what time these animals might arrive especially if they came by rail. In those days you more or less had to wait for all the passenger service trains before they'd shunt the cattle trucks in. Then in the summer time, if we had an extraordinarily good trade, such as holiday makers coming down, a lot more than expected, we'd probably sell out. One of the chaps, even two, would have to come in Sunday morning and kill half a score more sheep or lambs ready for Monday and Tuesday's trade. That often used to happen. We didn't have any humane killers those days. You pole-axed your bullock, hit him just below the horn and of course you'd go right into the brain. That was that. He'd go down naturally and then we used to pith them. That's a cane you put in the hole that you'd just made in the head, pushed it right in. That used to break the spinal cord. An instantaneous death then.

I could kill and dress a sheep when I was twelve and could help on beef quite a bit because I had to. I'd be standing up in the slaughterhouse watching the chaps

146

and my father would come up – he was a bit of a task master as they were in those days – and he would say to me, 'Oi! Come on, standing there! Get hold of a knife and get to work.' That's what happened; that's how I grew up. I used to have a pet lamb, kept him out the back and used to use it for getting sheep into the slaughterhouse. You know what sheep are, they'll follow one another. One day this lamb, he got what we call blown, that's eating too much green meat, clover and that sort of thing. All done up in a bundle, it used to get heated and blow their bellies out, right out. Of course, if you could get there in time to nick them with a knife the gas came out and you could save them. The smell nearly poisoned you! But if you weren't able to do that it just killed them. That's what happened to my lamb. One of the chaps came down and said the lamb had got blown up there. My father said to me, 'Go on. Go up and see him.' He was too far gone to stick him and that was the first time I'd ever killed a sheep or lamb. That was my *pet* lamb but I still had to do it. Of course, I never had any time like other boys to go out to play. Always had to do something. As a matter of fact I often got in trouble because I wasn't able to do my homework. I used to say to my father, 'I've got my homework to do, Dad.' 'Never mind about that. Get up in the morning and do that.' That was that and of course even if I got up in the morning I couldn't concentrate. All I'd get was a penny or twopence. I had to think myself lucky if got it and I had to save it, more or less, in my money box.

Adjoining the slaughterhouse was a cottage where the horsekeeper-cum-foreman used to live. There were five chaps and this horsekeeper. A good 'un – he'd got to be good, a real tip-top butcher, both slaughterman and able to talk to the customer – he'd get about £2 a week. An ordinary chap like the slaughterman, roundsman, they were round thirty bob and the one apprentice about ten bob a week. He had all sorts of jobs to do. Mother used to be in the desk, take the money, do the books. There was always a certain amount of housework she had to do but we used to keep two girls. Of course in those days the chaps used to live in. They'd got their own lodgings, we didn't sleep them but we fed them, all that you couldn't sell in the shop more or less. For breakfast, they'd get scrag of mutton or sheep's head.

You'd open about six to half past in the morning. First thing was to get the salt beef up on great big trays. In winter time, when it's cold, brine is very, very cold and you'd got to dive around in there, the tanks were pretty deep, and get out the different joints. Weekdays you'd close about eight, half past eight. Friday was around ten o'clock. Saturday'd be about twelve midnight. We used to do more trade after eleven o'clock than we done all the afternoon because the pubs used to shut then and the old girls came out for their shopping. It's true! More often than not before the chaps got away it was half past twelve, one in the morning. Mind

147

you, the poorer classes, they used to turn out good customers at times because they'd have all the odds and pieces you had to cut off. Perhaps you wanted half a pound of steak. Some people insisted on exactly half a pound and if you cut nine ounces, well, you had to cut the little bit off. They came in for two or three pennyworth of these pieces, little odds and ends, trimmings, pieces – mince wasn't popular in those days. Or you might give them neck or breast of mutton, that sort of thing. Farmers and labourers used to buy a lot of fat pork. Back fat – pure fat. We used to put it in dry salt, pack a layer of back fat, salt and so on. That'd stop there for weeks and weeks until the fat was a light pink. The labourers would take a chunk of this back fat and a piece of bread in the fields and it would last them all day long. One of our chaps did a country round. It was a long job and he'd be gone all day more or less, especially in the hopping season when he sold quite a bit of meat to the old tarts and hop pickers. Sold a lot of sausage meat and sausages then. Friday was a big day for him. He never got back until about eight at night, in winter time just the same, and I bet you nine times out of ten Friday night he'd be half sloshed when he got back. But he never made a mistake with his money. A good old sort he was.

Myself, I used to have to ride a horse with a basket of meat to Broadstairs and also do local jobs, delivering different joints on horseback. At Broadstairs there was a big boarding house and they had a lot of meat. I'd ride with the basket, a big butcher's basket, on my thigh but when I got to this house I couldn't get off. I had to ride up a rough old path where a brick wall went along and rest the basket of meat on top of the wall so that I could get off the horse. Then, when I'd got off I had to wait for somebody, the postman or milkman, to lift it down for me. That went on for a long time before this landlady came over and told my father he'd have to send somebody else instead of sending a little boy like that. Then instead of riding over I had to put the horse in the cart and drive over. I didn't like that as much because before, after I'd delivered the meat, I used to cut right across the fields, gallop all the way and right over the gate at the bottom straight on to the hard road. I wouldn't do that now for a thousand quid!

We did a lot of lightships and quite a lot of fishing smacks. What we called the Trinity boat, the steam boat that used to take the lightship crews and their stores out, lay right along at the end of the West Pier, close to the lighthouse. That was her permanent berth all my childhood days. These lightship crews had to take their own meat and we got quite a lot of their business. It was done in wooden pails, hinged so you could latch and lock them. These were filled up with salted meat that would last them their tour of duty, keep as long as you like. If the tide was out the boat would be right down low and these pails had to be lowered on a pulley. Right along the end of the pier when it was blowing a gale the horse had to stand there. I was scared out of my life he'd run away and jump in the harbour.

Monday as a rule was off day. Never used to do their rounds except you might have one or two to call on. Of course, the hygiene laws weren't quite so strict as they are today but it didn't make no difference, they used to clean the shop out every day after the morning trade and then on Monday have a real thorough clean out. Floor an' all, you know, was scrubbed because it was a wooden floor in those days with sawdust. We had gas inside the shop, ordinary flame just covered up, and then each end of the shop, at the front, you had these brass arms, gas arms, which folded back when you wanted to put the shutters up. My father and some of the chaps did the window display every day. Dad would tell them what he wanted and where to put it because he was the governor and so he had it as he wanted it. At night it all had to come in again, pulled up on the tackle to go down to the ice box. Up it came again next morning. There was no refrigeration, only this ice box, and we had to have four or five hundredweight of ice put in every other day. Some of it was made in the town but the majority of it used to come over from Norway or somewhere in big blocks the size of a table. And we used to have big slate brine tanks in the cellar too for pork, beef, bullocks' tongues, ox tongues and so on.

The best rump steak in the world was 1s 2d a pound! Best loin of beef 8d, brisket 4d, flank 4d, ox liver out of the best bullocks 4d. There were two prices of pork sausages. Nothing but legs of pork in them – absolutely all leg with a little bit of back fat, the best ones used to be 9d a pound. In the others you used perhaps a bit of neck, bit of belly and that sort of thing, they were 8d. They had proper skins too, you know, guts. We didn't clean them though, a gut man came round to different slaughterhouses and took them away to do them. Haslets – liver, lights, heart, tongue, caul right round it, that's a correct haslet – they were sold in the shop. Used to make lovely tasty haslet pies too, onions, sage, potatoes all cut up in big tin and then the caul right over the top. The fat soaked right through and cooked it. Very tasty. Bladders? You'd even blow them up and fill them with lard.

My dad died in September 1902. I was fourteen in the December. Well, of course, I had to leave school then and help mother keep on the business. She did it for about twelve months, perhaps two years, but it wasn't really a business for a woman to run so she sold out, lived in private for a couple of years and then went into the hotel line. I stopped at home for a little while and then left and got a job in Margate. That'd be about 1903. I was assistant slaughterman and I got sixteen bob a week. I had to pay 12s a week for my board and lodging and that only left me four bob to do everything with – buy my clothes, shoe leather, the lot. One day I said to the foreman, 'Don't you think it's about time I dressed me own sheep, Tom?' He said, 'You can't dress sheep to suit my governor.' Well, I thought, I got to find out so next day instead of going to dinner I went straight to the slaughterhouse and I got three of these sheep done before he came back. 'Well, there you are', I said. 'See if you can find fault with those.' Saturday, going home, about midnight this was, walking down the road with the foreman, I said, 'Wait a minute Tom, I've got to go back I've got two bob too much.' The governor then was quite a big church man so this foreman said, 'No, don't bother him now. Leave it till Monday morning.' That Monday I told the governor before he went to market. 'Oh, that's all right Charlie', he said. 'I think you done very very well with the sheep. Beautifully done.' Best rise I've ever had in my life that was, it really was.

At fifteen and a half I went to Chatham dockyard. Just inside the gate there was what we called the victuallers' yard, a biggish slaughterhouse. Before much frozen beef was about, nearly all the ships' stores were home-killed and it used to be done in this yard. They'd be killing beef all day long, bullock after bullock. Cor blimey! There was some work there! We got paid so much a week for dockyard hours, seven in the morning till five or six at night and after that we used to come on to overtime which was two bob a bullock. Two bob a bullock! And there's five of us in a gang. If there was a big commission and you'd got to put tons of meat on board you had to keep killing till they had enough. You worked all through the night sometimes. The chaps I worked with used to take half gallon jars of beer with them because that was very, very hard work. The hardest work I've ever done in my life I did there. It was such blimmin' hard work at the dockyard and I craved after having a horse that I joined the cavalry. Didn't have the hard work there, and that was that.

### Notes to Chapter 9

[1]Scola, 'Food markets', pp. 159–67; see also Baines, *Lancashire* for Liverpool and other industrial towns; Alexander, *Retailing*, pp. 43, 121–3.

[2]Vincent, *Pollbooks, passim*; Hennock, *Fit and Proper Persons*, p. 198.

[3]Perren, *Meat Trade*, pp. 17–25, 32–42, 151–4; R. Perren, 'The meat and livestock trade in Britain, 1850–70', *Economic History Review*, 2nd series, XXVIII, 1975, pp. 385–400.

[4]Booth, *Life and Labour*, VII, p. 201.

[5]Perren, *Meat Trade*, chapters 5 and 7.

[6]W. E. Bear, 'The food supply of Manchester, II, animal produce', *Journal of the Royal Agricultural Society*, 3rd series, VIII, 1897, pp. 490–2.

[7]Perren, *Meat Trade*, p. 89.

[8]J. T. Critchell and J. Raymond, *A History of the Frozen Meat Trade*, 1912, pp. 7–9; B. McNamee, 'Trends in meat consumption', in Barker *et al.* (eds.), *Our Changing Fare*, pp. 80–2.

[9]Critchell and Raymond, *Frozen Meat Trade*, chapter 17; Perren, *Meat Trade*, pp. 165–9.

[10]Meat Combinations Inquiry, report, pp. 9–15.

[11]*Ibid.*, pp. 8–9; Perren, *Meat Trade*, chapter 10; R. Duncan, 'The demand for frozen beef in the United Kingdom, 1880–1940', *Journal of Agricultural Economics*, XII, 1956–7, pp. 82–8; R. H. Hooker, 'The meat supply of the United Kingdom', *Journal of the Royal Statistical Society*, LXXII, 1909, 304–76.

[12]Farmers too publicised misrepresentation, S. B. L. Druce, 'The sale of foreign agricultural produce as home produce', *Journal of the Royal Agricultural Society*, 3rd series, X, 1899, pp. 396–400; Perren, *Meat Trade*, p. 196.

[13]Critchell and Raymond, *Frozen Meat Trade*, pp. 209–10.

[14]Meat Combinations Inquiry, p. 215.

[15]Jefferys, *Retail Trading*, p. 196.

[16]Perren, *Meat Trade*, pp. 63–8, 88–9, 133–4.

[17]Bonner, *British Co-operation*, pp. 112–13; *Tradesman and Shopkeeper*, 23 August 1902, p. 11.

[18]A. J. Jackson, *Official History of the National Federation of Meat Traders' Associations*, Plymouth, 1956; Meat Combinations Inquiry, pp. 211–15; Sel. Comm. on Sunday Closing, pp. 73–4; Deputations at Home Office, pp. 28–32; Perren, *Meat Trade*, pp. 155–6. On inspectors' qualifications Return on Inspection of Meat in various parts of the country, P.P. 1904, LXXXII, pp. 727–32.

[19]Jefferys, *Retail Trading*, p. 183; Perren, *Meat Trade*, p. 156.

[20]Meat Combinations Inquiry, p. 6; see also Chapter 6.

[21]*Ibid.*, p. 6.

[22]Critchell and Raymond, *Frozen Meat Trade*, p. 316; Interviews with Robert Dale, fisherman's son (1891–1975), Whitstable.

[23]Jefferys, *Retail Trading*, pp. 188, 201.

[24]J. B. Short, *The Butcher's Shop: a study of a country butcher's business*, Oxford, 1928, pp. 14–15, 23–31; University of Kent Oral History Collection – many respondents refer to butchers 'almost giving it away' on Saturday evenings. On Lancashire, Roberts, 'Working-class standards of living', pp. 313–14.

[25]*Modern Meat Retailing*, Feb. 1937, p. 62.

[26]H. Levy, *The Shops of Britain*, p. 53.

[27]Interview with Reg Clarke (born 1892), publican's son, Wingham, Kent.

# CHAPTER 10

# *Greengrocers — 'working men'*

The paucity of references to greengrocers and their produce in studies of food consumption and retailing could be taken as an indication of their insignificance.[1] Except for potatoes, popular demand for fresh produce was limited for much of the Victorian period and was adequately met by market traders. Even the wealthier classes exhibited a remarkable reluctance to incorporate much fruit and vegetables into their diet before the 1870s. Throughout the century, it is true, many country dwellers grew their own but until well into this century it seems that the urban working classes were either deprived of access to them or refused to allocate their scarce resources to buying them. Published working-class budgets and weekly diet sheets scarcely mentioned fruit or vegetables and if they did their significance was played down by commentators. Pessimists, now as then, emphasised the monotony of the working man's diet, its stodginess, reliance on cheap, filling carbohydrates, some singling out the lack of fresh produce as one of the 'unfortunate effects' of town life, only removed when 'canned vegetables came to the rescue in the second quarter of the twentieth century'.[2] Even those who have emphasised the increasing spending power of the working classes have tended to argue that it was channelled, at best towards protein-rich foodstuffs like meat, but more commonly into less nutritious items like tea, sugar and margarine or into conspicuous expenditure on consumer goods. Oddy, for example, concluded that 'environmental, physiological and psychological factors in working-class life', including a prejudice against milk, fresh fruit and vegetables, meant that rising real wages failed to bring about any marked improvement in diet before 1914.[3] John Burnett, too, concludes that 'fruit, green vegetables and fish were still insignificant items' in working-class budgets in this period.[4]

This view is difficult to accept. While conceding that the very poor could afford little more than potatoes, that a significant but unknown percentage of the country's expanding fruit output reached the consumer as jam, that oranges, nuts and grapes remained luxuries given only as presents at Christmas or to invalids, and that the working classes were deeply suspicious about new fruits like bananas and tomatoes, the latter reputedly cancer-inducing – even so, the evidence points towards a substantial market for fresh produce by the Edwardian period and to an increase in small specialist retailers to service it. Failure to appreciate this earlier can possibly be attributed to the patchiness of information on imports, the fact that these shopkeepers were invariably small men and easily overlooked by those mesmerised by company shops and co-ops, and to an excessive concentration on the plight of the very poor in Britain. Significantly, even in East London, the 'abyss' of late-Victorian society, Booth found that the bottom tenth of society – 'at all times more or less in want' – ate 'greens sometimes' while in the largest group of working-class families – 'representative of the way we live now' – with 'fully paid labour in regular employ', one third to one half of all families surveyed, meat and vegetables were eaten daily as part of a varied and wholesome diet.[5] Further surveys of working-class budgets in 1903 and 1904 suggest (given the relative cheapness of fresh produce, the price of which had not risen since the 1870s) that consumption was in fact considerable. Out of a total weekly food bill of 22s 6d the average family spent 2s on potatoes, fruit and vegetables, the last two accounting for half of this and showing a high income-elasticity of demand. An immediate pre-war estimate showed a healthy average per capita annual consumption of 61lb of fruit, 60lb of vegetables and 208lb of potatoes.[6]

Recent oral evidence collected by historians confirms this impression of a growing working-class demand. People regarded vegetables as 'a cheap nutritious, enjoyable and essential part of their diet'. In all but the central urban areas, they were able to resort to non-market sources, scouring the surrounding countryside for 'free food' in the hedgerows and fields. Allotments, increasingly common, yielded crops which were shared or sold to neighbours.[7] These were especially common in model villages whose promoters frequently stressed the uplifting nature of gardening as a 'rational recreation' and consequently made land available at the outset for the inhabitants.[8] Even where such sources were inaccessible vegetables were regularly used in various stews and hot pots to supplement cheap cuts of meat, bones or oddments; these were part of the staple diet in working-class homes, even those with simple primitive cooking facilities.[9] Greengrocers and small general shops offered 'two pennorth of pot herbs. That was an onion, couple of carrots and turnip. Potatoes and greens you bought and cooked separate. Mother'd put split peas and all sorts of vegetables in the stews.'[10] Purchasing in such small quantities was generally preferred to bulk buying by many on the grounds that it eliminated possible waste or deterioration and was very convenient in houses which had no adequate storage space. Vegetables were also essential accompaniments to Sunday dinner and greengrocers regularly opened in the morning to service the huge demand.

Incomplete though they are, the figures for the supply of fruit and vegetables also show a remarkable increase from the 1870s. Farmers, hit by low cereal and hop prices and aware of the shift in demand, diversified. In the twenty years after 1875, English orchards expanded by forty per cent and the acreage devoted to market gardening more than doubled from just under thirty-nine thousand to nearly ninety-three thousand. Small fruit cultivation, only in 1888 listed separately, also doubled in just seven years. Carrots, cabbages, peas, beans and sprouts were incorporated into normal rotations to provide quick cash crops. Regional specialisation developed, with Kent and the Vale of Evesham earning reputations for high-quality fruit. Intensely cultivated market gardens near railway stations on lines feeding large cities became commonplace. Early problems, especially inadequate protective packing for soft fruits, overloading of wholesale facilities and frequent gluts were gradually overcome and a sophisticated distributive network established.[11]

By 1896, Manchester's fresh produce market at Shude Hill dealt in fruit and vegetables from all over the country, even handling Kentish strawberries on the same day that they were picked. The municipally owned wholesale and retail market there extended over four and a half acres but, due to the 'enormous demand . . . even this space is not nearly large enough for the constantly growing trade, and, in the height of the season, great quantities of produce are stacked on the sideways of the adjoining streets'.[12] London's Covent Garden was similarly overstretched. There were, in addition, thriving local markets up and down the country where farmers still occasionally sold direct to customers. Foreign supplies were increasingly sucked in, although mainly to meet the requirements of the wealthier classes. Greatly aided by its new canal, Manchester drew on produce as far afield as North America (apples), the Canary Islands (potatoes), Spain, Italy, Egypt (onions), Algeria (peas), Germany, Holland and France. Nationally, the country's fruit imports rose from negligible quantities to over thirteen million hundredweight by 1905.[13]

Although market traders and street salesmen still remained important, a new race of shopkeepers progressively dominated the distribution of this produce in the towns. The precise numbers involved remain unclear since those listed as 'greengrocers, fruiterers and vegetable dealers' in the census also included wholesalers and workers, but an upward trend clearly suggests a remarkable increase in the retail sector. Between 1891 and 1911 no other category of food dealers or workers matched their rate of expansion, the United Kingdom total rising from just over forty-seven thousand to in excess of eighty thousand, confirming fresh produce dealers as the largest group of food dealers behind grocers, bakers and butchers, ahead of milk retailers, fishmongers and provision dealers. Furthermore, these figures exclude both general shopkeepers who also sold small quantities of fruit and vegetables as part of their trade and members of retailers' families involved in the business. Greengrocers fell squarely into the small shopkeeper category. The 1891 census figures for England and Wales show over sixty-five per cent of men and women over the age of ten involved in the trade returned as employers or in business on their own account, a figure only exceeded by costermongers and street sellers with seventy-five per cent. Other trades contained a much lower proportion of employers and proprietors. Even allowing for the probable inclusion of many general corner shops, only forty-three per cent of grocers fell into these categories. The figures for butchers, bakers and drapers were even lower at thirty-nine, twenty-eight and twenty-three per cent respectively.[14] Booth remarked of greengrocers that 'most of them are . . . in a small way of business' and 'stand low in the social scale. No other business can be started with so small a capital and little skill or knowledge of any kind is required.'[15] The Fruiterers' deputation on the Shops Bill in 1910 emphasised that 'We are all working men' who 'look forward to and depend upon the industrial classes's custom'. Consequently, they opposed larger traders' attempts to institute Sunday, early or even half-day closing. 'If you cut short our selling time,' they argued, 'our means of existence are crippled . . . You will find that the great majority of those who are making the demand for all retail shops to close at the same hour are the wealthiest and company shopkeepers and it would make it harder for the enterprising independent tradesman who works his own shop.'[16] Relying largely on family labour, however, they supported the government's proposals for a maximum working week for employees and they joined in calls for restrictions on street traders.

Although greengrocers challenged other tradesmen, especially but not exclusively grocers, by selling proprietary goods as sidelines, in their own specialist sphere they were mercifully free from the competition of co-ops, multiples or large retailers, all of which made negligible inroads into the trade.[17] There are fairly obvious reasons for this. The diverse nature, unevenness of supply and variations in quality of the produce, combined with the large number of dispersed suppliers, made the bulk purchasing, common pricing policies and centralised control, on which multiples relied, very difficult to attain. Above all, the highly perishable nature of the stock and consequent chances of significant amounts of waste jeopardised the narrow profit margins on which company shops operated and discouraged heavy investment in premises. Customers' unwillingness to carry their heavy purchases any distance also gave the small, local man an inbuilt advantage in the market and tended to reduce the level of competition. On the other hand, it was easy for the individual proprietor, working his or her shop, to set up in business. He needed little capital or skill; the trade demanded little more than long hours. Cheap, unskilled assistants could be hired and sacked at will to meet seasonal demands if family assistance was inadequate.

The absence of eye-catching retail giants in the fruit and vegetable trade and the incomplete figures for the supply of fresh produce have undoubtedly led to misconceptions about working-class diet and the neglect of the greengrocer. He will, however, remain an elusive prey for the historian. Patchily organised as a trade, dealing in unlabelled and little advertised products, suffering few legal restrictions on his trade, exempt from the prying eyes of factory or shop inspectors by virtue of his lack of equipment and reliance on family labour, unacquainted for many years with the taxman, unaware of the dubious advisability of keeping accounts, he has left few records which can be used to track him down. Only a few photographs and the memories of his daughter, Mrs Ellen Bryan, born in 1896, remain to help us reconstruct a picture of one such business, that of Mr Bennett, fruiterer and greengrocer of Henry Street in the quarter of Chatham known as Luton. Even his shop premises have long since been demolished. Like many aspiring small shopkeepers he conceived of trade as a ladder for social mobility. A labourer, lacking education or training, a chance windfall gave him sufficient capital to rent the premises; from there he never looked back. When his children were old enough to run the shop, which he by then owned, he graduated to a state of semi-retirement, sitting on the Board of Guardians, mixing with local councillors, drinking at the Conservative Club, driving out in pony and trap, engaging a daily maid and, after his first wife's untimely death, marrying a lady who obviously shared his pretensions and view of a local shopkeeper's role in society. To some extent his airs were little more than outward show, his success a sham. He explained to his offspring the importance of keeping up appearances. Symbolically he could not resist the temptation to buy the wealthy's second-hand, quality clothes, outwardly visible status symbols in the community, while the interior of his house, which neighbours were not invited to see, remained bare and uninviting.

His success was as much his family's as it was his but they did not share the rewards to the same extent. Their diet was, as might be expected, good, but otherwise life was hard, almost penurious. His wife and children worked the shop, his son eventually managing it entirely, but they received no regular remuneration and were surprised after his death to discover the extent of his wealth. His daughter's attempts to break away from the slavery of the shop were not viewed favourably since they threatened his source of cheap labour. Ingeniously he fostered Poor Law children before his own were old enough to help to circumvent even the minimal legislation of 1886 controlling juvenile shopworkers. Indeed, he appears guilty of many offences which the wealthier traders accused small shopkeepers of committing: exploitation of family labour, poaching of other shops' trade by diversifying into coal, sweets, tinned foods and even haberdashery and, of course, excessively long opening hours. Sunday afternoon closing was effectively forced upon him only by a family revolt.

His style of business was simple. 'He just put the stuff in it and people used to come and buy.' Window display and shop fittings were rudimentary and storage space at a premium, the pavement being used for display purposes. The only processing of produce on the premises was carried out by his enterprising first wife who converted surplus stock into wines and ketchups. Supplies were easily obtained locally from wholesale markets or even directly from farmers who brought their wares into the shop in times of glut in an attempt to dispose of them. Travellers were resorted to only for delicacies. An interesting feature of the business, however, was his wholesale activity, supplying general corner shops in the area, indicative of the widespread nature of the outlets for fresh produce. Credit seems to have been sparingly given. Items were sold by volume rather than weight, a device which allowed the greengrocer to give judicious short measure. We can also glean a little about working-class shopping habits and diet from the recollections, the eye for a bargain or 'speck' fruit, their yearning for fresh vegetables on Sunday. Mr Bennett's success was based as much on their regular custom as on his business talents and labour, and his social rise would not have been possible without such a large and growing working-class market.

--------

### 66 *A greengrocer*

My father never went to school. But it was funny, though he never went, he got his fourth-class certificate in the army. He could read and write but he didn't need to do a lot of writing. But he was a good mathematician without being able to put it down. He could work things out and scale things out.

Well, I can tell you how he got into greengrocery. He left the army and went in the dockyard but he left because it was only £1 a week and he bought a whole houseful of furniture for £5 and sold it and made enough money to start a little business. It was really a general business, but from there he branched out into the shop, 63 Henry Street. He rented it up to about 1910, then he bought it for £200. It was practically a new shop when he went but it's not there any more, all been pulled down.

He didn't need any equipment other than the shop. He just put the stuff in it and people used to come and buy. Greengrocery, wood, coal, practically anything that was saleable he sold. Afterwards he did a lot of haberdashery too. He had two windows you see, one in the main street and one in the side. We had sweets there for years and then he sold other things, tin cans as well, and put them in there. Coal we used to go to the wharf for, just off Sun Pier. We sold that in little peck baskets that just used to hold fourteen pounds of coal. That was 2*d*. We'd stack them up and sell them in no time at all. But oh, greengrocery, my brother used to have two days for wholesale. Tuesday and Thursday were wholesale deliveries, then it used to take him the best part of Saturday to Castle Road, Luton Road and Henry Street. We never used to deliver any further, just in the main street and round about. Quite nice people lived on Luton Road that called themselves 'class', nearly all business people, but Henry Street was working-class people. He took boys with him to knock at the doors. It was all little shops that used to have a bit of greengrocery, a few potatoes and cabbages. That's really how my father got his living.

The New Luton Arches, that's where he used to go and buy all his produce. That was the general market, twice a week, usually Tuesdays and Thursdays. Sometimes we used to go up to the market in the Rainham Road. Dad would say, 'Up early in the morning!' Half past three we'd walk to the Star public house on the Rainham Road. People from Rainham and all down in Upchurch used to bring their produce there with their horses and vans. If there was a shortage, the further you walked the cheaper you'd buy. You caught the market gardeners coming in you see and you'd get your stuff before they got to the market and found out there was a shortage. They always used to deliver it to the shop for you. Well, if there was a glut of anything then you used to get them ever so cheap. They often used to come in and put a bushel of stuff down and say, 'All right. Get rid of it. Make what you can out of it and pay me next time I come.' And they used to have flowers. Pinks or garden flowers really. We used to sell them in the shop.

We didn't have to go up to London for a market, only we used to have travellers from there for nuts. My dad used to buy these in January for the following Christmas! A man, I can always remember his name – Mr Lomas – used to come. He used to hire a truck at the station then push it round with his samples. And travellers used to come and get your orders for groceries and things like that. Hearns were a big wholesalers in the High Street, but if the travellers came from London, they were always dressed in top hat, frock coats — gentlemen! They were a different class of people to the local people, because the farmers, local farmers, were just rough and ready. Oranges used to come in crates. Forty a shilling we sold oranges. And grapes from a wholesaler came in big tubs, all packed in cork. We had one of them for our Christmas bran tub, a barrel with sawdust where we put all leather tickets in with a sack over the top with a hole in it. You'd put your hand in and pull out a ticket. Whoever drew out the lucky number, they could spend so much in the shop. Sold a lot of grapes and stuff at Christmas time. For illness or Christmas times. Grapes were one of those things that people didn't buy, only on occasions. And dates always came in a block, a solid block. You had to dig them out when you sold them. Used to sell all sorts of fancy stuff at Christmas but it was unusual to have a lot.

We used to sell everything in the greengrocery line, but mainly just the ordinary local-grown stuff. Dates and soft things like that were sold by weight. We had big copper scales for them. But other than that it was pints, quarts, half gallons and gallons. We had wooden measures all fitted into one another. We didn't even weigh carrots. If people came in for carrots, they'd buy just one, or you used to give them thre or four for perhaps a penny. And watercress, we bought a whole pad of watercress for a shilling. When I was first taught serving in the shop you just used to guess it because it was so cheap. You grabbed a handful and that was a halfpenny. We got that at one time from Springfield the other side of Gravesend. We took the trap and got it over the weekend. We actually knew the people that grew it. Other than that we used to get it from Farley's in the High Street.

Of course we used to get a lot of waste. All the green stuff and fruit would go off. You had to throw it out. Couldn't do anything with it. It went on to the heap and used to be carted away for rubbish. If it was fit for pigs they used to take it for them. We used to have a big manure heap keeping horses, and a man used to come and take it away. You never sold bad stuff. Oh no, even then people wouldn't come and take anything that had gone rotten. What they bought, they wanted good. Anyway my father wouldn't sell cheap stuff. 'If it's not good enough to sell then it's not good enough for anybody.' No, he was a little bit funny about serving stuff that was below its capacity. The only thing that we ever sold in the shop was 'specks', and that we used to let the kids have the benefit of. Might only just be a little bit on the apple or oranges, but he'd sell it for speck. The kids used to come and buy ha'p'orths at a time, hold their cap up. Or they'd stand out the front picking all the speck out and eating the good part. Throw it all on the path. You'd have to go and wash it all down afterwards. But rotten ones my mother, my own mother, used to make wine with them. Oranges, apples, potato, parsnip . . . anything that didn't sell, she used to make into wine or ketchup. We had big crocks, stone crocks in the scullery where we had a stone floor, and she used to put it all in them. She used to put them all round the shop at Christmas. Raspberry wine was good, they used to say, in those days, for coughs and colds. People wouldn't buy mushrooms that were broken. We used to put them all in pans for ketchup. Didn't have all these patent things then. We used to do toast and put it on the top. So much water in it, then let it work off with the toast and yeast on top. She put all sorts of odds and ends in. And jam too. Made all our own jam.

Of course, kids used to put their hands round the corner of the door and pinch an apple or orange or something like that very often, but there was nothing really to worry about. Never had any real bother. Dad put a bottle of beer out every night for the policeman. There was a place in the yard where they used to keep the manure where he had a flat shelf on top of the wall. A crate of stout and a crate of ale came in every week, and a pin of beer used to be kept on top of the cellar stairs so that if anybody came in Dad could always give them a drink. Market gardeners, they'd have a drink.

We had big sheds at the back of the shop, but of course the van went in one part, the trap went in the other, the stables were there and rabbits were kept all the way round in hutches. We bred them for Christmas stock, so we didn't have a lot of storage room out there. We had rather a lot underneath the bins in the shop, but special apples like Worcesters, for times like Christmas, used to be taken upstairs and put under our beds. There was no special facilities for keeping them, they used to be in bushel baskets. Used to go to bed very often and put our hand under the bed and have an apple to eat.

We used to sell potatoes and things with the dirt still on them. If there was a big lump of dirt on them you'd break it off but otherwise you always sold them with the dirt. Never used to bother. I still prefer potatoes bought with the dirt on them. You buy this stuff all washed and put in plastic bags, it goes green. A potato with the dirt on it had been preserved in a clamp and naturally dried off properly. And we were brought up never to throw fruit. They would always be gently tipped so as not to bruise them before people got them.

My father never had a bank. Everything was done with cash in those days. Always cash, and he always kept it indoors in an iron safe. When he died we found a few hundred sovereigns there actually. He'd covered them with dust and layered them with pieces of wood. My brother sold the sovereigns for half a crown each to a man we always called 'Puddingy Hook'. He was a horse dealer. My father never ran accounts or books. He just settled up each day as he went along. At the end of the week all the coppers – it was only bought in penn'orths and ha'p'orths in the shop, you see – went into a bag. We used to do them up in shillings and roll them up in newspaper and tie them round, and we'd change them with some of the travellers probably. They would take that on your bill and then their bosses used to bank it. We used to keep our money on the mantelpiece in the living room at the back as we used to take it. We had farthings at one end, the coppers in the centre, and any silver or gold at the other end. I remember getting into trouble when I was only about seven. I gave half a sovereign away for a farthing, someone must have put half a sovereign up where the farthings were and I gave it away as a farthing change. I knew who I gave it to but they didn't let on.

My brother and I had to work in the shop. When I was six my father taught me how to use a chopper and chop up wood in the cellar. A merchant used to come round and he'd bring in logs and I had to chop the wood up and tie it up in bundles with a tarred string. People used to buy a halfpenny bundle to light their fires. And we had to deliver the stuff when we were quite small too. At one time I knew the street from one end to the other when I used to go out with my own basket and deliver the stuff. In fact, I've got one hip larger than the other where I used to carry a basket. And coal, I delivered in hundredweights or half or quarters in a wheelbarrow. I've carried a hundredweight too. My brother, who was five years older than me, he worked in the business all the time. Actually he took it over when my mother died and father broke his leg in the same month. My brother just took over the round, we had a maid in and we worked the shop. He was thirteen years, ten months so they let him leave school. I was nine years old. Father never actually did any more work after he broke his leg. He had an awful bother to get it to heal. All my dad was was the gentleman at home, going in and out to serve in the shop and doing the buying for my brother until he was old enough to do it all himself. He used to go to the Conservative Club nearly every afternoon, playing cards and drinking, I suppose. He let me have two years' apprenticeship at dressmaking, but he taught me that I could go in his shop and I was home till I was eighteen working in the shop. I used to do needlework in between to make myself a bit of pocket money because he never gave either of us a weekly wage of money or pocket money. As I say, I'd just get in the middle perhaps of making a silk blouse and somebody would come in for two pennyworth of dates. You hands would be all sticky! Or potatoes – used to have to go and wash every time. So at eighteen I really went to work on him and told him I was leaving. I only got ten shillings a week then but he never took any money off me.

Lots of things stopped when my mother died, ketchups and wines and all that. I think my father began to neglect everything when my mother died but he was introduced to my stepmother and I suppose that just made him pull himself together. She was a very nice person really, but she wasn't domesticated. She was a lady in her ways. She used to go in the shop – well she had nothing else really to do. As it all came off the shelves we used to string different sized brown paper bags up and hang them on the top shelves.

There were poor people in the area where we lived. To us, I suppose we were well off because we kept a shop. And my dad always had a method, he used to say, 'If you've only got 2*d* in your pocket, don't tell anyone.' You didn't have to let anybody know whether you were poor or whether you'd got it. That was his method. I think he'd been brought up a little bit that way. He just liked to keep up appearances. He made us keep it up, but, well, we never were as hard up as they were really. I've never known what it was to have to go near, not when I was young, though he was very tight with money. He never gave us pocket money. If we wanted any clothes or anything we just used to tell him and he used to give us the money to go and get them.

But we were just that little bit above the very poor. We weren't in want for anything. Always had plenty to eat and drink. Father considered himself just that much above the working class really, but I mean we learned to mix with everybody, whatever class they were. We were allowed to play out in the street, I mixed with any of them. It didn't make any difference. My parents didn't worry. I used to go in quite a lot of houses. One house especially we used to go into, when they finished with their breakfast in the morning the mother used to fill the teapot up with hot water and leave it on the dresser, then when the children were thirsty they used to go in and drink it as cold tea. And there was one family never had shoes. One of the kindest women that you could meet but Dad used to spend all his money in the pub. They had straw beds to sleep on and every year they used to have new. She gave us the old ones for our bonfire. No, I mixed with all of them, and we all went to school together. We were friends with all of them, never made any difference with the people. We got our living by their trade, and we weren't kept aloof from anybody. Some of them were tougher than others. The men used to come out of the pubs out in the streets and fight, but we never took any notice. We were always friends with all the neighbours. But we didn't have them in our house, only perhaps one or two of the girls that I was friendly with, perhaps for tea on a Sunday. We never went visiting unless it was anything very special. If there was a children's party, they'd give us an invitation but otherwise you never went out with parents, not mixing. Well, I should say Father was middle-class really. He'd been brought up quite decently, and although he had to work for his living to a certain extent, he did mix up with the élite of the town at the time, the mayor and leading tradesmen.

162

All those side streets, you know, it was a very poor area. People that were out of work used to go to a food kitchen at the town hall, and kids used to go down to the dockyard and beg bread from the men coming out if they had got anything left over. My husband can remember doing that when his father was out of work. 'Any bread left sir?' Of course, I never had to do that so I can't talk on it. But business people in those days were always willing to give anything if they thought people were really hard up. They used to give them tickets and there were certain shops they could go to. Hewitt that lived in Constitution Road, he would take all the grocery tickets. But you had to be really hard up. Father never took tickets but if he knew of anyone that was hard pushed he used to put them a bag of coal down or give them vegetables. Didn't used to charge for it. He always put vegetables in for one person in particular until she came in one day to buy a cabbage. They were a penny or threehalfpence each and she turned all his window over for this cabbage. A few days afterwards he saw her buying one off a chap that came round with a barrow. So he said, 'Well, if that's what you can do, that's what you can do in future.' So he stopped delivering stuff for nothing.

My father used to take the boys out of the cottage homes, orphans, before we were old enough, and keep them until they were old enough to go into the services. Boarded them and they helped in the business. I remember, after my mother died, coming home from school one day, and one of them came and met me at the bottom of the road and he took me into the High Street to a shop called Roger's, a toy shop, and bought me a big dog and a picture album. He said he nursed me when I was a baby in arms and he had to go with my mother and father on the van and keep me warm while they went cutting cabbages one frosty morning. Eventually my dad really blossomed out and he went on the Board of Guardians. Got mixed up with a crowd of, well, conservative people.

We never closed the shop, not for years until, well, the First World War. Half past seven in the morning till ten at night, every day of the week. I think I must have been about seventeen and we decided we were going to close the shop on Sunday if my dad would go to church. That's how we got the shop closed on a Sunday afternoon, but not in the morning. You took more money on a Sunday morning than you did all the week sometimes. Men used to go to the pubs, come out at lunch time, come in and buy stuff to take home for the afternoon.

The only time of the year that the shop was shut was the greengrocers' holiday on Whit Monday. They used to go to Upnor and put on a bit of a carnival effort, roundabouts, swings and stalls. I've still got a photograph of my father taken on a tin brooch at Upnor. Cost a few pence. They never had holidays like they do now. It was just an understood thing that they all had that one day out. The only holidays we children had was the Sunday School Outing in the meadow or sometimes as far as Herne Bay. Then when we closed the shop on Sundays sometimes we used to go out for a drive into the country.

We had a stable for three horses out the back but we used one for fodder, so we had one horse for the delivery round and one for the trap. Used to have a two-wheeled thing at first and then after my stepmother came we had the trap and then a four-wheeled one afterwards, rather a flash affair all done in black kid. We used to have to keep that clean and look after the harness for weekend. Horse medicines – father made all them himself. Never used to buy any. Of course he'd been in the artillery so he was in with horses. For cuts on a horse's knee – I always remember doing this – gunpowder and lard mixed together would make the hair grow again.

People used to come to us for heavy shopping, that they didn't want to carry home far, potatoes and greens, and then they used to go and get their other stuff in the town shops. So competition didn't really worry us all that much, you see. We just sold to the people round about. There was always somebody going round in the street though, taking all the odd stuff round. Barrows full of cabbages perhaps they'd bought off somebody. They might have been a little cheaper but not much different really, and my father wouldn't do cheap stuff.

You used to be able to get help for almost nothing. If you gave a kid a few sweets he'd come and do anything. He'd work all week for a shilling after school hours, and they'd go on the round on Saturdays. Boys used to come in – 'Can I help?' My mother used to have one boy come in and do the knives and forks. It turned out afterwards he was my brother-in-law. He said he remembered her putting the horse whip round him one morning because he was reading *Dick Turpin* instead of doing his knives and forks. And we normally had somebody round that used to come in all day, just someone round about. We used to treat them like somebody we knew, never really used them as a maid. They just helped do jobs in the house because my mother (not my own mother) never used to do anything in the house.

You could eat what you liked from the shop. Always had your pick. When strawberries or raspberries came in, we always had the first basket on our table for breakfast. And there was no shortage of meat either. Always had a big joint of meat for the weekend and in the week. My father would eat a pound of steak for his breakfast, or a pound of pig's fry. We had a cooked meal every day we did, but of course lots of other people didn't. We never went without anything really. I know during the war people couldn't buy things but we always had a supply of stuff sent in from the grocer. A seven-pound tin of corned beef and four-pounds of cheese every week.

My stepmother did dressmaking for about a year after she married Dad. She'd had two apprentices with her when my father married her. One finished her time but the other one hadn't so she had to do needlework until that girl finished her time. She came to our place and worked in the big room upstairs that they afterwards turned into a bed-sitting-room. Then she gave it up, because dressmaking wasn't no good at all. You used to only get half a crown for a boned blouse even in my time. She just didn't want to do it and there was enough money coming in to keep her. Of course she still made all our clothes. I was eleven when she came there and I used to sit and help do sewing and darning. That's where I got the idea that I wanted to do dressmaking. But I've known my father buy a second-hand suit just simply because it was nicely made. There was an old second-hand shop in Chatham. A man by the name of Samuels kept it. He always had gentry stuff in there. Real good suits, you know, brought down from London. That's where the fashion was. My father would go in there for a suit because he could get a good one for a lot less money. You could buy a lot of cheap stuff but you couldn't get good stuff. That was the only way you could afford quality.

My father bought a lot of second-hand stuff in those days. My stepsister and I had plain, ship's lino on the floor in our bedroom that came off the boats in the dockyard. We had ship's carpets all upstairs, dark red with a tiny blue design. They used to cover the rooms right over, and we never had hoovers. Used to put tea leaves on the floor, damp tea leaves, then brush it all up. Stop the dust rising. And we never had wardrobes, only chests of drawers. Downstairs we had a big room behind the shop and a very big kitchen with a stone floor. There were only chairs and a big wooden table that we used to have to scrub in there. It was a general room. The front bedroom was eventually made into a bed-sitting-room so that if we'd got company we could always take them upstairs. It was furnished with armchairs and settee, and a round table with a coloured cloth with odds and ends on it, pictures and prayer books and things all laid out.

No, I don't remember we ever got fed up with running the shop. We enjoyed the company. We enjoyed seeing people, and we learned to mix with everybody, whatever class they were. And you were never lonely, not when you could talk to anybody.

### Notes to Chapter 10

[1] Jefferys devotes only five pages to them: *Retail Trading*, pp. 244–50.
[2] R. S. Sayers, *A History of Economic Change in England, 1880–1930*, Oxford, 1967, p. 10.
[3] D. J. Oddy, 'Working-class diets in late nineteenth-century Britain', *Economic History Review*, 2nd series, XXIII, 1970, p. 322.
[4] Burnett, *Plenty and Want*, 1968 ed., p. 210.
[5] Booth, *Life and Labour*, I, p. 157; VIII, pp. 428, 432 quoted in Mathias, *Retailing*

*Revolution*, pp. 24–5.

[6]Burnett, *Plenty and Want*, pp. 130, 210–11.

[7]Roberts, 'Working-class standards of living', p. 314.

[8]S. Constantine, 'Amateur gardening and popular recreation in the 19th and 20th centuries', *Journal of Social History*, XIV, 1981, pp. 392–3.

[9]S. Meacham, *A Life Apart: the English Working Class, 1890–1914*, 1977, p. 78; University of Kent Oral History Collection, *passim*.

[10]Interview with Mrs K. Baker (born 1904), Canterbury coalman's daughter.

[11]C. S. Orwin and E. H. Whetham, *A History of British Agriculture, 1846–1914*, 1964, pp. 272–3; A. Torode, 'Trends in fruit consumption', in Barker *et al.* (eds.), *Our Changing Fare*, pp. 119–22.

[12]W. E. Bear, 'The food supply of Manchester, I, vegetable produce', *Journal of the Royal Agricultural Society*, 3rd series, VIII, 1897, p. 208.

[13]*Ibid.* pp. 208–27; Torode, 'Fruit conumption', pp. 125–8.

[14]'Others' have been excluded for the purpose of calculations. For mid-nineteenth-century shift to markets, Scola, 'Food markets', pp. 164–5.

[15]Booth, *Life and Labour*, VII, pp. 226–7.

[16]Deputations at Home Office, pp. 127–8 – also representing National Federation of Small Shopkeepers.

[17]Jefferys, *Retail Trading*, p. 245. Co-ops had two per cent of the market by 1920, multiples, one per cent.

166

# CHAPTER 11

# Saddlers
# — the horse's tailors

The retail saddler is almost always himself a practical man. He works in his own shop. and his men work alongside of him. He is one of the few surviving illustrations of the medieval workshop. His tools are simple and the work is good, there is none of the hurry, noise and bewilderment of machinery; and there is no mystery in production; for every passer-by may look in through door or window and watch the men at work.[1]

So wrote Charles Booth's able assistant, G. H. Duckworth, of the London saddlers in 1895. Specialisation was evident, with brown and black saddlers, harness makers, saddle-tree carvers ('a different industry altogether'), horse-collar makers, whip and rug makers all being included under the general term 'saddler', but mechanisation had made little headway and 'no two shops could be found in London which practised the same mode of doing work'. Sewing and stitching machines were used by women in the East End producing horse rugs, but the rest of the trade required handicraft skills and, in the case of saddler-tree carvers, strong labour. Consequently many workers lacked industrial work discipline; saddle-tree carvers in particular remained 'on the booze' for several weeks at a time and observed Saint Monday, the 'tradition in favour of the practice [being] so strong that education has not been able to break it down entirely'. The anachronistic, rural flavour was strengthened by the influx of young country saddlers who flocked to London for temporary employment, the city's workshops preferring to take on such men to training their own apprentices. Pay and conditions were good and 'neither men nor masters have much cause for complaint' although female machinists in the sweated rug trade fared less well. The craftsman/retailer, selling goods from his place of work still dominated saddlery and enjoyed a good living.

That such 'medieval workshops' should thrive in London, the largest and most progressive commercial city in a country emphatically conceived of as an industrial, modern nation, sixty years into the 'railway age', is, at first sight, surprising. Yet, as F. M. L. Thompson has shown, late Victorian and Edwardian England was, despite all this, 'still at heart a horse drawn society'.[2] Between 1871 and 1901 the percentage increase in the number of horses exceeded that of the human population; the peak was reached in 1902 when there were around three and a half million horses in England. This explosion in numbers was facilitated by the massive influx of cheap North American grain from the mid-1870s which overcame a potential food supply problem, lowered the cost of feeding and maintaining a horse and reduced transport costs and general price levels. Allied with new machinery like the reaper-binder, the horse was more widely employed on the land, ousting labour-intensive harvesting practices.[3] By 1900 some two hundred thousand animals were kept purely for hunting, no longer the exclusive reserve of landed society but a popular pursuit for the emulative urban manufacturing and professional classes. It was in the towns, however, that increasing utilisation of horse-power was most noticeable, increasing short-distance personal mobility, improving distributive channels, facilitating general economic expansion. Over half a million private carriages vied for road space with fleets of cabs, horse trams, buses and railway companies' vans; the major rail termini in London alone provided stabling for over six thousand horses which were used for short-haul services for passengers and goods deliveries. Not surprisingly, in view of the complexity and competitiveness of the expanding distributive sector and shopkeepers' emphasis on delivery services, horses kept for trade purposes experienced the greatest rise in numbers, increasing by some sixty per cent in the two decades after 1890 and continuing to rise long after numbers elsewhere in the economy had begun to stagnate or decline.[4]

Such an explosion of numbers brought with it problems of pollution and congestion, but to the army of various craftsmen and retailers – saddlers, blacksmiths, whip makers, carriage makers, etc. – who pandered to the horses', or their owners', whims and needs, it brought prosperity and apparent security. By 1901 there were over thirty thousand saddlers in England and Wales, dispersed all over the country with only small concentrations in the West Midlands. The growing demand for their products, however, failed to induce major changes in the organisation of their trade or the widespread emergence of factory-made goods. A transformation had apparently been on the cards as early as the 1850s when Walsall began to consolidate its reputation as the 'chief seat' of the British leather industry. By the following decade the town's workshops provided employment for over two thousand saddle and harness makers and several hundred workers in ancillary trades while, in the last quarter of the century, sewing machines operated by women in what threatened to become a sweated industry, were replacing skilled manual labour.[5]

Despite the localisation of the industry and the consequent external economies of scale achieved, however, Walsall manufacturers failed to present a major threat to scattered, small craft workshops. Cost advantages were negligible since methods of working resembled those in traditional saddlers' shops, there being few mechanical aids which they could utilise. Brown saddles were 'made exclusively by hand, chiefly by men', work discipline was lax and the 'factories' themselves remained small, rarely employing more than fifty people and the majority fewer than twenty.[6] The decisive factor in the industry's development had also been a flourishing export trade; when the development of native industries in Australia, South Africa, South America and even Russia seriously underminded this from the 1880s, it was they, and not the retail saddler, who had to adapt their strategy to survive. The journal *Saddlery and Harness*, launched in 1891, exhorted retail saddlers to discard domestic production and buy Walsall's wares instead but it appears to have been remarkably unsuccessful. Its letter columns provide the reasons for this. Walsall goods threatened to destroy the skilled basis of the saddler's trade and did not provide satisfactory financial returns as compensation, failing to match the profit margins achievable on the saddler's own hand-made products which could also be tailored to meet customers' specifications. Furthermore, the proud craftsmen, rightly or wrongly, feared the dilution of their trade and subscribed to the uncompromising view of one of their number that 'factory stuff is nowhere', 'rubbish' turned out by 'sweaters and blacklegs'. Within eighteen months of its inception the journal's editor was forced on to the defensive, decrying 'the opprobrium which is thrust upon manufactured goods . . . Surely the subdivision of labour tends rather to improve than to deteriorate the quality of workmanship?'[7] The Walsall men lacked the necessary capital to expand vertically into retailing to provide tied outlets for their goods as shoe manufacturers like Freeman, Hardy & Willis had done, and, as they faced insuperable difficulties if they dealt through non-specialist retailers who were unable to provide necessary after-sales servicing or advice, they were consequently unable to compete with the knowledgeable saddler and were obliged to turn away from horse gear to the growing luxury and leisure market for leather goods, catered for in the main by high-class retailers, including department stores. They continued to exhort the saddler, however, to dabble in these 'sidelines' and 'to obtain the business for which he is more adapted than those who at present have the greater part of it'.[8] *Saddlery and Harness* carried reports and pictures of shops which heeded its advice on diversification, but many skilled craftsmen still clung doggedly to the belief, substantially justified in the 1900s, that the horse business was sufficient. Significantly, it was not until 1930 that the Master Saddlers' Federation, the nucleus for manifold local associations, changed its title very belatedly to include 'Leather Goods Retailers'.[9]

The massive pre-war demand for horse-related products, therefore, continued to be met largely by independent, skilled craftsman. Unlike his close relatives, the cobblers and shoemakers, eclipsed by mass-manufactured footwear and chain stores, he was never seriously challenged.[10] Industrial and retailing revolutions scarcely affected him; 'His shop, instead of being what it ought – the mart of a successful and intelligent tradesman – is little more than a workshop, and he a workman instead of a salesman.'[11] Although some aspects of the trade had been modified – leather was now bought ready prepared, whips were frequently made elsewhere, and a few machines, for stitching leggings in particular, were being used – the saddler retained many elements of his craft tradition, producing hand-made goods, utilising primitive often makeshift tools and equipment, relying on home-made materials such as dye and wax. Even the limited specialisation of labour noticeable in London was lacking in provincial and rural workshops. The saddler also employed his skills in servicing and repair work since few leather items were cheap enough to allow discarding when worn. This repairing string to his bow was also denied the unfortunate cobbler since cheap footwear could be so discarded or repaired by the wearers, the possession of a last and the purchase of grindery, often ironically from a saddler, being commonly referred to in oral history recollections.

Complaints about 'unfair competition' were not, of course, eliminated in this favourable environment, and village shopkeepers and travelling auctioneers were criticised for selling 'articles that really belong to the saddler' but he experienced little real threat to his livelihood from them. His other problems also niggled rather than threatened: the excessively long credit which customers expected, the alleged blackmailing by grooms to secure their master's trade, the unseasonal weather of the 1880s and 1890s which ruined the hunting, heightened agricultural depression and reduced farmers' ability to pay. Generally, however, the saddler was able to 'command a fair profit on the trade he did, selling direct to the customer and thus doing away with the middleman's profit' while his repairing and servicing roles provided 'the backbone of every country saddler's business'.[12] Those who were enterprising enough to deal in various manufactured leather products were also protected after 1906 by the Saddlers' and Harness Makers' Proprietary Articles Trade Association, one of the earliest successful price-fixing organisations.[13]

The demise of the skilled saddler who refused to diversify came as a result of a massive decline in the demand for his goods rather than from the competition of mass-produced substitutes, new retailing organisations, excessive competition or the dilution of his trade. Since his fortune remained inextricably linked with that of the horse, he succumbed rapidly to the second transport revolution, the blossoming of the automobile age which called forth its own skilled élite of service craftsmen: engineers, upholsterers, electricians, mechanics. Various manifestations of the change before 1914 – the popularity of the pedal-cycle, country doctors' predilection for cars, the affluent minority's dabbling with such motorised status symbols, the virtual eclipse of horse-drawn buses and trams – were unfortunately treated with disdain. Few, even among informed circles, believed that the novel, unreliable forms of transport would ever displace the horse so entirely. Although horse power survived well into the present century, its decline was relatively rapid when it came. As late as 1924 there were still more trade horses than there had been in 1871; the Great Western Railway at Bristol retained two hundred delivery horses in 1930 and the tractor did not monopolise farming much before the late 1940s, but overall numbers were falling rapidly from the early 1920s and the writing was clearly on the wall for the horse's parasitic hangers-on.[14] Attempts by the National Horse Association supported by various saddlers' organisations to prove the superiority of the horse were futile. Reassurances in struggling saddlers' journals that the 'revival of the horse' was imminent, that the 'direct attack on the horse will fail' and that 'he is safe because his economic value is definitely established' were hollow and unconvincing. In 1930 the London branch of the Master Saddlers' Federation acknowledged 'insurmountable difficulties in the changed conditions' and recommended that members should diversify immediately into travelling and fancy goods 'to make good any deficiencies of the staple trade', advice proffered by manufacturers thirty years earlier but obviously only partially heeded.[15] By this time, however, it was too late. The new consumer leather goods trade, including sports equipment – which had a special supplement to itself in the last edition of *Saddlery and Harness* – was firmly in the hands of specialist retailers more attuned to modern fashions and sales techniques. Working saddlers, with their outdated premises and inherited emphasis on utilitarian horse products, had little hope of survival away from the less competitive rural or small market town environment.

Charles Evernden's recollections highlight both the static nature of the trade and the events which overtook it. Born in 1899 and entering the trade immediately after the First World War, he was to be the last practising saddler in the Wealden market town of Cranbrook. The family business, founded in 1816 by his great-grandfather, a local man who had served his apprenticeship at nearby

Tenterden and in distant Bermondsey, was to survive for over 150 years but some of its durable products like the founder's original tool bag and his son's hold-all which he took on a visit to Australia in 1852, have outlived it and remain in the family's possession.

Although minor adjustments in the business had taken place even before 1914 – the rope-making being phased out for example – it is clear that until the late 1940s very little else altered. The Everndens remained craftsmen first and retailers second. Their premises, despite the impressive window display (see plate 23) were primarily a workshop where they and their men made, sold and repaired their own products. Other stock, purchased infrequently from wholesalers or other local craftsmen, was closely related to farming, general rural domestic needs and the horse business: gloves, rope, rugs, embrocations, boot powder, grindery and horse medicines for those wagoners who did not rely entirely on their own concoctions. To the end their trade remained primitive in its methods with machinery making virtually no inroads, the underlying reason for this, here as elsewhere, being a firm conviction that hand-sewn leather products were superior in quality and strength.

As the major horse owners in the area, the gentry and farmers provided the bulk of the custom. Consequently the saddler, like other rural tradesmen, was obliged to give long credit and to adopt a deferential stance, although the 'jumped-up gentry', first-generation landowners, sorely tried his patience. The lifestyle was obviously hard but no more so than other tradesmen's and it was not without its compensations. Remuneration was adequate, especially in the trade's heyday before 1914 when Mr Evernden recalled that the family enjoyed day trips to Hastings, participated in local social functions and survived on a plain but wholesome diet. Opening hours were shorter than most retailers though the working day was considerably longer especially when away on service work or during busy seasons. The shop environment was warm and inviting, the work satisfying and rewarding but, in common with other saddlers, it simply failed to pay its way in the changing conditions. By the 1940s he admits, 'I couldn't keep going on one man's work. I'd got to find a quicker way of earning money so I gradually let the saddlery go and started going in for hardware.' By then, the leather goods trade, as it was now called, was organised on sophisticated, commercial lines. Exhibitions and trade conferences were dominated by firms' representatives and high-class retailers. Old-fashioned craftsmen were largely absent, Mr Evernden recalling that when he attended, he seemed to be the only one with 'dirty hands'.

## 66 *A country saddler*

The general saddler used to make practically anything in leather. A tremendous variety. Can't think of *all* the things we did, to tell you the truth. There were dozens and dozens of different sorts of harness and parts of harnesses for a start. Some of the tradesmen used to keep best harnesses as well as the ordinary working ones, and farmers, they'd have a light outfit for taking them to market, but it was always the gentry who had the best stuff. One farmer might have a dozen, fifteen horses at least because they'd always have two or three teams and a few odd horses for general work. There was no amount of work there for a start. The collars had got to be relined every nine to twelve months to keep them in condition. The farmers'd contract once a year to do all this work, so much a horse for twelve month, and we'd go out round the farms. They'd find our food and men to wash and clean the harness but the saddler would do all the repairs, oil it up, keep it waterproof, even reflock it because after twelve months they'd only got a thin lining of this hard straw left so you'd got to reline it. The farmers were all right really because they made some good cider, some of them did, and they used to give us a bit. But that was hard work. They wanted my father to continue it again after the First War but he said 'No', he wasn't going to start all over again.

Anything in leather, though, you made it; didn't matter what it was. Before there were any motor-mowers they used to have a farm horse or donkey to pull mowers over the lawns of these big houses so we made horse boots so they didn't cut the lawn to pieces. They were three or four thicknesses of leather for the sole and they were devils to mend. Although they'd got a thick thread, after they'd been used, wet and dry, wet and dry, the stitches used to go and we'd got to sew them up. That really was one of those tough jobs. It got so hard that every time you stuck your awl in there it would break the handle off the awl. Couldn't help it.

That's another thing we used to make – leggings. Sheepskin leggings, button leggings, spring leggings, there were at least four or five different sorts we sold, and made, in the old days. They were very popular. Keepers' leggings used to have a buff leather, the workers' ordinary black leather and some of the farmers had big long ones come right up to their thighs to protect themselves from rough old hedges. A lot of men had best ones too for when they were dressed up for Sunday best. We had a proper leggings room in those days and it was about the only things we used a machine for because you could do finer sewing.

Gloves of all sorts, hide gloves, felt gloves. I've made hundreds. We used to make them of white felt for wood cutters' cuffs, single thickness for the right hand for holding the tool and a double palm for the left hand. No matter how rough the hedge is you'll never get a thorn through there and however wet and cold it is, winter snow, wet through, that was still warmer than any leather glove would be. And they weren't slippery; you could hold wet, slimy wood and no danger of it slipping out of your hand when you were chopping it. Sheepskin gloves too we made, fairly fine ones, but as a rule the tailor made the best ones, the proper chamois leather. Practically all the gloves were hand sewn.

When my great-grandfather and grandfather ran the business we had our own rope walk. We made all our own rope for eighty years until about 1899, just before I was born. I've got newspaper cuttings of those days which claim that we had the best spinner in the country but I think they meant county. He was the man who did the actual spinning of the ropes on the rope walk. This was in the garden, about 150 yards long, ten or twelve feet wide with a lodge [shed] at each end. After they'd got their hemp or manilla or whatever they'd throw it on hitchells and comb it all out one way and then the spinner, he'd take about seven pound round his waist and walk backwards down the walk spinning this thread over the poles until it had built up into ropes. When they began to get machines – they did it in Ireland because I've still got a catalogue of Belfast rope works for the 1890s – it was cheaper to buy it than make it but we still used to sell a lot of rope though. Always had about half a dozen coils of all sizes up to three inch. We supplied all the churches around with bell rope and clock ropes and put new ropes in slaughterhouses. We'd go out to farms putting new ropes in rick cloths, in fact, they used a lot of rope on farms and instead of having leather traces some farmers would have rope traces for shims [hoes] and ploughs. Then, even in my time, we went round mending tents. Benenden Chest Hospital, when that first opened, it was all under canvas, marquees. One winter, before I was born this is, it snowed and snowed and my father had to go over there for a week or more, him and another man, sitting all day in the snow sewing these marquees because the snow had split the seams open.

There were some queer things to sew in the old days, you know. I'll tell you one of the worst things to do was one of those old basket trunks. They were sort of wicker baskets, the big ones, with a curved top and lined with waterproof stuff, outside and in. The corners used to come off and you'd got to sew them back on, right through this wicker basket as well as the lining. You couldn't get at it any other way, it was a devil of a job. Then we had one man come up there from Benenden [a few miles away], he used to bring his wife's artificial leg up to be mended wrapped in a travelling rug. He didn't want anybody to see it. It was one of these hollow ones and he used to come up hoping nobody would be in the shop. Many's the time I put a new strap on that. Trusses were another thing you had to do. They'd got to be covered in chamois leather but I never liked doing them because they weren't always clean. But you learned to do everything because they'd got to take things to Maidstone or Tunbridge Wells otherwise. The trouble was when they knew you did it they used to tell somebody else! – I mean, it was nice to have the work but some jobs were not so good. I mended an elephant's foot one day! An *enormous* foot. Somebody had brought it back from India and they had it for an umbrella stand. The stitches had all come out at the back. And if a dog had a badly cut foot I had to make a boot for it, a surgical boot in leather so they could put a bandage on it and a boot to protect it. I've had people knock me up Sunday morning to get me to make one of them. And kicking straps too, whether for a horse or dog or anything else. You were expected to do any job as a saddler, never turned a job away. Tables, chairs, practically anything we'd cover; and bellows, I've mended many a bellows up to about four foot long. They used to have these old chimney corners, these gentry, where they had great, long-handled bellows, all carved. I had to re-leather them and I always put my name inside them when I'd done them.

For a lot of jobs in the old days we didn't even go and buy special instruments. They were all home-made gadgets. We used needles but we also used pig bristles, the shoemaker did too, because they bend round so where you've got loops or you couldn't go right through we used these instead. When we spliced rope or opened it out we used an old natural cow's horn instead of a marlin spike. That was nice to hold and it was sharp and wouldn't spoil the lay of the rope because the rope would go back into place. I have one now that's been in use for anything from 100 to 150 years but I wouldn't part with it. There's nothing to beat it for splicing. Sometimes you'd see these old horns with a hole in them, at the end, what they call a drenching horn. Nearly every stable had one and they put horse's medicine, or cow's medicine in there. It acted as a medicine giver. Another thing we used that they never use nowadays – quills. It's surprising how many uses a quill's got, you know. For example, a lot of big carriage whips, they'd break sometimes and if you got a goose quill – we always kept a stock of those, I've still got some now – you can split those up, they bend inwards, fit in the whip and make an invisible mend. You put them round a bend, covered them over with white paper and put black binding on it, cross stitches, and it looked quite nice. Made a new whip out of it so you'd have to look twice to see it'd been mended. Did that for about fourpence. We always stocked a full range of whips from the best carriage whips to wagoners' whips, about half a crown a whip. Shoemakers and carpenters, like us, always had a box of broken glass on their bench. Now you have metal scrapers but it's much easier to get a bit of broken glass, it scrapes just as well and is much quicker. You just threw it away and got another when it lost its edge. We'd also use old bones for polishing the edges. Shoemakers were just the same.

Of course, we made all our own thread and all our own wax. In my time we bought these balls of fine hemp and flax, very fine. You'd run it over a hook about two or three foot away from you and then rub it on a leather apron and it'd pull apart, unravel a bit. Then you put two, three or four threads, or if you'd got one of those lawn boots perhaps five or six, and you'd rub them on an apron to twist them together because it's the twist that gives the spin and strength. Then you'd rub wax up and down it, either black wax or beeswax, to give it a coat and it would come to a very fine single thread at the ends so you could put a needle on. Well, for brown harness you used beeswax. In fact, in those days, every woman would have a packet of beeswax in her work basket to take the curl out of her thread. Covered with wax, thread'll last fifty or sixty years. Most harness work was black though and so we used black wax. We boiled up Swedish pitch, resin and neat's foot oil then tipped it into a pail of water. We'd have two grades, one for summer and one for winter. As soon as you put this in the water it went like a great big football with a skin on the outside, so you bared your arms and kneaded it under the water till you could handle it. Had to be careful that you didn't split it open or the hot wax would shoot up your arm. Then you took it out of the water as soon as you could handle it, carefully pulled it and twisted it like in toffee making, then cut it off in slabs into a pail of water. If that was good wax it'd float and it was better for you too, in the winter time when your pail of water would be frozen stiff and you'd got to break the ice to get the wax out to use it. If your wax had sunk to the bottom you'd to get your hand down in the cold water, otherwise you could just dip your finger and thumb in. We had one saddler who worked for us, he could never make it float and he used to get so cross. Ours all floated but he never did discover the secret. I can only think that it was just a knack of how you twisted it to get air into it. It must have been that. But the trouble was you couldn't use wax like that when it was freezing hard, otherwise it all peeled off the thread, so you had to have a warm shop.

There were over three thousand stitches on one trace and it was all done by hand, you know. We used to do fourteen stitches to the inch on brown harness, riding stuff. That's pretty fine stitching when you'd only got a little gas jet to work by. Nowadays with a machine they can make a row of holes that can make the stitches look ever so nice but they don't put much thread and wax in them, only a fine cobweb and as soon as it rains of course the thread breaks or rots. We filled the holes right up though. I mean, you could cut the top of the stitches afterwards and they'd still hold because the thread was fitted in so tight the wax would hold them. We used a diamond awl to make the holes and you mustn't turn it a fraction out otherwise you were piercing the next hole and spoiling your leather and stitching. You'd be surprised how one bad stitch shows up too. If you pulled your thread just too much it would bury it and sink down lower than the others and that would show up as well. So, if you saw a bit of stitching you could always tell whether the saddler was trained or not. And every stitch was pulled individually. That meant you could always tell a saddler because the backs of his fingers, his little fingers, they'd got big cracks there, especially in the winter time, where the thread had pulled and cut it and made it bleed. You filled them up with wax. That's all you had. You used to get it, put it over the gas jet and make it hot then pour it into the cracks. Sometimes you might make little finger stools, leather ones, if it was getting very bad, just a rough finger stool with no tip on them, to save your fingers but hot wax was about the best remedy there was I think. It hardened your finger edges. You didn't want anything soft, you wanted something that would form a harder skin on it afterwards. Every trade had its mark like that, you know. The miller always used his thumb for testing the grain and he felt the grain so much that he gradually flattened the thumb out and he had what they called a miller's thumb. A baker, you could always tell a baker! He always walked like this [feet splayed out] because he couldn't stand close enough to his bench without turning his feet out. And the carpenter, he'd generally got a bit of a humped back where he was always sawing wood. Every trade'd got its own mark.

We made our own dye as well. We'd boil barrels of black dye for leather marking or to sell to farmers for marking hop pockets or horse rugs. Made it from copperas and nut-gall, the old oak apple and we'd boil up to forty gallons at a time sometimes. It was lovely dye – I mean it could *dye*! Better than all this spirit stuff. We sold a lot of it. People used it for blacking shoes too. If you'd got a pair of brown shoes and you took the grease off you could stain them black quick with that. And you never sent a horse rug out that you'd made without dying the name of the farm on it. It got pinched otherwise. If you hadn't got a pattern for it you made your own. You'd cut all the stencils out of cardboard, get a couple of laths, knock them on there, cut the full name and farm and everything else and dye it on the rug or whatever. We got quite artistic, quite skilled at doing these names.

Most of the trade was home-made horse stuff. You didn't really do much retail selling in comparison. Saddlery agents came down now and again but even after the First War you only bought stuff for the shop once or twice a year. Mostly they were a lot of preparations; different polishes, harness preparations and embrocations, quite a variety of bottled stuff. Some of them were very good but I never could pronounce the names of some of them, they had about twenty-four-letter names some of these things. I remember Bickmore's gall cure. That was a thing we used for horses if they were rung, had broken skin perhaps from using a horse collar that ought to have been relined and that gave them sore shoulders. Also a lot of saddler's shops in the old days used to have these great big Vanner and Prest clocks, like parliamentary clocks. We had a coupon clock like this from the 1890s. This harness preparation called Molliscorium, we sold it for 2s 6d and 4s 6d , used to give coupons with it. Of course, wagoners and coachmen bought the dressing but they'd no hopes of getting the clock because they'd never used enough so the saddlers would give them so much for their coupons and have the clocks. I've still got ours. Only been done up once since and keeps perfect time.

Then we used to have about twelve different colours of boot top powder for the turnover tops of the coachmen's and footmen's boots. White, grey, all different shades of pink, red. My early days we stocked dozens of sponges, all types. Honeycombs galore, Elephant ears, Turks' heads — used the little Turkish bits for cleaning saddlery. Then we sold buckets and bellows. We dealt with one firm who kept twelve or thirteen wood carvers making bellows all day. Oh yes, and we sold a tremendous lot of mats. Most of those we bought. There used to be one or two local men, a blind man was one of them, they made some rope but mostly mats, doormats. Trugs, Sussex trugs made in willow, we got them mostly from Burwash or Hailsham. They used to go up to — what was it now? — a bushel I think was the biggest size. Then we sold bait sieves. They were like round sieves but were made with a cane base for feeding the horses. Funny thing too, until I retired in 1970 I still remember we ordered ox-muzzles. Used them for horses but they were still listed as ox-muzzles, nets to fit over the nose to stop them eating the fruit perhaps when they were shimming [hoeing]. We used to make and sell nets and snares too. I've never made them myself, I had too many jobs to do and we could buy them cheaply by then, but we had used to make them. In my days we got them from Bridport I think and we sold dozens of skeins to country people to make their own. It was a very popular pastime, netting rabbits. Plenty of farmers caught hundreds of rabbits. They said they paid better than the crops and that they didn't get as many crops of wheat a year as they did rabbits! Carriers used to call every week and pick up fifty or sixty rabbits, perhaps more, at a time. And snares, several gross in one day we could sell on Saturdays as a rule, single snares. We made them at one time but afterwards we bought humane ones with an eyelet in them so they didn't choke the rabbit, make them bold eyed. One firm we bought from, they kept a dozen or so girls on making snares all the year round. On machines this was. They must have made millions.

In those days shops weren't like they are now. The selling part was so small really. Ours was a workshop and shop combined and it had two counters, one special one for serving customers and the back one where we worked. It was like that till after, well, it was the 1920s before we did away with that because it got a bit dusty and dirty what with the flock and work in the saddler's shop. If you went into a shop you knew what it was because all the shops had their own scent. You could go in with your eyes shut. I still think the saddler's shop was the best scent of the lot, different leathers, they've all got that little different scent and those blended with Stockholm tar went well together. In the shop we always had, hanging from the ceiling, rows and rows of hemp, ropes, lines, halters, clothes lines, hair fillets, brushes and brooms. You couldn't see the ceiling. Must have been a tremendous weight hanging there. When the fashion came that everybody must keep their ceilings clean, have them painted and the rest of it, we just kept our stuff hanging up there.

We used to go to Benenden every week, twice a week initially. We had a workshop there which my grandfather started. He used to rent one of the cottages right in the middle of the village and used the big room for a workshop. The man who lived there had it rent free for taking our work in. Then Lord Cranbrook wanted it for a wagoner so he built us a workshop, matchboard lined, oak outside and corrugated iron. We went over there in the afternoon and stopped there until we finished our work, mending up horse collars and sewing until well into the evening. The trouble was, sometimes, people would get home from work after dark and instead of coming straight up to the shop they'd have their tea, clean up ready to come up the pub and then bring their work up. I've been there till twelve at night and my father's been over at Benenden till three in the morning and still had to be at work at seven next morning. And you never had much to eat there. The woman who had the cottage next to the workshop used to bring up a cup of hot tea at five o'clock but we never got any more till we got home. In the winter time the only heat we had was two Duplex lamps, oil lamps, and as soon as we got over there we'd put these lamps on the floor to warm the shop because the wax would be too cold to work otherwise. Cor! Good old days they were!

Farmers, the devils, wouldn't pay their bills some of them. They didn't want to. They were notorious for that. I know my father one day, he got hold of one old farmer by the beard and he said 'If you don't pay me, I'll pay you.' A usual thing then was to get all this credit on your books and you often had to wait twelve months before you got your money. Michaelmas generally, that was the usual time when they would pay you but sometimes you could even go several years before you got it. Even the Earl of Cranbrook, we used to have his account, he only paid once every six months and sometimes he'd go twelve depending on the steward. But you got more trouble when you had somebody come down from London, perhaps take a farm, have a few fields of cabbages, fruit, vegetables for selling at Covent Garden. They'd try to knock you down every time. They were a damn' nuisance. I know I had one particular one, he never wanted to pay the proper price for anything but he had to whether he liked it or not. I told him to take his work back to London where he could get the price if he wanted to.

There was one old lady customer, she used to come along with her coachman and footman and she wouldn't even get out! She used to slash our window with her whip and make us go out to her and see what she wanted. She wasn't popular, no. But the old Earl of Cranbrook used to come in and sit on the bench I've heard my father and grandfather say. Some of the other gentry would too, I know, because the men played a trick on one of them. He'd come in and sit on the bench so they slipped a bit of wax on it. He sat on it and when he come to get up he couldn't because his seat was a bit warm and it stuck him to it like a great lump of glue. He took it in good part. I don't believe in all this looking down on wealthy people. I mean, you find some bad ones, but they were really like the father of the family, the whole village looked up to keep them going and they used to look after everybody. Christmas time, they used to see that everybody got a Christmas dinner, didn't matter who they were. If anybody was ill they used to go round and look after them. People couldn't find fault with the Earl of Cranbrook's family at all. I've got a letter from Lady Cranbrook in about 1880 wishing my grandfather a very happy birthday and sending a little gift, yet she only knew him through being the saddler who did work for her. And they rebuilt the church at Benenden, restored it all and refurbished it inside. They built a club house for the village, and two or three wells in the parish, and they built a school and chapel in another little hamlet just outside the parish. Everybody depended on these people to do all this and they used to do it freely.

Before the war, right up to 1914, my grandfather kept four skilled saddlers on, an odd man to collect work and deliver it and a woman in the shop to do book-keeping. She was generally one of the family, an aunt I think. There were still three or four of us there between the wars but after the second war it gradually got worse, dropped off, and then there was only my father and myself. He was old, over eighty, so I ran it myself. Then I thought, blow this, I can earn more money than I am at this sort of thing. I'm not going to spend the rest of my life working for nothing. Remember, I'd got two lots of coach houses and stables and workshops and I had to work all day and night, it seemed just to pay the rates and taxes. In the old days they could manage, but I couldn't keep going on one man's work. So I gradually let the saddlery go and started going in for hardware. It soon paid me to give it up altogether. I was sad then in a way. It was restful sitting in the workshop even if you were on your own.

## Notes to Chapter 11

[1] Booth, *Life and Labour*, VI, p. 154; the section which follows draws from pp. 153–65.

[2] F. M. L. Thompson, *Victorian England: the Horse-Drawn Society*, 1972, p. 8.

[3] D. H. Morgan, *Harvests and Harvesting*, 1982, pp. 17–18.

[4] F. M. L. Thompson, 'Nineteenth-century horse sense', *Economic History Review*, XXIX, 1976, pp. 65, 80–1.

[5] E. Tonkinson, 'The Walsall and Midlands Leather Trades', University of Birmingham, M.Comm. thesis, 1947, especially chapters IV, VI, VIII; J. G. Jenkins, 'Saddlery and allied trades', *The Victoria History of the County of Stafford*, II, Oxford, 1967, pp. 235–8.

[6] Tonkinson, 'Leather trades', pp. 37, 22–3.

[7] *Saddlery and Harness*, Sept. 1892, p. 42; Dec. 1892, p. 109.

[8] Tonkinson, 'Leather trades', p. 46; *Saddlery and Harness*, Jan. 1906, pp. 3–4.

[9] *Saddlery and Harness*, July 1930, p. 7.

[10] Jefferys, *Retail Trading*, chapter XIV, 'The footwear trade'.

[11] *Saddlery and Harness*, Oct. 1891, p. 50.

[12] *Ibid.*, Oct. 1891, pp. 49–50; Oct. 1892, p. 80.

[13] Macrosty, *Trust Movement*, p. 255.

[14] Thompson, 'Horse sense', p. 80.

[15] *Saddlery and Harness*, Jan. 1930, p. 3; July 1930, pp. 3, 6.

# CHAPTER 12

# Pawnbrokers
# – the working man's bankers

Despite the acknowledged importance of the pawnbroker in the daily life of working class in the late nineteenth and early twentieth centuries, surprisingly little has ever been written about him. He was essentially an urban creature, rural areas lacking the necessary local clusters of potential customers with the pawning habit, a money-lender rather than a salesman, but still requiring premises to store the goods taken as security for loans. As we shall see, however, many diversified into general or second-hand trading too.

No other tradesmen have collectively received such a bad press. Although endearingly referred to by regular customers as 'uncles', critics have endowed them with Scrooge-like qualities. They have been maligned as parasites on the needy, aiders and abetters of petty thieves and subsidisers of spendthrifts and excessive drinkers. 'The great majority of people', commented Charles Dickens, 'are inclined to look upon a pawnbroker as a being who is not entitled to the least sympathy or friendly feeling . . . They regard a pawnshop as a sort of spider's web, into which poor flies, in the shape of human beings, are decoyed, while the pawnbroking spider laughs and grows fat at their expense.'[1] There was the implication, too, that there was something a little unsavoury and indelicate about making money out of loans to the poor and shiftless on the security of their 'napery and drapery', rumoured to be inseparable from offensive odours and 'livestock'. The social respect accorded in some degree to most tradesmen has been only begrudgingly bestowed on the pawnbroker.

The advancing of loans on the security of goods and chattels, the age-old basis of pawnbroking, has rarely been viewed as anything other than an evil by the state, a business prone to attract unscrupulous, undesirable characters. In many western European countries from the sixteenth century onwards it was actually run as a state monopoly, but in Britain it has always remained the domain of private individuals subject, however, to tight legal controls and supervision.[2] Even during the heyday of economic *laissez-faire* in the mid nineteenth century the pawnbroker was hemmed in by a multitude of petty restrictions, obliging him to keep details of all transactions and make them available for inspection, controlling his charges, even limiting his hours of business. The growing demand for small, short-term loans, however, spawned many illegal, unsupervised 'dollyshops' and money-lenders which threatened to destroy and undermine the licensed trade's existence and jeopardised its already insecure social standing. Partly as a result of pressure from the Pawnbrokers' National Association and Pawnbrokers' Defence Association, therefore, a House of Commons Select Committee was established in 1870. The Liberal government's ensuing Pawnbrokers' Act of 1872 can be seen as an attempt to protect the public from unscrupulous money-lenders but it was also far from ungenerous to the trade.[3]

Under this Act the pawnbroker's freedom of action was carefully circumscribed. He was not allowed to advance more than £10 on a single item unless he was also in possession of a money-lender's licence. The statutory maximum period for a loan was extended to twelve months and seven days after which the client forfeited his pledge if he had failed to redeem it or renew the loan by paying the interest due. However, only items on which the pawnbroker had lent 10s or less became his outright property. Higher-valued goods had to be disposed of at public auction, although the pawnbroker was allowed to fix a reserve price to ensure that he did not sell at a loss. Even then, for a period of three years after the disposal of the goods, the pawn ticket holder was entitled, on payment of 1d, to examine the pawnbroker's books and to claim any profit on the sale over and above the sum loaned to him after deducting accumulated interest, storage and auction charges.

Nevertheless, as its critics pointed out, this was not a measure designed to impoverish or abolish pawnbrokers. On loans up to £2 in value $\frac{1}{2}d$ interest on 2s, or any fraction of 2s, per month could be charged, this amounting to, at the very minimum, a hefty twenty-five per cent over the year, more if the item was redeemed regularly or valued in fractions of 2s units. In addition the pawnbroker was allowed to charge a fee for the ticket issued to the pledger, $\frac{1}{2}d$ on loans up to 10s, 1d above that amount, and, if the pledgers desired, an additional 1d for special storage of clothing – hanging boots or clothes to prevent creasing or laying garments out in drawers rather than racking them in tightly bound parcels. For loans over £2 and under £10 there were no restrictions, the pawnbroker being allowed to draw up a contract with his client fixing the interest rate, ticket charge, storage fee and period of loan. On balance it is not surprising that pawnbrokers did not object overmuch to the Act.

183

Those in the 'city' trade relied on long-term, substantial loans on jewellery and plate but the majority were 'industrial' pawnbrokers dealing primarily with small value pledges rarely amounting to more than a few shillings. Clearly, even with the generous charges fixed by law, they could thrive only if they had a large turnover of such pledges. Their success in achieving this – for in the heyday of the trade immediately before 1914 an estimated seventy-five per cent of articles were pledged for a week or less – probably contributed more to the popular image of pawnbrokers as poor men's parasites than any other single factor because it grossly inflated the true rate of interest which they charged. For a man's Sunday suit, a common security, pledged each Monday for 4s and redeemed each Saturday throughout the year, the pawner paid out 4s 4d interest, 2s 2d ticket fees, and probably a further 4s 4d hanging fees, a staggering 10s 10d interest and associated charges on the 4s advance. The same suit left in pawn for the maximum statutory period of one year incurred only 1s interest, ½d ticket fee and 1d hanging fee; total 1s 1½d.

The industrial pawnbroker, therefore, relied on his customers' inability or unwillingness to survive without the pledged items for more than a few days, on their willingness to see their possessions go 'up the spout', the popular name for the lift in pawnshops which took articles up to the storage area and down again in rapid succession.[4] By doing this he was open to the charge of making money out of others' misfortunes or personal failings including their continuing inability to live within a weekly budget. To some extent this is true, although it is a picture which needs careful qualification.

In the first place, we must recognise that convenience and logic might explain the working-class practice of frequenting the pawnshop so regularly. Without full-length wardrobes it was sensible to pawn Sunday best attire for the week if it was to be carefully hung. Valuables might be safer in the pawnbroker's than at home; they were at least insured. Migrant workers found it cheaper to pawn the tools of their trade if they returned home each weekend than pay a retaining charge on lodgings. Over a longer term mothers obtained credit on unwanted baby clothes.

Secondly, in a society where, despite the increasing standard of living, many lived close to the breadline and where provisions for the unfortunate were decidedly sparse – voluntary associations like friendly societies for those in regular employment, charity or degrading poor relief for the rest – 'uncle's' willingness to advance relatively generous sums on household items far in excess their market value to regular, or trusted customers was an important quasi-social service and was valued as such. As his nickname implies, he was viewed as part of the neighbourhood and kinship mutual assistance networks on which the urban

184

working classes relied so heavily.

Thirdly, it was rarely the very poor or destitute who paid the grossly inflated charges. These either had nothing to pawn or were not in a position to redeem regularly what they had. Similarly, it is worth noting that the pawnbroker was not encouraged to deal with drunkards or thieves. Their pledges, too, were unlikely to be redeemed and tied up valuable storage space and financial resources, while if discovered in possession of stolen goods it was the pawnbroker who was most likely to be prosecuted. He would certainly lose his licence, his passport to limited respectability and legitimate business.

The most plausible defence of the trade makes play of the fact that not one of the many possible reasons for pawning can be directly attributed to the pawnbroker's existence or his active crusading or advertising. He was not the *cause* of working-class poverty, financial ineptitude, drunkenness or crime. Nor was it *his* moral campaigning which convinced aspirers to respectability among the working classes that it was imperative to dress up at weekend to maintain social status. The inestimable burden on those sections of the working classes barely able to maintain the trappings of respectability or emulate their neighbours' lifestyles was the real cause of the pawnbroker's prosperity. Contrary to popular belief, therefore, 'uncle' thrived in times of high employment when his aspiring, consuming, but financially inept customers were consistently able to redeem their pledges. In depression his warehouse filled with unredeemed low-value second-hand clothing and household utensils which, by law, he could not dispose of for over a year. His income was almost non-existent, his cash reserves dwindled rapidly and the goodwill of his regular customers was jeopardised by his inability to lend as generously in their time of greatest need.

Possibly in an attempt to insure themselves against such an eventuality or simply to ease disposal of unredeemed goods, most pawnshops also had a 'front shop', so called because the entrance to the pledge department was usually discreetly hidden around the back of the premises. Here the pawnbroker sold a diverse mixture of new, cheap and second-hand clothing, drapery, jewellery, household fittings and furnishings. It was not uncommon for successful pawnbrokers eventually to open entirely separate premises as clothiers, house furnishers, jewellers, milliners, drapers or even boot and shoe retailers, this business subsequently becoming the major preoccupation rather than a mere adjunct to pawnbroking itself, especially when this began to decline after the First World War.

The number of pawnbrokers' licences issued rose dramatically in the late nineteenth century, reaching a peak of 5,089 in 1913–14. After this numbers fell steadily until by mid-century there were only 1,654.[5] It is not difficult to unravel

185

the reasons for his demise. On the one hand working-class demand for his services dropped. State provisions for personal misfortunes, the expansion of other forms of institutionalised credit, the breaking up of tightly knit urban communities which had looked within their ranks for mutual assistance in times of need, the possible expansion, rather than the erosion of the concept of respectability to exclude pawning as an acceptable habit, and, especially after 1945, higher wages and full employment – all these are in some way responsible. Costs have also risen while interest rates and charges have not. Higher returns could be made from straightforward retailing, cashing in on increased working-class spending power directly rather than lending to those less well placed. Recruits to the trade have consequently been rarer, staff more difficult to find. Financial rewards were meagre, social status diminished, the work unpleasant.

Both those whose accounts follow left the trade after 1918 largely for this last reason. Mrs Freda Clout (née White, born 1902), the eldest daughter of a Gillingham industrial pawnbroker, after assisting in her father's furniture shop, established on the proceeds of his pawnbroking, took up nursing as a career in 1918. Louis Loynes (born 1902) entered the trade only because, as a boy, he was unhappy at home and sought a situation where he could live in. His experiences in London pawnshops during the war years amounted to a life of confinement and monotony illuminated only by occasional Sunday outings or daydreams about tackling burglars single-handed. After a short spell in a draper's shop which he found more amenable but still unsatisfying, he set himself up as an artist, a following in which he spent the rest of his life.

These recollections do little to challenge the stereotyped picture of the pawnbroker as at best a hard businessman, at worst a miserly rogue. His invalid wife's condition did not deter Mr White from moving out of good-class residential accommodation to live in the 'awful hole' above his newly acquired High Street shop; his daughter still considers that he sacrificed his wife for his ambition. His household economies amounted to penny-pinching meanness. He was indifferent, or blind, to the social embarrassment this caused for his family. His reputation for tough bargaining and dealing, not always strictly legal it seems, was fully deserved. Louis Loynes's memories are less critical but they still illustrate how rules were bent, customers' addresses ignored, clothes not folded or hung. The meagre board and lodging he received seemed scant reward for his services.

The ambiguous social standing of the pawnbroker and the gradations within the trade emerge clearly from these extracts. Loynes's stepfather, an accountant, considered his entry into industrial pawnbroking, although potentially remunerative, to be socially degrading. Mr White's daughters on their way to private school were mercilessly ribbed in the street by children of the same class of people who were at other times embarrassingly intimate with their father. Although his pawnbroking and retailing ventures relied on others' craving for such items as lace curtains and pianos, Mr White clearly had no great yearning for the trappings of household respectability himself, even turning the hallowed front parlour into a clothing workshop. Mrs Clout had difficulty coming to terms with this parsimony and his obvious success as a businessman and leading freemason of the town.

Finally, the accounts shed light on the day-to-day affairs of the trade; the long hours which pawnbrokers, flying in the face of the majority of retailers, fought to maintain,[6] the daily fluctuations in custom, the employment of children as cheap labour, the pavement displays with the temptations they presented to pilferers, the variety of expedients resorted to to dispose of unredeemed pledges and the special relationship with the police. Louis Loynes's experiences do not bear out the contention that they were 'the best unpaid detectives in London' but there is certainly nothing to suggest that they actively encouraged crime as some critics suggested.[7] Easily overlooked, however, is the fact that, with a few exceptions, pawnbroking remained a skilled male profession. Apprenticeship to the trade was common and it was illegal to allow anyone under sixteen to take pledges in unsupervised. Mr White worked his way through the ranks and in turn took on an apprentice. Louis Loynes was officially one, and the luckless hero of Walter Greenwood's *Love on the Dole* had to struggle hard to avoid becoming one in the 1930s.[8] The skills did not, as in most other trades, involve manual dexterity or salesmanship. They centred around evaluating the customers themselves. There were no fixed 'prices' or pledge values for specific items; their value depended upon the pawnbroker's assessment of the pawner's willingness and ability to redeem and the speed at which he or she would do so. Items from comparative strangers, even high-value luxury items from regular customers, were not treated as favourably as weekly necessities like Sunday clothes, cooking utensils or tools of a trade. On these, which had an intrinsic value to the pledger far in excess of market value, he could lend heavily, but to do so without fully evaluating the chances of redemption or the risks of overburdening the customer with large debts which they were unable to pay off, would have been financial suicide. Competition in the trade was consequently limited, a newcomer outbidding established tradesmen (the equivalent to undercutting in most retail trades) at his peril especially since he was less sure of his customers. There is truth in the old saying that a pawnbroker knew his customers' financial positions better than they did themselves; such knowledge was, after all, as essential to his survival as the baker's ability to produce bread was to his. It was his job to know.

### 66 *An 'industrial' pawnbroker*

My father went from Southampton to London, to Bethnal Green, to a pawnbroker's to training when he was ten years old, and he and the other boys slept on the counter. They had no bedroom, they went from counter to warehouse to put their clothes on. They had their meals in a room overhead where there was an old girl, an old housekeeper, who used to prepare their meals. She used to turn them out on Sunday mornings and they were so hungry, he told me, they used to go to eating houses and stand over the gratings to get the smells from the kitchens. She let them in again at six o'clock at night and I think they were given a mug of cocoa and some bread and then banished to the store room again, the warehouse, to spend the rest of the evening until it was time to go to bed. If they weren't up in the morning they used to open the door and let the customers in the shop with them on the counter. He had 5s a week and he sent half a crown of that home to his mother, who was a widow. He paid so much for his laundry and the rest was his. That's what my father told me, indicating to me what a lucky child I was.

Well, he then got a job as a pawnbroker's manager at 121 High Street, Gillingham with a man named Sams. He was then married and had a young family – I was about four or five – and wanted to better himself, so he left the manager's job and started on his own in rented premises in the other end of the High Street, number 89, a place that had been empty for some time. It had been an undertaker's and it had a huge warehouse place at the back which I found out afterwards was where they did coffin making and that sort of thing, so he could use that for his pawnbroking warehouse, you see. Anyway we went there.

The shop used to open from eight o'clock every morning until about eight at night, Monday, Tuesday and Thursday. They had a half day Wednesday. Friday was nine o'clock and Saturday ten o'clock. My father and the staff, they had relief dinner hours, perhaps leave the boy or the man in the front shop and they had a particular way of knocking. We lived upstairs and they used to knock on the stairs for the old chap if he was needed, but they didn't do much pawnbroking business in the middle of the day. It was mostly morning, late afternoon and evening.

On Monday morning it was terrible, the noise, on the front of the shop. There were literally dozens of these people, anything from little boys to old women, waiting for the pawnbroker's to open to take the children's shoes out of pawn and put father's Sunday suit back in, because the kids couldn't go to school until

188

mother had got their boots out of pawn. They used to pawn everything under the sun, everything you can think of, from false teeth, locks of hair, even a false leg with a boot on it. We were very naughty children. At the weekend, if the leg was in, we used to go and fetch it and stick it under a table or something with the boot hanging out so that somebody might think that we'd got a burglar when they went into the room and saw this boot hanging out. Most of the stuff was small stuff. If anything was in for a pound that was a big thing. Mostly they were in for half a crown, five bob, because even that was a lot of money in those days, I mean it was a lot of money to get paid back.

Some of these customers were boozers. Terrible! They'd never got any money, didn't matter what you did for them, they'd never have any money. There was one old Irish lady though who used to come in regularly. Beautiful-quality stuff she used to bring you, but where it came from we don't know. But we hated her. If we heard her in the shop we wouldn't go down, but conditions were so bad that we had to come downstairs from the living quarters through the shop to go to the toilet out the back. So we had to go through with all these people in, we had to walk through the back of the counter. She, especially after out mother had died, she used to embarrass us by saying 'Ah, the little darlin', ah, there's a little darlin'.' So going through the shop the 'little darlin'' used to scoot through!

When the ships came into Gillingham, Chatham dockyard, the sailors were allowed out before they got their leave passes and they used to go out and have a proper booze up, spend most of their money. Then they used to come to the popshop before they went home to pawn things they'd brought home for their wives and their mums. I've seen the most beautiful Maltese lace scarves and mats, sort of Duchess sets, you know, dressing table sets. And those that had been to India brought in the lovely coloured shawls, embroidered shawls, little ornaments like those ebony elephants with the tusks. Of course, they never were redeemed because they had to wait until they went on board again. They never did get the money for it.

Widows had no other way of living hardly. One family in particular, the woman did feel it, she had to resort to pawning things. My father realised she was a genuine case and she used to have our washing to do, to take away. She had two or three boys to bring up so the eldest boy my father trained in the pawnbroker's and then he managed the front shop afterwards. We used to call him the mouse because he used to make funny little noises. He was killed in the 1914–18 war.

Of course, pawning, it didn't pay for the customers, because they used to have to pay so much interest. They paid us I think $\frac{1}{2}d$ for the ticket, a duplicate ticket with the pawnbroker's name printed on the top and a number. They would come in and give their stuff to the man. He'd value it. She'd say she wanted five bob and the man'd say, 'No, only four bob.' So she'd say, 'Oh, I'll take that.' Then the boys behind the counter used to fill these tickets in with the amount it was pawned for, and the articles, and the person's name and address. The ticket was torn in half, they had one and the other ticket was pinned on to the parcel they had pawned. They had wrappers, really old pieces of rag torn into squares, and they were done very tightly, rolled very tightly and pinned with huge pins. I should think they would be four times the length of an ordinary pin and three times as thick, and you had to have quite strong wrists to get them to pin these tickets on the parcels and then secure the parcel with one end of the wrapper. Then he had this huge warehouse out the back where all these parcels were stacked. They were stacked on racks by numbers, so that if anybody came in to redeem one, you looked at the number and the date on it and you went to the warehouse and, if they'd been stacked properly, you found your parcel quite easily. When they were redeemed the other half ticket was brought in and you took the two halves and pinned them together and then you had to go through the book and cross off those that had been redeemed, because every one of these tickets was entered into a book in numerical order.

The business of pawnbroker was conducted there with a front shop with second-hand clothing, jewellery and new men's clothing, generally working shirts, trousers, boots — Army boots — and socks, hosiery and all sorts of things — table cloths, old mohair table cloths and the velvet pile too, things for the home, well not exactly furniture but heavy furnishings. The local men, dockyard men, were keen on Navy flannel shirts, like the sailors used to wear, but they couldn't get them, the only way outsiders could get them was to have them copied, so my father employed a woman and she used to make these shirts up out of what they called Navy flannel, sort of white flannel with very short wide sleeves and a square neck piped with navy blue dungaree stuff. She worked over the shop in a room with a big machine, in one of our living rooms really. She made so many dozen of these things a week and did the bookkeeping for the pawnbroking as well. Then they used to have working men's clothes, what they called police trousers. They were very heavy navy melton cloth. He used to buy those and shirts, very heavy calico woven shirts, wholesale. They were all done up in bundles on the front of the shop with cheap new mats, carpets and chenille table cloths, and those big red hankies with spots on them that were very strong and that they used to take their dinners to work in, all hung up by their corners to make an outdoor display. Of course, second-hand clothing always sold very well but any jewellery my father took in pawn he used to sort and value, put them into two or three different piles. One lot went to Birmingham to a place, Nathan's in Vyse Street, for renovation. It used to come back very nice looking pieces of stuff.

The other stuff that wasn't any good, that was old fashioned or anything like that, he sold by weight and it went and was melted down. That went away by registered post to these people, or sometimes a traveller used to come and collect the stuff. But other stuff, which was cleaned up was put back into stock as it was.

On the whole of this outside display there were just big arc lamps with very awful smelling long carbon sticks in them. I think they called it carbide. Well, the old ladies used to wear capes in those days and they used to come along with their capes on and just whip these parcels of trousers and towels and things all outside the shop, just whip them up and hide them under their arm under their capes! Then of course the pawnbrokers had to catch them if they could. They were very friendly with the local police though – they knew one another by Christian names – and every week the police brought a list of stolen goods in and that used to be very useful. And the pawnbrokers had their own newspaper, called the *Pawnbrokers' Gazette*, that used to come by post. That used to publish details of stuff stolen in big robberies and from pawnbrokers. It was through that paper that they were able to catch up with a burglar they they'd had in a shop that my father's first boss managed at Sheerness. Father saw the description of the stuff and he said to his governor, 'Look, this looks like some of our stuff', and they followed it up and it was. They used to do all sorts of things, the thieves. The outdoor show used to have to be fetched in at night and the front shop was stacked high with everything in it. You could hardly get through to get out of the front door. On one occasion a man got in and hid himself up, got himself shut in at night so that he could have a go at the safe. I remember the police caught him in the end and he admitted in court how he'd got in the night before.

Our living accommodation above the shop was very bad. Terrible really. There was a fair-size room, looking out on to the front, that was supposed to be our sitting room, front room and all the rest of it, but this woman, the one I was telling you about who made the shirts, she was installed in there with a machine. That used to be packed up at weekends though and we used to use it then. Then at the back was a room with a sink in it and a fireplace and a black iron gas cooker. We used to feed and all in that room. There was just a round wooden table which five of us sat round, a bureau bookcase and an armchair where my father sat and read his paper. Never had carpets, only lino. Leading from there was a small back bedroom which my father used and a winding staircase to two apartments at the top. The front one wasn't so bad – it had a little dormer window and the housekeeper that looked after us when mother was ill, she slept in that part and one of my sisters had a cot in a corner. The other room had no window. I wonder we ever survived. We had little old iron beds, like hospital beds in here. In the summer it was furiously hot. And the fleas! I used to be kept home from school in

191

the summer because the fleas bit me so. I used to get jolly great blains. Used to do the boards with turps to keep these animals down. It was really awful. And it's unbelievable how awkward things were in that place. They did have to work hard to keep the place clean. The housekeeper used to cart washing down the night before into the house next door which was empty, that the old man had either bought or rented, into the back kitchen of the place next door to do the washing. It was an awful hole to live in but I heard my father criticise other people that bought their own private houses and moved out of the High Street. He always said that once a man did that his business suffered. His business was his life. They said – with his ambition he sacrificed his wife. My mother had T.B., but father, being an ambitious and selfish man, moved her and the three small children from Priestfield Road to these terrible living conditions and it was too much for her. She was in bed all the time there in a water bed which a nurse used to come every so often and change. Mother never survived it long. She died in 1910 of T.B. No, his business was his life.

He was in with all the business people, and he was a freemason. Nearly all the tradespeople were freemasons, there were three or four lodges in town. We went to lovely parties at Christmas time and they were held in what was called the Masonic Temple. We went in our best clothes and our white party stuff, silk frock and mittens and a fan. You always took a fan, and little boys used to go in evening suits. They used to serve the most beautiful food catered for by a local baker who was also a freemason. His name was Thorne and I always remember him because he was so good to mother and always sent mother some special soup and iced pudding when they had these installation banquets, marvellous seven-course banquets. They would all help one another. In the lodge there were two gentlemen, two local grocers. One was manager of a firm called Camburns and the other had a private business. Well, one week it was Mr Hills's turn for the grocery order, whether you wanted him or not, and next week it was Sid Cornelius who was manager of the other place, whether you liked his bacon or what have you. You couldn't buy your groceries anywhere you wanted to!

But my father had some very funny ways and he was a very hard bargainer. I've heard him argue with travellers – mind you, some of them did need to have somebody that could stand up to them! And he was very, very careful, in fact he was Scroogey with his money, even after he married again. I know he got rid of certain assistants because he thought they were being too generous with the customers. I suppose gas must have been expensive because he always used to be on about burning it and not letting the flames come up round the kettle because it didn't do any good and it wasted gas. One thing in particular I remember. The convent we went to closed down. I was school-leaving age so I left and was put in the business but my two sisters were sent to Rochester Grammar School. Well, you know, when you go to a school like that there are certain clothes, uniforms and things that you've got to buy. Well, instead of buying the proper ones he racked his brains to get things made out of old materials and they weren't the same, you could see they weren't the same. My sisters were very embarrassed by it because these other children all went in proper uniforms and they had these sort of made-up things. Before my mother died we had a housekeeper and she was wonderful to us and our mother. She had many rows with my father over the way he treated us. What was odd was that it was a struggle to squeeze money out for clothes for us yet he was determined to pay school fees which were quite heavy in those days, a guinea a term for the three of us. I think it was that my mother was a schoolteacher and it was her wish that we went to a private school. He'd promised her that. My father was a very strict, narrow-minded man and he had a very violent temper. If we did anything wrong he used to stand us in a row and thrash us, cane us with our hands out, and if we flinched we got an extra one. At the end of this performance we used to be told to go to bed and we used to run for our lives up the stairs because he used to cane our legs all the way up the stairs. I never loved my father. I mean I respected him, but I always feared him.

In the town father was Uncle Fred. The bloke along the street, the other pawnbroker, was Uncle Sam. I used to be most disgusted as a child. We used to walk to Gillingham church on a Sunday and when we came home we'd meet some of these old customers of my father's and he always used to raise his hat and say, 'Good morning, Mrs So-and-so', and I used to be so disgusted when these old women used to shout out, 'Morning, Uncle Fred.' I was reprimanded for making comments about these old girls. And we had a terrible time as kids going to school. You see, the convent we went to and the one other little private school were the only ones other than what were called Board Schools and when we were about eight or nine years old these other kids all used to shout out 'Popshop'.

Anyway, my father did very well indeed, so much so that he bought a doctor's house that was going along the other end of the High Street and had it made into a first-class house furnisher's. There was enough living accommodation at the back and we even had a bathroom which *was* something and *two* toilets, one outside and one indoors. By then, I mean he was getting on a bit, getting on not only in age but in finance and he was doing quite nicely. He put a manager in the pawnbroker's and he used to work between the two. They had a queer-looking telephone sort of communication line from shop to shop and if the manager got anything in that he was dubious about, say some jewellery that he was wondering where the party had got it from, he would contact the old man. After I left school I went in this business for 10s a week. I was only about sixteen or seventeen so I had to do it, I couldn't refuse. I used to look after the shop and clean the plate glass windows – because the men had gone to war and the boys couldn't do it – and every second or third day the errand boy from the pawnbroker's used to march the book along to the office in the furnisher's to me and I used to have to check all the tickets off when they were redeemed as well. I was told I was a very lucky girl because I had 10s a week to buy my own clothes, I was fed at home; but I was the general skivvy as well as being in the business and booking and serving in the shop.

They used to do a big trade in big lace curtains in those days in this furnisher's shop. I don't know why quite, whether we had a special source for them or they were extra good. He always had two or three pianos on the front as well and it was nothing to sell three a week. They used to go from £30 to £50 according to condition. During the war people went piano-mad and I can remember him buying seven second-hand ones from Leicester which all came down by rail. He was always very chary about credit. We always had to check and make certain about it. One thing he impressed on me in the business – no credit for Navy or Army officers, because they were such bad payers and they used to move about from place to place and you couldn't catch them. No credit. He was most emphatic about that.

He'd also one or two 'sidelines'. He'd buy property, say a house, and sell it again without the deeds being changed. And another thing he did. Just after the war they had dockyard sales when they were refitting the ships. All the stuff that came out, wash basins and tables, chairs, even buckets and bowls and everything else, was put in sales in Chatham dockyard. My father and the local auctioneer were in league together and it used to be worked that they were knocked down, the lots, to my dad and then when dealers from London and anywhere wanted anything they had to do it through him you see. He used to buy stuff there and sell it again on the spot without touching it! He even had a cinema built, although that was later on. No, he wasn't badly off at all when he went.

---

**66** *A London pawnbroker's apprentice*

Lots of boys left school at thirteen, got jobs as errand boys and got very good money. During the war there was a great shortage of boys and you could get lots of jobs, but not to live in. I wanted to leave home. I liked the idea and my stepfather wanted me out because of these damn' kids around him. He'd got a big family, you see, so he wouldn't argue. So I left home and my twin brother left home and we got into a pawnbroker's where we could sleep and live. My stepfather said we should get into jewellery, because there's money in jewellery but, although there were a few that did, very few, jewellers wouldn't take you on to live there, but pawnbrokers did because they had all that stuff in pawn and they had to keep boys there all night for burglars. Anyway I went to one pawnbroker's for a year and then I went to another one in Hammersmith where I got more money. I started off at 3s 9d a week and later on got 5s. If I got into a lower-class pawnbroker's I could have got a lot more but I would have had to work a lot more and they said to me, 'You don't want to work hard, do you?' I didn't mind work. I wanted the money. I wasn't afraid of work. So they said, 'Well, you don't want to be a working man, do you?' There was plenty of work for everybody in the war. There was a rule everywhere – all my friends in the pawnbroker's, both pawnbrokers, and visitors to pawnbrokers, they all agreed on one thing. When times are bad pawnbrokerage is bad, when times are good, pawnbrokerage is good. Now people who aren't in the trade think the reverse. They think when times are bad the pawnbrokers are doing well. I never found that at all. When times are bad and there's a shortage of money, the pawnbrokers have it rough too. When times are good and there is plenty of money about they go to the pawnbrokers.

If people pawned jewels or watches they could come into a special little cubbyhole which was set aside for them, but if they had clothes or sheets they had to come into the back part where there were cubicles and they'd get in there and chat. I could pick up a lot of things listening to them, all the scandal and so on. We had to take everybody's name and address, but that was guesswork. We guessed their names and guessed their addresses. Put anything down on the pawn ticket. Well, when they'd got the ticket, whoever had that ticket could get the things out of pawn, so it didn't matter what name was on the ticket or what the address was. It was only a legal matter. By law you had to ask. At the beginning I used to ask their full name, how did you spell it and so on, get their full address – 15, 15 what – but after a while you got tired of all that. You just scribbled out any name, Marie Louis, any name, any address, Buckingham Palace, any address you like. They never argued, came in a week later and redeemed it.

Pawnbrokers used to say, the law is that you lend a third of its value, but we always lend the whole value and we only want them to get it out. We lent the whole value of anything. Now, I was supposed to be an apprentice and I tried to take things in pawn. They'd say 'Now you do this parcel.' I couldn't assess the value of anything at all. I'd just make a guess. 'No, no', they said. 'No, 9d for this, 1s 6d for that, 3s for this. Let this go it's a towel', and so on. People often wanted more but we used to lend very high so very often that they didn't argue.

Pawnbrokers liked it if stuff was redeemed. I said to them once, 'What does the three balls stand for?' and they said, 'It's two to one you don't take it out, two to one you don't redeem it.'

But pawning was very uneconomic. People'd pawn the same thing again and again and all the time they're paying what amounted to thirty-odd per cent interest per year. They didn't realise that. It was all in halfpennies and pennies. Now if they'd borrowed something to go on with they could've stopped pawning, but they never did, they always pawned. They'd have to take it out next week, take out the husband's Sunday suit of clothes, bring it back on Monday again. They never gained by it. It doesn't pay to borrow money and keep paying interest and every time they took it out of course they paid more interest. If they'd left it in they'd have paid less but they kept taking it out. They pawned for a week or part of a month, a halfpenny in 2s with a penny for the ticket and a penny for the drawer to keep them tidy. You charge a penny for that. They'd say, 'Put it in the drawer. Keep it nice won't you? You won't get it rumpled.' 'Oh, yes, we'll keep it in a drawer, especially yours, yes. One penny.' There was no drawer. You just dumped them in their proper place with a number. And boots, if you parcel them up they get cramped and get spoilt, so they had to be hung up. We had to charge a penny for hanging them. They never got hung up at all. They were kept wrapped up in a cloth and went with all the others.

Every year a chap called and he made notes of everything in pawn that was 'out of pawn', that is to say, they had been in pawn for a year and a week, unredeemed stock. He would make a list of it all and he would give us a cheque for that plus so much per cent and take the lot away, the pawnbroker's price plus five per cent or ten per cent, I can't remember which. So we never did any sales. But in the East End outside the pawnbrokers' there was a great stall and they could sell things very cheap that way. When people had an evening dress or an evening suit it didn't mean that they'd gone to the tailor to get an evening suit made, it meant they went to a pawnbroker's and got one, or hired one. People would die off, you see, and the butler used to pawn the clothes and not redeem them.

Every morning a huge bundle of paper, roneod off, came from the police. It came every morning, bonk, a great wad of paper and it went straight into the waste-paper basket. I went through some of them once and they were a long list of objects which had been stolen, including bicycles. Well, I thought, we ought to watch that because a chap might come in with something. But the manager said, 'Well, we did that years ago, but after five days we got so tired of seeing the thing we put it in the waste basket.' All that was wasted you see, but I remember a chap did come in with six watches and I said to him, 'We don't take those sir.' 'Why not?' 'We don't take those.' 'Well, what do you take?' 'Nothing sir, nothing from you', because I could see he was a pickpocket. Who would have six watches to pawn unless he was a pickpocket?

We had a fierce dog which was always getting stolen, but he'd got his name and address on and he knew his way back. They'd steal it in order to bring it back and get half a crown reward. They'd manage it somehow. It wasn't fierce during the day, it was only fierce when strangers came in at night. It would bark its head off and show its teeth when strangers were about, but in the day it was quite normal, quite happy. I had to bath that dog every Saturday. I hated that job. The dog slept under the counter among the cloths for wrapping parcels up with. I slept on the counter on a mattress. During the evening people would knock on the door or ring the bell on some pretext trying to get in but we had chains about and we had to take care they didn't get in. They couldn't get in. I used to wish they would. I used to think, if only we had a burglar. Forty years after I'd left I read in the papers that that very shop had been burgled. They weren't sitting on the counter any more. I think it's against the law. Two burglars got in, got hold of a chap with a pistol, made him go down stairs into the kitchen and stole what they could. I thought, well, if they'd made me go downstairs there was an iron railing, I'd have gone into the passage, I could have caught hold of their legs easily, made them fall down the stairs. How they got away with it I don't know. But I never got a burglar.

For a while I had a boy with me, a boy companion, but he got a job in munitions. A boy could always get in munitions. There was money in munitions. We used to have every Sunday off while my colleague was there, then every Thursday afternoon off. There were no amenities at all. I just used to wander the streets, too proud to go home, too proud to tell my people in the pawnbroker's that I wasn't going home and wouldn't have something to eat. So I wandered the streets with nothing to eat. When I came home at night they said, 'Haven't you had your tea, Louis?' I said, 'Yes, but it was a long time ago', and made some excuse, so they made me a cup of coffee and gave me a slice of bread and margarine. So I thought, well, that's something, last me till breakfast. But I used to steal the dog biscuits. The dog had better food than I did, and I used to steal these biscuits and get into the park and eat them in the park. They were very good. My colleague, he came from a good family, and he put up a stink. There was a row about it because he didn't get enough food, but I was too proud to argue.

What I liked about the first pawnbroker's in Earls Court was the museums in South Kensington. That was a wonderful world opened up there. They were free and I went in there. It was nice and cosy and everything to see. Wonderful things to see. I loved that. I've been a museum fan ever since. I got my culture there if you can call it culture. On the way home I'd get into a cinema which opened at six o'clock or so for fourpence. I'd get in there and have a sit down. But really it was a dreary life. In 1918 I left and I got better money and better food, better lodging, twice as much of everything and less work in this wholesale draper's stores. There were thousands of fellows and thousands of girls, plenty of people and plenty of social life. The hours of work were much less, much more leisure. I got 10s a week instead of five, easy work and plenty of amenities. I stayed there for a year.

## Notes to Chapter 12

[1]C. Dickens, 'My uncle', *All The Year Round*, n.s., XXXVII, 1885, pp. 245–51.
[2]Anon., 'Pawnbroking', *Quarterly Review*, CLV, 1883, pp. 106–33.
[3]For a detailed description of the 1872 Act and its passage, A Hardaker, *A Brief History of Pawnbroking*, 1892; Select Committee on Pawnbrokers, P.P. 1870, VIII, pp. 391–714; 1871, XI, pp. 377ff.; 1872 XII, pp. 1ff.; III, p. 689.
[4]The phrase is first recorded in J. H. Vaux, *Flash Dictionary*, 1812.
[5]A. L. Minkes, 'The decline of pawnbroking', *Economica*, XX, 1953, pp. 10–23.
[6]See p. 94 above.
[7]The alleged involvement of pawnbrokers with organised crime led to detailed official investigation in the early 1880s. Select Committee of the House of Lords on the Stolen Goods Bill, P.P. 1881, XII, pp. 119ff.; 1882, XIII, pp. 703ff.
[8]W. Greenwood, *Love on the Dole*, 1933, chapter 4.

# CHAPTER 13

# The village shop
## —a department store in miniature

The stereotyped proprietor of the village general shop has been the wife of a labourer or a penurious widow attempting to eke out a living from its meagre turnover. Some writers automatically refer to the shopkeeper as 'she'. Consequently, the shop has invariably been assumed to be small, clean and tidy, but hardly business-like, ignoring the usual rules of shop management. The shopkeeper provided more of a social service, giving credit and furnishing a meeting place for the interchange of local gossip. The work itself was easy, involving long periods of inactivity; no one could possibly be overworked there. In the famous little post office at Candleford Green Flora Thompson enjoyed 'long, quiet intervals in which meals could be taken in comparative peace, or reading or knitting were possible'.[1] W. H. Simmonds's treatment of rural trading verged on the romantic and condescending. 'In our broad village street the cottages stand back from the road half-hidden among the lilacs and gooseberry bushes, and over the door of one of them we read the notice "Post Office".' The window display, little more than a collection of oddments, was 'entirely shut off from any but the mounted passers-by by a large clump of lupins growing a yard from the window'. This, 'the old and rural and quiet', he contrasted with 'the new and "up-to-date" . . . the bustle and hum and smartness of a first-class shop in one of the largest of our busy commercial cities'.[2]

Such shops certainly existed. At Corsley in Wiltshire in 1904, 'at least three women kept shop, in addition to other occupations or to supplement the earnings of their menkind. One of these does a good business, but little is done by the others.'[3] 'Progressive shops', as Wallace Arter (born 1898) calls them, were also lacking in his childhood village of Bishopsbourne:

The village shop was rather a funny arrangement. It was the passageway of a cottage between the pub and some farm cottages. You went in the front door weekdays, and an old lady used to come forward, you would order what you wanted and she went poodling off somewhere in the back room to a row of shelves. If she'd got it she brought it and you paid for it. The room to the side was a sort of store room and we kids used to peep through the window and see the wonderful things in the jars and the boxes that could be bought if you'd got any money. Now it was a very small house, and the old lady who kept it had got two unmarried daughters and a son who came home sometimes, so when they shut the shop on a Saturday night, there was an immediate transformation. Back in the window that we used to look through to see the sweets on display would be a big aspidistra in a pot, there would be lace curtains up each side of the window and curtains drawn over the shelves inside. The old piano was pushed out from somewhere, from an odd corner, and Sunday evenings they used to treat themselves, and the village, to songs round the piano, what we used to call a 'scorpion match' because, in sharp contrast, on Saturday night, next door they usually had a sing-song in the pub, in the bar parlour, which was only two bricks' thickness from the shop. My goodness! they used to go straight through your head sometimes, some of those songs.

The only characteristic common to all village shops, however, was their rural setting. They ranged from the pathetic display of goods in a front-room window to the thriving business not unlike a primitive department store, appealing to a broad spectrum of local society, offering personal attention and an impressive selection of goods – drapery, haberdashery, hosiery, grocery, toys, hardware, medicines. Such a business called for considerable skill and tact to succeed. The shopkeeper was expected to be knowledgeable about a diverse range of trades which in the towns still required some form of training, if not apprenticeship. He was also expected to be equally at ease with gentry and agricultural labourers and yet, by virtue of his occupation, he was excluded from both of their social circles. The degree to which village traders met these challenges must have varied considerably.

Much of the stock of the village shop of 1900 would have been found on a hawker's back or in a Cheap Jack's cart a hundred years earlier. Groceries, especially high-value, low-bulk items like tea, hosiery and haberdashery were distributed by packmen while hawkers often operating from fixed premises in towns and possessing a pony and cart hauled drapery, crockery and hardware around rural areas.[4] Although it was still possible to succeed as a hawker in the late nineteenth century, as Michael Marks's rise demonstrates, the opportunity for, and benefits from, itinerant trading were gradually being whittled away.[5] Items such as pins, thread and reels of cotton were carried by tramps to disguise their begging. Other hawkers sold foodstuffs like fish ('a wonderful change from bacon') for which regular supplies and, consequently, outlets were lacking in the countryside. From the descriptions we have these fish sellers appear to have been colourful characters. Wallace Arter again:

> There was an old lady from Canterbury named Olive, surname was Olive, who used to push an old pram loaded up with fish – not fresh fish, only kippers and bloaters – call at every house, pass on all the scandal, have a cup of tea, possibly sell a couple of bloaters and push on back. If you wanted fresh fish there were an old man named Clements who came round and cleaned up the fish on a little wooden slab. God knows what sort of living they made.

William Nichols (born 1898) also has recollections of a similar hawker:

> Every Saturday morning – and this was the only fish that I knew of – this man, they used to call him Fishy, walked from Strood, four miles, with a barrow with fish on. On one great occasion the visiting football team was short of one man and they picked Fishy to play in goal. The most amazing performance you ever saw; he let about twenty through!

The expanding rail network which had served initially to increase the distances which hawkers could travel, ultimately assisted the rural shopkeeper more, allowing him to obtain supplies from wholesalers and manufacturers by making use of the postal services or dealing directly with the new breed of travelling representatives. Suppliers tended to prefer traders with fixed premises to hawkers; they were more likely to develop the potential of the local market, to place regular orders and to prove creditworthy. Enterprising wholesaler/retailers in towns who allowed the rural shopkeeper discount on purchases to secure his custom came to view village shops as equivalent to branches, permanent outlets for their own goods. Simultaneously, the expansion of retailing from fixed premises in urban areas robbed itinerants of their valuable winter trade. By the end of the century, therefore, hawking had been reduced to a fringe activity in retailing. Most traders travelled only short distances. Only gypsies with their pegs and lucky charms remained of the old-style itinerants; their trade now belonged to the village shop.[6]

The creation of a national postal service requiring permanent bases throughout the country for its efficient operation further assisted the village shopkeeper. A post office demanded that someone be on the premises continuously but the salary paid, especially to those in charge of non-money-order offices, was insufficient to maintain an individual, let alone a family. The sub-postmaster or mistress, therefore, looked for an additional source of income which did not involve working away from the premises; not surprisingly they relied on retailing. Conversely, the existing shopkeeper found it worthwhile to obtain a licence to run a post office since nothing acted as a better advertisement for his shop. The local population were drawn towards his premises for mail or stamps with increasing frequency as literacy spread and expanded the use of the postal service. Dealing with the mail he also became personally acquainted with all the villagers. Even in the shops which did not operate a post office, stamps were often sold unofficially to attract custom. Trade directories reveal that many sub-postmasters were also listed as retailers or traders – bootmakers, chemists, stationers and, most commonly, grocers or simply shopkeepers.

These favourable developments, however, did not mean that village shops necessarily prospered or that they were local monopolies. In most villages like Corsley, there was 'no lack of competition for the custom of the labouring classes'.[2] Before 1914 this competition came not from infant mail order businesses which later destroyed much of the rural drapery trade, but from town tradesmen. As early as the 1840s there were reports of labourers' families walking in, especially on Saturday evenings, from areas close to towns to take advantage of the shopping facilities there. They brought prams, carts or simply troupes of children to carry their purchases home. Many urban shopkeepers, especially grocers, butchers, bakers and drapers, keen to increase their turnovers, began to offer country deliveries once the farm labourers' real incomes began to rise from the 1870s. Of these the grocer presented the greatest challenge to the village shop since he offered a wider variety of products, lower prices and direct delivery to the customer's door. Leonard Coombs (born 1901) recalls here how his father, Charles, handled a potentially dangerous situation which faced their long-established family business in Ickham, one of a cluster of villages five miles east of Canterbury.

My family has lived here since 1750 and throughout that period all my forefathers were grocers in this particular property, and there were brothers who were also bakers in the village. Now, when my grandfather had the business he was also clerk to the Seaton mill in the parish and he wasn't interested in the grocery and so he left his wife to look after the business. The demand was small and we gave no delivery service in those days. This is back in the 1870s, 1880s. Well, my grandfather died in 1896 and the business came to my grandmother as one of the executors of his will. She put my father and an aunt of mine into the business to run it on her behalf, so the business continued to be run under the name of J. Coombs, my grandfathers name, you see, John Coombs. My father had had no training, none whatsoever apart from what he learnt from his father and grandfather.

Now my father found that he was really up against quite an element of competition round here. In Wickhambreaux the grocer had a horse-drawn van and, therefore, he was giving a delivery service and he was coming into Ickham and seizing a part of the custom of the people who lived here. He was also delivering paraffin oil. Then a frightful thing happened because all of a sudden a German grocer in Canterbury High Street, his name was Schlenker, suddenly began coming round these villages twice a week in a horse-drawn van with an oil tank on the back of it delivering candles, paraffin oil and also undercutting in the groceries. My father really had to put his thinking cap on and see what he could do about it, because the figures in his accounts show that the business was at a very low ebb when he took over. So, on the day that Schlenker was due, to forestall his arrival, he would deliver paraffin oil on a carrier bicycle in five-gallon drums. Then he went out and sought for custom – he didn't do it round the other villages, but if anybody moved into this part of the parish, he immediately called on the day of their arrival and sought their custom explaining that he could give a delivery service which he then did by buying a hand-truck. The result was that the business began to grow, and about 1910 we had our first errand boy.

Well, then my brother next to me left school in about 1915 and he suggested buying a little Omega motor cycle which horrified my father very much. At the back of it he strapped on a grocery basket and piled it up with goods and he would go into the other villages and deliver to people. Then, after the war, we eventually got our first motor, an Austin Seven, private tourer, which could be converted into a little delivery van by taking the hood off and putting a business part on it. Now we run two vans and do a delivery service of a five-mile radius round every village within the area.

The once familiar horse-drawn carriers' vans, providing regular links with nearby towns, also performed a multiplicity of retail roles.[8] Charles Coombs employed his to fetch supplies from wholesalers. The Crowhurst family who between 1911 and 1916 kept the village shop at Upchurch, a few miles outside Rainham, relied almost exclusively on theirs for supplies from Maidstone. 'We used to have a carrier next door to us, Simmonds. Then he died, so we had to go over to Rainham. After we'd shut the shop at eight o'clock we used to walk there and give the carriers there the notes ready for the morning to take to Maidstone. They'd bring them back the next afternoon. That's how we got everything.' The carrier, however, was a mixed blessing to the village shopkeeper. His urban counterparts advertised country deliveries by carrier and other country people could for a few pence, either travel, usually at snail's pace, into the town or delegate responsibility for shopping to him. Doris Gambrill (born 1898), the daughter of a carrier from Waltham, a village high up on the North Downs, recalls here some of her father's tasks.

He went every day except Thursday, because that was early closing day so it wasn't worthwhile. Monday he fetched the coal and then Tuesday, Wednesday, Friday and Saturday he went to do the shopping and take the passengers. He used to bring out meat and groceries, and parcels on approval when he was buying for other people. He'd bring boots and shoes for them to try on, then whichever pair they wanted they kept and gave him the money and he'd take the others back to the shop – Hiltons, Freeman, Hardy & Willis, all those places. He used to take us to Canterbury and have us fitted. The van used to be piled up with parcels because there were seats all round and then the parcels were put in underneath, you see, and all stacked up on the back. There was a village shop but there wasn't everything you could get there. In fact, although we had bakers, there used to be one old lady, I don't think she ever wanted anything else from Canterbury only a loaf. I always remember I had to keep telling my father she wanted a cottage loaf, 'And it must be nice and crusty', she always used to say. I can hear her voice to this day.

In Shorne, the village where Bernice Baker (born 1884) grew up and spent nearly all her life, the publican doubled as carrier, travelling into Gravesend twice a week:

> You paid him two pennies for doing your shopping. I know the two pennies used to go up separate: 'That's for Mr Welch.' Then a list you'd give him and he'd say all right. He would go to the draper's and get things if it was written out. He'd buy you a new saucepan if you wanted one, tin kettle ones with the handles over which we often used to hang round the fire-place, the same sort of thing that we took to Cobham Hall to get our soup in the winter. Even medicine, he used to go round the chemists' shops and get people's medicine made up for them. It wasn't doctors' prescriptions; they'd write down what they wanted and the old chemist used to make it up for them. They all knew what the old people wanted. Some of those things must have been in the families for generations. Mostly they could make their own, but they wanted other things to mix with it.

The village shopkeeper, therefore, faced competition; survival and prosperity were by no means guaranteed. He responded by trying to service the needs of all sections of the community, being willing to oblige anyone. At the Crowhursts' shop, 'You couldn't ask for a wrong thing. If we hadn't got it my brother would say, "It'll be here by six o'clock tonight" and somebody had to go to Rainham and get it,' Boot repairs and hair dressing were additional services which they offered. Other shops allowed urban tailors to use their premises as bases for village trade. The gentry and clergy sometimes felt a social obligation to patronise local shops but to make sure they were pledged personal attention, first-class merchandise, credit and regular deliveries. Farmers, widely regarded as 'the worst payers', were handled with caution. At the other end of the social scale the trader also had to cater for the basic requirements of the labouring classes, to deal in pence rather than pounds, to give credit to those in need.

An estimate of the nature and scope of one family business, that at Ickham, can be attempted using scanty documentary evidence which has survived in the shop and Leonard Coombs's recollections. In 1910 his father obtained a mortgage and bought the business outright from his mother for £267 17s 0¼d. In exchange he received stock valued at £217 8s, book debts (money owing) amounting to £81 9s 3½d, and cash in hand and at the bank of £16 1s 11d. He also inherited debts totalling £47 2s 2¾d which were owed to various suppliers. The value of the stock was arrived at by a meticulous stocktaking. Each item was painstakingly entered in pencil, in no obvious logical order, in a small loosely backed notebook still in the family possession.

It is clear from his stock of drapery, haberdashery and hosiery that he supplied his customers with cloth and necessary goods to make their own clothes and household fittings. The drapery side of the business attempted to cater for all possible uses but leaned towards the cheaper end of the market. There was angora, cretonne, worsted, shirting, muslin and nainsook, galatea for children's sailor suits, flannel and flannalette, drill, twill, print cloth, a variety of linens — buckram, apron linen, drabbet, Holland and American cloth — oil baize, calico, 'unbleach' or cheap calico usually for making up into sheets, and a selection of linings. For working with the material he provided thimbles, pins, reels of silk and cotton, thread, embroidery thread, crochet hooks, buttons, hooks and eyes, elastic, tape, webbing, frilling, torchon lace, binding and insertions.

Ready-made items of clothing were limited to small items, underwear and hose. In addition to shirts, underpants and vests, corsets, busks and busk protectors, a wide range of hose, babies' socks, gaiters and shoes, blouses, aprons, pinafores, bibs, capes, scarves, shawls, gloves (including leather ones), leggings, handkerchiefs, ties (silk, lace etc.), belts and braces, he stocked an extensive selection of hats, collars and cuffs, articles of clothing which, possibly more than any others, labelled their wearers socially. There were felt hats, sailors' caps to match the children's suits, motor hats (four at a cost price of $3s\ 11d$) for the pioneering ladies, 'tamys', servants' caps, bonnet fronts, fringe and bun nets and a choice of veiling, including widow's weeds. Collars and cuffs were distinguished more by their material than their use; linen, Eton collars for 'best', lace collars, easily scrubbed rubber collars and cuffs for boys and servants. Numerous personal accessories sold included purses, hat-pins, studs, brooches, slides, umbrellas ($1s\ 6d$ each), an enormous variety of coloured ribbon, together with a range of grindery — shoe buckles, laces and ties, caps, tacks, blacking and brushes.

Household goods and cleaning equipment constituted another 'department'. Diverse brushes were sold: stove brushes, laundry brushes, tar brushes, scrubbing brushes and even sweeps' brushes, together with a variety of brooms and handles. Domestic lighting requirements were met with a stock of lamp wicks, candles, lamp glasses and shades, Duplex burners, and night lights. There were carriage candles for late travellers too. Ironmongery was not in evidence but metal polishes and Brasso were. For multifarious domestic needs there were cans of paraffin, hearth stones and whiting ($56$lb at $\frac{1}{4}d$ per lb), sand for scattering on brick floors, polish, leathers, string, rugs, mats, string bags, wooden spoons, a fire screen, picture wire and 'seccotures'.

In addition to 714 postcards, note-paper and envelopes, he offered a varied choice of specialist stationery: birthday and greetings cards, exercise books, memo pads, calendars, carbon and blotting paper. Writing implements and equipment included fountain pens, lead pencils, slates and slate pencils, ink and marking ink, while among the oddments could be found an album, 'books', photo-frames and dessert papers. The proximity of Christmas also meant that he had a small number of paper chains, Christmas tree decorations, wreaths of holly and toys, among them the usual hoops, peg tops, aunt sally, diabolo, ninepins, drawing slates, dolls (dressed, undressed and rag), rubber rings, rattles, a pop gun, a money box, playing cards, darts, crayons, pistols, caps, animals, ABC blocks, doll's furniture and a rubber ball. Other items reflected contemporary fashions: *Ally Sloper*, a motor, magic lantern and banjo. Five trumpets, some mouth organs and a drum, doubtless more popular with the children than with their parents, were also in the shop along with quieter pastimes: a Noah's Ark, mechanical monkey, tea set, building bricks, and blow football. Chocolates, chocolate dates, caramels, sherbet, mints, peppermints and sugar candy comprised the small sweets section.

There was a chemist at Wingham, a larger village nearly two miles away, but Charles Coombs purchased popular patent medicines, hygienic aids and chemicals from him for re-sale in his own village. Keating's Powder, a famous treatment for preventing or destroying lice and fleas, Ozo, a headache powder, Epsom salts, camphor, magnesia, zinc ointment, Vaseline, embrocations, camphorated oil, castor oil and various unclassified 'pills' were in his shop in 1910 along with small quantities of alum, aniseed and nitre. Large stocks of soaps, scented and unscented, branded (Lux, Sunlight) and unbranded, tooth powder and brushes, sponges, nail brushes and scissors, cold cream, hair oil, curlers and a collection of different combs were stocked for customers who valued their personal hygiene and appearance, while those who wished to improve their odour could do so by purchasing some of his scents and perfumes. Starch, blue, fuller's earth, carbosil and Hudson's soaps, and lengths of clothes lines were all available for washing day. There were babies' bottles, teats, dummies and a bath for the expanding family. Tobacco addicts could call for some of his Condor shag, or clay pipes, while $2\frac{1}{2}$lb of snuff was in store for those who preferred nasal pleasures. Bird lovers and poultry keepers were able to purchase bird seed, sand and bran. Cycle oil was kept for the stray tourist or fortunate local owner.

Branded and packeted grocery goods were relatively common. Epps's and Cadbury's cocoa, Mazawattee, Nectar, Tower and Golden Petal teas, Cerebos salt, Keiller's jams, Harvey's and Club sauces, Bisto, and Bird's custard powder were singled out individually in the stock list, possibly as brand leaders, but none of the biscuit firms which supplied the shop were mentioned by name. Many items, however, still arrived requiring processing in some way. Salt required chopping up, sultanas and currants needed cleaning ('one of the jobs the boys had to do'), sugar was sold either as demerara, granulated or in 'pieces', while tapioca, sago and rice, all popular, filling Sunday desserts, desiccated 'cokernut', and flour from the local mill, all came in bulk and required packaging. Apart from tea, the only beverages sold were lemonade, cream soda, and coffee. 'Ground coffee was not used at all, you could say, by the poorer people, but the coffee was bought in the form of beans by the bigger houses. It was quite expensive. Many grocers, of course, roasted their own. We hadn't got a roaster in our shop, but we used to grind it for people if they wanted. Most of it was done privately in their houses.' A surprisingly large selection of spices, herbs, flavourings and condiments were sold: 'currie' powder, peppers (black, green and red), ginger, cloves, olives, anchovies, tarragon, angelica, cinnamon, arrowroot, caraway seeds, lucca oil, pickles, relish, chutney, mustard, vinegar and unspecified 'essences'. Breakfast cereals, a recent innovation in the food line, were absent from the shelves, only oatmeal for the filling — and therefore very popular — porridge was stocked. Also absent, apart from biscuits and hard 'fairy cakes', was any confectionery.

With the possible exception of butter and margarine, nothing in the shop could be classed as perishable, and very little stock was obtained locally. The cheese was all American or Canadian. The only milk sold was in tins, Nestlés' condensed. Apart from sides of bacon, meat and fish could only be bought in tins: mutton, beef, rabbits, salmon (8$d$ a tin) and sardines. Beans and peas were supplied dried. Fruit, too, was sold in tins — pears, pineapples, apricots and tomatoes — as jam, or, in the case of sultanas and currants, dried. Bananas and oranges were enjoyed for a short spell at Christmas but even then only the big houses or customers who had contributed throughout the year to the shop's Christmas club could afford them. They were strictly rationed in the shopkeeper's family. 'My father always called them a luxury. We were allowed to have half a banana, never a whole one. And grapefruit, you never saw a grapefruit. I didn't know what grapefruit was until I was quite old.'

During the summer months fresh produce was sold in the shop but never on a systematic basis; most of it came from the shopkeeper's garden or was bought in from cottagers.

We got very little off the farmers. Very little. The farms used to sell direct to the people. For instance, we all had to go to the Treasury Farm in this village to get our milk. You would at the same time buy your eggs and cream from them, and those who could afford it would buy their butter. We sold practically no vegetables yet today I should say that probably thirty per cent of business consists of vegetables. It's a tremendous trade, simply because nobody in the country seems to go in for growing vegetables. But then most people were self supporting and, of course, there were poorer people in the village who got a copper or two by selling them to a neighbour and so on. But there wasn't a great demand for them in those days.

Paradoxically, since the village shop rarely provided an outlet for farm crops, people in the fruit-growing areas of Kent were often unable to purchase any of their local farmers' produce. Benjamin Harrison, a shopkeeper from Ightham better known for his geological and archaeological investigations, pondered on the absurdity of this situation in his diary: 'Two young cyclists came in, and asked whether I could tell them where they could get some cherries or other fruit. Alas, I could not. One of them was a splendid sort. She said, "It is so tantalising to see the fruit as we ride along and yet to be unable to buy any".'[9] Bernice Baker encountered the same situation in her village:

My mother used to go down to Shorne Ifield, there was a big farm that was Lord Darnley's then, and they used to pick raspberries for market. They were never sold in the village. They all went away in tubs, therefore I think they went to the jam factory. But you could never buy any. They didn't sell any fruit in the village, it all went up to the London markets. Unless you'd got a tree in your garden, then you never had any of those fruits. That's why the children used to pinch fruit. Apples you could buy, but only the drops. All the picked ones were sent to London.

The wide range of products which Charles Coombs sold obliged him to deal with many suppliers, some of whom, his creditors, were listed in the stocktaking of 1910. Crescens Robinson of Bristol, supplier of wrapping paper and stationery used in the shop, was the only manufacturer listed and was the most distant of his creditors. Pollard, the chemist at Wingham, who also supplied him with newspapers, was the closest. Most of the others were traders in Canterbury: Steddy Brothers, linen drapers and general warehousemen, Fortescue West, linen drapers, George Nash & Son, broom and brush makers, Williamson, the owner of the tannery, and Cox & Scott, wholesale grocers and provision merchants. It becomes clear from Leonard Coombs's recollections, however, that these were suppliers who were dealt with only irregularly and therefore paid infrequently. Consequently many of the major wholesalers and manufacturers were excluded from the list. Biscuit manufacturers, for instance, and the Anglo-American Oil Company, who supplied the paraffin, were paid regular 'journey money' when their travelling representatives called. Leonard Coombs takes up the story:

Initially, he had all his groceries delivered from Dover; Richard Dickeson, a very fine firm of wholesale grocers in the Market Square, Dover. We dealt with them for very many years – my grandfather had dealt with them. Travellers came up to take my father's order. If they came round in a horse trap they were driven by a coachman, and they were known as the gentlemen of the road. They were very courteous and

208

very excellent people. I could speak highly of all of them. Poorly paid but they had to keep up appearances. Dickeson's had the first car that appeared in Ickham, a chauffeur-driven car which was completely open. It was rather like a wagonette, a round tub affair with the chauffeur sitting in front with two oil lamps on either side and a huge motor horn which was sounded by pressing a rubber ball. This traveller arrived wearing a bowler hat, sitting almost on the top of this car, rather than in it. It was tremendous. As a small boy I was privileged every time he came to go and sit out there and wait for the magnificent experience just to press the ball of the horn so that it might sound. Then I well remember a team of four lovely horses drawing a van with a white cover over it bringing up simple things like cheese, bacon, fats, blocks of salt and sugar. All these things had to be broken up and packed in the shop, so we were constantly buying, from the paper manufacturers, bags and satchels for putting it in. Very often it used to occupy a Monday night, weighing up tea, sugar, soda and suchlike ready for the week.

Then in the early days of this century my father had a traveller call on him from William Laurence Limited, Maidstone, and he bought from this firm his cheese and butter and one or two other miscellaneous foods. But the cheese was a speciality with them because they always sold mature Canadian cheese, and it was on the reputation of this and of their New Zealand butter that my father built up the business as a high-quality provision merchant. Now, William Laurence's had no transport at all in those days, and, therefore, all the cheese and butter came down by rail in crates from Maidstone to Bekesbourne and then we used to pay a local carrier to bring it to us here. History was quite made when William Laurence's decided to use the first motor lorry that came into the area as a provision van. It caused quite a sensation every month [c. 1908–10].

The bacon merchant was Denny's Dry Cure, an Irish firm. That was a super bacon, absolutely different from today. It came originally from Dickeson's, then we gave the trade to Maidstone. But we also had another string to our bow – Warren & Reynolds in Orange Street, Canterbury. They used to smoke their own bacon in a huge room, with oak cuttings.

My father could not compete with the price he had to pay the wholesaler for margarine, because the Maypole Dairies had a wonderful place in St George's Street, Canterbury where they used to sell it at a terribly low price. Every so often for every pound you bought they gave you a pound. So, when I was at school in Canterbury, my father used to say, 'Keep your eye on the Maypole and if they're giving away an extra pound, let me know and I'll give you the money and you buy 12–14lb and get your double-weight.' Then I would bring it out here and he could compete.

Now the drapery, how did we get the drapery? Well, there were two sources. First of all we had wholesalers who would call on us; a Maidstone firm called Marchant & Tubb. They were very flourishing and provided most of the underwear and drapery section. Hambrook's there supplied some habersashery. The second source was for us to go into Canterbury. We had an account with drapers there on the understanding that they gave us a discount on what we bought and then we could sell it at their price out here. Sometimes when I was at Simon Langton school I had to go out in my dinner hour and buy for my father. It was a little shop, (run by the West family,) a remarkable affair because you went down three or four steps to it. When you got inside there were three quaint people and they were all miniatures, almost like dwarfs. To reach the top shelf they had little ladders they had to climb to bring down the sheeting, unbleached calico or whatever it was I wanted. It fascinated me no end. They would price it out for my father and put it down to his account, then I would bring it home or he would send the local carrier. That's how we got our drapery. Then there was a brush manufacturer by the name of Nash we bought from, and if I wanted a particular kind of tobacco, I went to Mr Pettit, the tobacconist, who was almost next door, and so on.

Records of the daily takings in the shop for the years 1896–8 and 1917–29 are the only other documents to have survived.[10] Incomplete and fraught with pitfalls though these are, they nevertheless do yield considerable information. Incidental interests of the shopkeeper himself and exceptional weather conditions, such as droughts or unseasonal snowstorms, are noted. 'Armistice' is gladly recorded alongside the entry for 11 November 1918 while 'Influenza prevalent' less happily explains a significant drop in receipts two weeks later. For national celebrations such as the Diamond Jubilee, 22 June 1897, and the peace celebration of 19 July 1919 the shop closed. No reference is made to the General Strike of 1926 nor did takings for the period deviate from the normal pattern, but the following week they fell considerably.

After allowing for price changes there can be little doubt that the volume of business increased over the period. In 1897 and 1898 receipts were fractionally over £700 per year. Just over twenty years later, in 1920, they were £4,715, an increase of over six hundred per cent in a period when prices and money wages rose by less than one third of that figure. No rise in population occurred to account for this. In fact, Ickham's population fell steadily until 1911 and dramatically over the next ten years while those of nearby villages also stagnated. The success was due partly to the enterprise of its owner, assisted, in his son's view, by the effects of the war which reduced outside competition and encouraged people to trade regularly with their local stores in the hope of obtaining favourable treatment and by the rise in real wages of the local labourers. The potential for expansion would seem to have been exhausted by 1921, however, and for the next six years receipts fluctuated approximately in line with retail price changes.

The annual variations in trade were firmly wedded to the farming cycle in the locality. In the late 1890s business was slack from October right through to July; Christmas merely checked the decline in takings which continued to plummet to a trough in the spring. As summer progressed local employment became more regular and with opportunities for women and children to work on the land and supplement the family income business steadily improved. Some of this upturn doubtless involved the settling of debts incurred at the shop during the winter months but cash trade was largely responsible for the subsequent enormous rise during August and September when clothes and provisions for the next winter were purchased.

Although the same seasonal variations persisted in the 1920s they were less marked and business was not so concentrated in the few summer months. March, April and May remained particularly poor months, September outstripped all others, but weekly receipts deviated far less from the average for the year. In the shop's financial year 1896–7, which Charles Coombs chose to calculate from 1 May to 30 April, weeks when takings were twenty-five per cent less than the yearly average amounted to one-third of the total; thirty years later, during 1926–7, only four such weeks were experienced.[11] Similarly, the number of weeks when receipts exceeded the average figure by twenty-five per cent was nearly halved. Two developments contributed to this change. First, there was, as the number of cheques received over the year indicates, a noticeable increase in the number of affluent customers who paid accounts regularly throughout the year. Secondly, the financial situation of the farm labourers improved. On a national level, despite erosion in the years just after the war, real wages were twenty per cent higher in the late 1920s than they had been before 1914 and, with the decline of the practice of laying men off without pay during inlement weather, earnings became more regular.[12] Nevertheless, trade still peaked during the summer months when overtime and piecework were more common.

The exceptional rise in takings from late August and the subsequent equally spectacular fall were adequately explained by Charles Coombs's brief comments in his account book: 'Hop picking begins' and 'Hop picking ends'.[13] Not only did this peculiarly Kentish seasonal task provide regular employment for local women and children, school holidays being scheduled to coincide with it, but hordes of townfolk, including Londoners, flocked into the countryside, lodging in specially constructed huts provided by the farmers. Shopkeepers, in common with the rest of the local population, viewed this annual migration as a mixed blessing; not everything the visitors left the shop with was paid for. Many shopkeepers resorted to erecting wire barricades around the counter, passing goods out through a little cubby-hole. To protect their regular customers from being infected by the visitors who – not surprisingly in view of their living conditions – were none too clean, they sometimes segregated the two groups, either constructing a partition across the shop or serving the newcomers through an outside door. Until machines replaced hand-pickers in the late 1950s, however, rural shopkeepers willingly suffered these inconveniences because they were more than compensated for by the boost their trade received. Indeed, as

211

Leonard Coombs recalls, they often found it worthwhile to extend their range of stock:

> Well now, during the hop picking we had an influx of about two to three hundred people from London, Deal and Dover, and they lived in huts down in the meadows, so the amount of business suddenly increased. As the premises were so small, we had to use the outer part, which is still known as the shop kitchen and which has double doors, and on the top of the copper just inside the door we used to stack loaves of bread which were brought in from the local baker. We probably had two or three deliveries a day from this baker of about 100–150 loaves and then we served them over the side door because it avoided all this bulk being stored in the rather confined space of the shop. Another problem with a packed number of customers in the shop was that shoplifting became very easy and so, prior to their arrival, most of the things which were hanging on hooks were tied down by string to make it more difficult for them to lift them off. A little trap door was put through the gap between the end of our counter and the shelves so that nobody could pass behind to the back, and that served as a little serving hatch as well. The business was open from six in the morning up to ten at night, and usually it was packed once the work ceased in the evening. We didn't deliver to the hop gardens because there was no necessity; the hop fields were so very, very near to the village and the people had to pass the shop to get to them. So they had no difficulty in getting supplies, and they could always send children in if they wanted something during the day.
>
> I remember distinctly my father ordering special stock. Wooden barrels of broken biscuits, huge barrels which stood five feet high, came from Peak Freans or Huntley & Palmers. They were sold off at a very cheap rate. Then we used to have great casks of golden syrup or black treacle. People brought jugs and jam jars and we used to fill them up. Oh, and we used to have quite a number of cheap jams. Everything was very cheap; second-quality stuff. That was all laid in some weeks before the hop pickers arrived. After they'd been paid at the end of hop picking then we did a roaring trade in drapery, but they didn't buy that until they'd got their final payment.
>
> I'll tell you another very extraordinary thing. One or two of the hop picking families were regulars; they'd been coming year in and year out and they were trustworthy. My father knew them very well and so he was able to give them credit and when they paid up at the end of the season he gave them a glass of wine each. I think that was a rather nice gesture. Then, of course, where there was real necessity with a few of the local labouring people during the year, very poor families, or families who had met with disaster and had been hit by two or three deaths, so he used to say, 'Now, don't pay me. Don't worry. When hop picking comes and you've earned your extra money then, then pay me.' So we used to pick up quite a lot of money from them. It was a very busy and a very hectic time.

In his diary, Benjamin Harrison had complained bitterly on one occasion about an undesirable consequence of running a small, village shop; for fifty-four years he had spent every Saturday behind the counter. Charles Coombs's figures show why this is necessary. In 1896–7 Saturday's receipts accounted for over fifty per cent of each week's total during nine months of the year, the proportion rarely falling below forty per cent in the other fifteen weeks. Such a situation was indicative of a business relying on a clientèle existing at near-subsistence level, struggling from one weekend to the next, possibly borrowing for short periods in the week and settling up each pay day. Significantly, the importance of Saturday trading varied inversely with the seasonal pattern of trade, diminishing from late July to early October when customers had ready cash, but increasing, sometimes to as much as seventy per cent of the week's total, during the winter and spring months when scarce employment and depleted savings re-imposed a hand-to-mouth existence. During these difficult months, mid-week daily receipts dropped dramatically, sums as low as 4s occasionally being recorded in the ledger. Monday, domestic washing-day, remained perpetually slack throughout the year.

By the 1920s, although this pattern still persisted, the over-riding importance of Saturday's takings had declined. The typical weekly pattern now resembled more closely that previously found only during the peak season. In the financial year 1926–7, for example, Saturday's trade accounted for over half the week's total receipts on only nine occasions, a positive indication of the increased prosperity of the community, the growing proportion of business done on account, and the importance of the weekday delivery services. Not surprisingly, since Wednesday had been established as half-day closing, takings for this day were now significantly lower than any other, while Friday's share of the weekly total had increased marginally as it became more widely regarded as the accepted pay-day.

Although the leisured class looked down on him because of his trade and labourers looked up to him because of it, the village shopkeeper's social standing in the village was never clearly defined and depended to a large extent on his own choosing. The Crowhursts, an ex-farm worker's family, considered themselves on a level with their working-class customers. Others, like the grocer's family at Candleford Green, were disliked because 'they had ideas above their station in life'.[14] On financial criteria Leonard Coombsargues that his father did not qualify for entry into the 'middle class' until 1930 when the taxman first acknowledged his existence, but he suggests that his family associated itself strongly with middle-class values and lifestyles long before then. Unlike urban tradesmen who were able to form their own separate social circles, however, the village shopkeeper was condemned to virtual social isolation despite appearing to be the most gregarious member of the community, mixing freely with all classes in the course of his business. His only consolation, though it is doubtful whether he viewed it as such, was that an active social life was effectively precluded by the long business hours. Leonard Coombs concludes this picture of his family's shop with a few thoughts on these long hours, exacerbated by the system of customers' personal accounts, and on his family's social position in the village.

During the First World War there was no competition from the surrounding towns, chiefly owing to lack of transport, and my father was really able to build up the business so that we supplied the whole of the village, including the big houses. With them you had to go out and ask for the order, come back and pack it, then go out and deliver it, and then probably give a month or three months' credit, so there was always a lot of money outstanding although, of course, they were very secure. If a customer had a monthly account, that was a very exacting business. The work was three times what it need have been. If that customer paid cash the transaction would have been ended, but if she had a monthly account, first of all you served her, secondly you went and entered each item in the shop ledger, probably twenty to thirty items, and then at the end of the month it was transferred individually into her own account book so that she had an accurate record of all her purchases. The amount of labour and time taken! My father would possibly settle down on a Monday as a slack day and get the accounts out but later it was usually shared between us. When I ran the shop with my brother in the 1930s, there was probably thirty to forty accounts and it was nothing to have two hundred items that a person had bought in a month. It took a whole day, so something desperate had to be done. I mean, we were working eight days a week instead of seven! I remember that we decided that instead of writing out every individual item, the customer would have a bill given to her on the purchase of everything and then we would enter it into the ledger as 'goods' and then in her account at the end of the month as 'goods' so she could check up the date of her invoice with the date of entry in her book to see that it was correct. Some people took quite a dim view of that and more or less said they wanted a detailed account because they lost their bills. But we won in the end. It's now an accepted thing.

Our family would be, I suppose, what you would call the middle class in the village. The people we looked upon as those we could easily mix with and invite into the house or go into their houses, would have been the schoolmaster and his wife, a local butcher (a friend of the family), and a local baker. Then, of course, we had friends in the other villages, such as the manager of Margate Water Works at Wingham, the local builder there, the schoolmaster at Wickhambreaux and the people who kept the mills round here. That was our circle. But we had very little time for socials. Chiefly it was in the form of whist drives. You met them there or at a concert, but to have people into the house was not very convenient because people had got big families. In our case there were six of us in quite a small space and so it was not very easy for mother and father to invite people in.

We didn't have much to do with the gentry, not socially. The rector and his wife were very nice people but they belonged to the gentry section in those days. The same with the people in the big house opposite: very pleasant people so you never felt embarrassed with them, but you would feel embarrassed if you were invited to one of their dinner parties. I think those sorts of distinctions still hold today. When all's said and done you mix with people who are compatible don't you? You're friendly with everybody but you couldn't make them intimate friends.

214

## Notes to Chapter 13

[1] F. Thompson, *Lark Rise to Candleford*, Oxford, 1945, Penguin ed. 1973, p. 406.

[2] Simmonds, *Practical Grocer*, I, p. 30.

[3] M. E. Davies, *Life in an English Village*, 1904, p. 129.

[4] Alexander, *Retailing*, pp. 61–68 esp. 75–80.

[5] Rees, *Marks and Spencer*, p. 5. For a further instance of successful progression see G. E. Evans, *From the Mouths of Men*, 1976, pp. 41–2.

[6] For vivid descriptions of hawkers see Penn, *Manchester Fourteen Miles*, pp. 173–5; Ashby, *Joseph Ashby*, p. 201; Davies, *Supertramp*, pp. 174–6; Hindley, *Cheap Jack*.

[7] Davies, *English Village*, p. 192.

[8] A. Everitt, 'Country carriers in the nineteenth century', *Journal of Transport History*, n.s., III, 1976, pp. 179–201 is the best survey of carriers' networks.

[9] Sir Edward Harrison, *Harrison of Ightham*, 1928, p. 253. This is a diary entry for 30 July 1903.

[10] These, along with the stock book for 1910, are still in Mr Coombs's possession.

[11] 1896–7 has been chosen as the first year under Charles Coombs's management; 1926–7 since earlier figures for the 1920s were distorted by rapid price fluctuations. Unfortunately no profit or loss figures are available.

[12] B. R. Mitchell and P. Deane, *Abstract of British Historical Statistics*, Cambridge, 1962, pp. 344–5. This figure is a national one; rural labourers may well not have benefited to the same extent.

[13] For hop-picking see M. Lewis (ed.), *Old Days in the Kent Hop Gardens*, West Kent Federation of Women's Institutes, 1962, rpt., 1981; Winstanley, *Life in Kent*, chapter 6; A. Bignall, *Hopping Down in Kent*, 1977; Charles Warren, *A Boy in Kent*, 1937, pp. 34–57.

[14] Thompson, *Lark Rise*, p. 463.

# AFTERMATH: SURVIVORS

The half century before 1914 witnessed the emergence of radically new methods and forms of retailing in a wide range of trades and over a broad geographical area. As was the case with early nineteenth-century industry and retailing, however, contemporaries' and later historians' obsession with progress and large scale organisations may have caused them inadvertently to misrepresent the nature and extent of such change. From their accounts one might conclude that multiples, co-ops and department stores had all but annihilated the private trader by 1914, only a few corner shops remaining in the back streets of working-class areas. Business histories like Peter Mathias's excellent account of Allied Suppliers, Lipton's successors, have charted the speed and magnitude of growth of such firms.[1] Despite its broad title, *Retail Trading in Britain, 1850–1950*, James Jefferys's influential volume is really concerned with the spread of multiple retailing. Official Co-operative histories, now as then, glory in the movement's progress. Charles Wilson has posited the distributive trades' transformation and the consumer industries' meteoric development as proof of the continued existence of successful, aggressive British entrepreneurship, previously considered by many economic historians to have been laid to rest in the later decades of the nineteenth century.[2]

The existence of these innovations should not be confused with their rate of diffusion or overall significance. Tucked away in Jefferys' work is a sobering comment: 'The revolution in distributive trades was ... far from complete by 1914. Some of the characteristics of this revolution were, in fact, still confined to small sections of a few trades ... Many trades remained highly skilled and the family tradition was by no means dead.'[3] The preceding chapters have confirmed this. According to Jefferys, by 1910 there were fewer than twenty thousand multiple shops in chains of ten or more in the United Kingdom and, whether we accept the 1911 census figure of a grand total of 607,300 shops or the Inland Revenue Commissioners' listing of 310,000 shop premises rated at over £20 per annum, it is clear that these newcomers still comprised only a very small percentage of total outlets. There were also significant differences between trades. Over 13,200 multiples were concentrated in grocery, meat and footwear, accounting for 9–12 per cent, 10–13 per cent and 29–34 per cent of each market. With a couple of exceptions their share of other markets was still negligible. Department stores had only between 1.5 and 3 per cent and co-ops 7–8 per cent of the national market, the former making most inroads into the women's clothing market (10 per cent of sales), the latter into grocery (20 per cent) and household goods (11–13 per cent). Together, therefore, large-scale retailers were significant in certain trades but elsewhere the private shopkeepers, despite their misgivings, still dominated retailing, accounting for over eighty per cent of total sales.[4] The most interesting feature of the distributive trades was not the emergence of such giants but the much larger, and not as observers seemed to think, smaller, number of general and specialist independent shopkeepers of whatever standing or skill. As one columnist remarked in 1911, 'The crushing process has not succeeded in anything like the extent that was anticipated, and in a quiet way, many retailers are making a very comfortable living'.[5]

Although independents' share of the market has declined and British retailing exhibits a greater degree of concentration than any other country's, the survival of the private shopkeeper has been more striking than even the most cautious Edwardian pundit would have predicted, so much so, that by the 1940s economists were debating whether or not there were 'too many shops'. The first official Census of Distribution in 1950 listed over 583,000, an average of one for every hundred members of the community. Proprietors with just one shop enjoyed 45 per cent of the market; multiples, defined more generously than Jefferys as two or more outlets under common ownership, had 38 per cent, co-ops twelve and department stores a meagre five per cent.[6] Numbers have only fallen significantly since the 1960s. By 1980 there were 345,100 outlets but the vast majority of them, 280,000, were still run by individual proprietors or were part of small multiple chains of two to three branches; together these enjoyed 45.8 per cent of the national market and employed over half the labour force in retailing.[7] Nor should we assume that all the reduction in numbers has been borne by the independent sector. Larger multiples, co-ops and department stores have all shed outlets, partly in response to rationalisation schemes, partly as a result of falling profits.[8] Most of the independents who have disappeared would seem to have been the small, unskilled general shopkeepers. In some respects the nineteenth-century private specialist trader of moderate means is coming back into his own in many trades, the large-scale supermarkets and discount stores having effectively replaced the small-scale general retailer. Most of the old skills are now obsolete, displaced by new ones unheard of a century ago – stock control, accounting, purchasing and selling techniques – but the answer to the question posed by the pessimist tradesman in 1902 who asked 'Shall We Survive?' must be a qualified

217

'Yes'.[9] Experts now agree that the independent shopkeeper will continue to play an important, not just a residual, role in the distributive sector.

All this suggests that rather different questions ought to be asked by historians of retail development. Instead of concentrating on the factors encouraging the growth of large-scale retailing, we ought to ask why this did not grow even faster given the lack of legal constraints on it. Why have small, private traders been able to co-exist alongside their Goliath-like competitors for so long? To what extent was their 'fight for survival', individually or collectively, a contributory factor? Are there any 'market imperfections' which have shielded them from unrestricted, cut-throat competition or do we need to examine each trade on its merits? All that is presented below if a brief introductory evaluation of possible factors.[10]

### Shopkeepers' attitudes

Shopkeepers themselves like to believe that their prosperity can be partially attributed to their own efforts and abilities, that their collective survival is the result of a multitude of individual, unrelated initiatives to combat larger competitors' challenges. Hard, honest graft, supplemented by careful pandering to customers' requirements and above all that elusive, indefinable, unmeasurable 'goodwill', all these are presented as the essential ingredients for, if not success then a comfortable continued existence. There is obviously some truth in such a belief and it is one which numerous hopeful recruits to trade cherish.

They also value social and psychological rewards which find no place in the balance sheet or the economic textbooks. Consequently smaller shopkeepers accept a lower financial return on their investment, whether it be in the form of capital or time, than strictly rational economic logic would deem to be the necessary minimum. This, too, has contributed to the continuation of what in strictly utilitarian terms are uneconomic businesses. As in the nineteenth century, running a business has continued to be regarded as a passport to freedom, an escape from the drudgery and subordination of wage-earning. Mr Polly's view is still that of many: 'In a shop there's this drawback and that, but one IS one's own master.' For Miriam, his wife, the idea was attractive because 'A shop's such a respectable thing to be'.[11] Independence and respectability have remained powerful counterbalances to possible financial disincentives. 'The possession of the business is not merely a matter of calculating profits', observed Hermann Levy in 1949. 'The possession of a small shop means an independent livelihood, though such independence may mean any amount of worry, drudgery, vexation and insecurity ... Many shops which should go out of business remain alive by changing hands. The acquisition of a small shop has always been, and remains, a particular attraction to many people. The owner is, or appears to be, his own master. His social position is affected and in his view enhanced by not belonging to the wage earning class.'[12] More recent, detailed sociological surveys have confirmed the continued existence of such views.[13]

In some specialist trades, however, the drawbacks of shop life are compensated for by involvement with the stock itself. This is especially true of developing leisure-related trades. Sports shops run by ex-athletes, art and craft centres operated by artists, woodworkers and potters, photographers, book dealers, model shop proprietors – many of these are drawn in by the transformation of individual interests and pursuits into full-time occupations. Their specialist knowledge and skills enable them to project themselves as experts in their respective fields, to merit respect and custom from less informed but interested sections of the public. Their specialisation also allows them to draw trade from a wide area and to offer services and goods which the more impersonal, larger general retailer, stocking only quick moving items, cannot. Their desire, in some cases their need, to retain personal contact with the products of their trade deters them from expanding.

It is not enough, however, to show that some shopkeepers have valued non-economic criteria which have persuaded them to remain in businesses with poor material rewards. Individual abilities may explain, too, why some succeed where others fail, but they do not demonstrate why it has remained feasible to earn *any* living from small-scale retailing, why market conditions have allowed this avenue to remain open at all.

### Restrictions on competition

It is worth recalling shopkeepers' collective restraints on free market operation championed on an increasing scale from the 1900s by these apparently committed individualists. Clearly personality, goodwill and service take on a greater significance when larger competitors' ability to utilise major weapons in their arsenal is restricted by widely accepted rules dealing with competitive behaviour, sometimes enforced by a third party. Small shopkeepers, unlike their counterparts in Belgium, Germany or France, have not been able to rely on direct, open state assistance in the form of laws outlawing or restricting the development of super-stores, but they have undoubtedly benefited from government restrictions on opening hours and on manufacturers' resale price maintenance policies.

The question of legal opening hours remains complicated and contentious. There is currently an attempt to abolish all restrictions on trading hours championed from the House of Lords by Lady Trumpington. The battlelines and the arguments are familiar ones. The move is supported by the public and small shopkeepers, opposed by larger employers and by U.S.D.A.W., the shop assistants' union. The debate is not just about convenience, costing and the inadequacy of the present law but about principles. 'But there is something else which is at issue here', argues Lady Trumpington, 'and it is the issue of personal freedom, the freedom of consenting adults to trade when they wish and not when the state tells them to do so'.[14] Whether the abolition of restrictions would result in longer evening opening hours and seven-day trading, and who would benefit from it if it came about, is far from clear. There is no doubt that as it stands the law is widely flouted especially by small general shopkeepers and that they are not prosecuted for their offences. Despite some early evening extensions and the occasional discount stores opening on Sunday, larger establishments have resisted the temptation to extend their hours and they might well continue to do so if a legal free-for-all is established. They have no guarantee that their volume of trade would increase sufficiently to offset their extra overheads. Should they open longer hours, however, if seems likely that the small shopkeeper, at present effectively free to trade as he likes, would be the ultimate loser. If he extends his opening hours his personal freedom would be further eroded; if, in the short term, he increased his share of the market by this move then there is no doubt that his larger competitors would respond. All that can be safely stated is that the law legitimises and strengthens a widely agreed restrictive code of conduct regarding opening hours which emerged as a result of controls imposed in the First World War. Only its repeal will demonstrate how much voluntary agreement there is in the retailers' ranks and the small shopkeeper is ill-advised to support this.

More significant and unequivocal in its effects was the rapid expansion of resale price maintenance. The proportion of consumer expenditure on price maintained goods rose from an estimated 3 per cent in 1900 to 30 by 1938 and 50 per cent by 1955. Its application was limited to standardised, branded products of uniform quality where the manufacturers were able to adopt a national pricing policy and enforce it by instituting boycotts on price cutters, but, by mid-century, these encompassed tobacco, confectionery, books, newspapers and journals, electrical goods, motor cars and petrol, photographic equipment, gramophones, records, radios, pharmaceutical goods and some furniture, hardware, groceries and, of course, milk, the price of which was regulated by the Milk Marketing Board. Small retailers were consequently encouraged and supported by fixed, protected profit margins while larger competitors were unable to increase their share of the market by offering the lower prices which their greater efficiency made possible; consequently they, too, turned to service, improved premises and 'free' gifts or simply enjoyed inflated profits.

Resale price maintenance, however, suffered considerable setbacks in the 1950s. Some discount stores blatantly flouted fixed prices and suppliers, anxious to secure a larger share of the expanding market, hesitated to enforce sanctions against them. Informed public opinion also slowly became more critical of it. The 1956 Restrictive Practices Act outlawed collusive price fixing by manufacturers and the Resale Price Maintenance Act eight years later banned its individual enforcement unless suppliers could argue that its retention was desirable for at least two out of a possible five reasons, one of which was that abolition would seriously reduce the number of retail outlets and inconvenience the public. Although price competition has been reintroduced into many areas of retailing, possibly at the expense of the small, inefficient shops, resale price maintenance still exists on a number of goods – medicines, books and magazines – while in some trades recommended retail prices are commonly adopted or more emphasis placed on product differentiation. This is true even of super-stores which prefer promoting their own brands to engaging in debilitating price 'wars' over long periods. 'There is more reluctance to use price competition in Britain than in the US, so that the danger of predatory price-cutting is much less and the desire to use price competition in a legitimate way, entirely in the interests of consumers and of the best allocation of resources, is, unfortunately, much more muted ... The tendency is for economies of bulk buying to yield higher profits rather than lower prices.'[15]

### Market imperfections

The independent shopkeeper, however, even in trades where price competition has made some inroads, has benefited from other market imperfections which have provided valuable protection against larger rivals. Most relate to the nature of consumer demand and the nature of the products being sold. Irrational consumer purchasing habits, mismanaging of time and money, inexplicable loyalty to certain retail outlets – these to some degree have assisted the independent trader, especially the neighbourhood general shop. Convenience and ease of shopping, too, economising on time, travelling and effort, have allowed widely dispersed retail outlets to survive. Improved means of transport may have afforded people easier access to city centres, or, in more recent years, to out-of-town super-stores, but the same improvements have encouraged suburban growth, increasing both the distance between the homes and the concentrated retail centres, and the cost of bridging it. As far as regular purchases, especially of bulk items, are concerned, the fact that local shops may not be as price-competitive is more than outweighed by the time, labour and expense involved in travelling to take advantage of larger competitors' possible price reductions. Sometimes these can compete by offering delivery services but the cost of these erode to some extent the price and cost advantages they possess. Centralised retailing areas, especially in large city centres, have consequently become populated with shops selling high-priced, low-bulk goods which are bought irregularly. Purveyors of fruit, vegetables, bread, even meat, and for slightly different reasons tobacconists, confectioners and newsagents, have all benefited from the nature of demand for their products, customers making regular, comparatively small purchases and placing ease of access above price in their list of priorities.

The need to be close to the source of regular custom may explain the continued existence of a large number of shops but it does not rule out the possibility of these being parts of multiple chains. To understand why many have remained in private hands we need to concentrate more on the nature of the product being sold.

As we have seen, multiples and large-scale retailers rely heavily on standardised, manufactured or pre-processed, non-perishable products for which there is a steady demand and a guaranteed regular source of supply. If any of these conditions are not met, then large-scale operators hit problems and the small man comes into his own. In greengrocery, for example, a trade which has remained relatively easy to enter, multiples have made very limited inroads, usually only on a local basis, the perishable nature of the stock, its irregular supply and variable quality rendering it unsuitable for such retailing methods. Despite widespread refrigeration the same factors apply in the meat and fish trades. Newspapers and journals, perishable because of their preoccupation with current events, fall into this category too. Similarly, wherever it is possible to distinguish differences in quality, or where a large range of a very specialist stock with limited appeal needs to be held, where the price is of secondary importance to the consumer who desires to obtain something unique or specific, then the private trader can also survive. In clothing, consumer taste for originality and/or fashion leaves an opening for the boutique, personal tailor or dressmaker. Carpet, lighting and jewellery shops rely on similar appeal. Where there is a strong element of service involved in the sale of a product or its after-sales care, then, here too, the private trader comes into his own, in hairdressing, bicycles and motor-bikes, electrical goods and, of course, milk deliveries. In baking and catering and increasingly in craftwork, art and pottery where part-production or processing could still be required or is still possible, then he is also able to retain a significant share of the market. There is always room, too, for the specialist catering for a narrow section of the public, often geographically dispersed over a wide area.

222

Chain and department stores may stock leisure items that have a quick turnover and wide appeal for example, but for the committed sportsman, fisherman, model railway enthusiast, photographer or hi-fi fanatic for whom price is of secondary importance to quality, the private, informed trader still provides a valuable role stocking slow-moving lines, providing detailed knowledge and advice. It is difficult to see how anything other than mail order firms working through specialist magazines can displace these.

What the future holds is difficult to predict, depending as it does on so many immeasurable and unknown variables. The complication of Value Added Tax has reputedly deterred many from entering or continuing. Increasing price competition either from multiples or mail order firms seems poised to spread into areas previously the domain of the skilled specialist shopkeeper. Frozen and convenient foodstuffs encouraging cheap, bulk buying may erode greengrocers' and butchers' shares of their respective markets. Major city centre redevelopments, the shopping precinct with its high rents and rates, may also discourage the independent. Relatively cheap private transport is still promoting out-of-town bulk buying at the new breed of super-stores. All these, indicative of a rising standard of living, could well militate against the small man; but a fall in real incomes could also hit him hardest, making people even more price-conscious, less willing or able to pay the extra for personal service or product differentiation.

Conversely, it is possible to point to more favourable signs. The continued surburban sprawl and increasing cost of public and private transport may well revitalise the smaller local general shops, even minor shopping centres. Consumer taste, admittedly within a restricted section of the population, would also seem to be shifting from the bland uniformity of standardised, mass-produced goods, searching instead for those hinting at originality or possessing elusive 'traditional' quality, craft or hand-made goods for which they are willing to forgo price advantages. Hand-made pottery and furniture, art and craft products, 'real' bread, and health foods all appear to be becoming more popular, expressing some dissatisfaction with the general range of products on offer through popular retail outlets. Growing leisure time, especially if accompanied by a stable or rising real incomes, could further advance the trade of specialist dealers offering individual products and services. Butchers already seem to have adapted well to the home-freezing industry and greengrocers appear to be relatively unaffected by the limited range of relatively highly priced frozen vegetables and fruit on offer. There would in short, always seem to be a place for the enterprising private retailer, whether in general trading or in skilled, specialist areas, who is willing to adapt to changing tastes and levels of expenditure, even if his choice of trades and his chances of becoming large and successful remain restricted. The old 'traditional' retailer of the mid nineteenth century has survived only in very rare cases without experiencing some change in his practice and custom, but his place has been filled, to a greater or lesser extent, by a variety of new, skilled men who, like him, rely on factors other than price for their appeal.

### Notes to Aftermath

[1]P. Mathias, *Retailing Revolution*, 1967.
[2]Wilson, 'Economy and society', *Economic History Review*, 1965.
[3]Jefferys, *Retail Trading*, pp. 36, 39.
[4]*Ibid.*, pp. 14–30.
[5]*Retail Trader*, 12 April 1911, p. 4.
[6]Yamey, 'Evolution of shopkeeping', p. 31.
[7]*Retail Business*, April 1982, p. 12.
[8]*Retail Business*, April 1979, pp. 6–10.
[9]*Tradesman and Shopkeeper*, 20 December 1902, p. 208.
[10]For a more detailed examination of the subject see J. A. Dawson & D. A. Kirby, *Small Scale Retailing in the U.K.*, Farnborough, 1979; M. Hall, *The Small Unit in the Distributive Trades*, H.M.S.O., 1971; A. D. Smith, *Small Retailers: Prospects and Policies*, H.M.S.O., 1971.
[11]Wells, *Mr Polly*, pp. 114, 116.
[12]Levy, *Shops of Britain*, p. 10.
[13]Bechhofer *et al.*, 'Small shopkeepers'.
[14]'You the jury', Radio Four, 11 April 1982.
[15]Hall, *Distributive Trades*, pp. 41–2.

# INDEX

Lough, Thomas, 91, 97
Lovett, William, 25
Lubbock, Sir John (Lord Avebury), 73, 91, 94, 143
Ludlow, 124, plates 14, 17
Lydd, plate 25

Macclesfield, 10, 101
machinery, dearth of, 65–6
Macphie, John, 83
Maidstone, 121, 175, 203; traders in, 208–9
mail order, 35, 45, 83
Manchester: markets and shops in, 5–6, 12–13, 121, 141, 143, 154; trade associations in, 75, 77, 88; politics in, 11, 27, 29
manufacturers' gifts, 134
Margarine Act, 1887, 63
Margate, 45, 137, 149
markets, 5–6, 95, 121, 140–1, 143, 154, 158
Marks and Spencer, 5, 39, 200
Married Women's Property Act, 1870, 29
Marshall, Alfred, 39
Master Bakers' Protection Society, 75. See also National Federation of Master Bakers' Associations
Master Saddlers' Federation, 170, 171
Masterman, C. F. G., 73, 97
Maynard's 39
Maypole Diary, 39, 124, 209
Mazawattee Tea, 59, 206
meat: chilled, 141; frozen, 38, 43, 90, 141ff. See also butchers
Menzies, John, 38
Merchandise Marks Acts, 64
Metropolitan Grocers' Association, 77, 122
middle class: demand, 2, 8, 34–6; shopping habits of, 3, 53ff., 123, 127ff., 143, 180, 214. See also credit, deliveries
milk sellers, 41, 155
milliners, 9, 14, 68, 185
Morris Beef Co., 141
motor transport, 60, 66–7, 78, 171, 203, 209
multiples, 36–9, 53, 68, 89, 90–1, 120, 124, 155, 166, 216–17. See also under separate trades
Municipal Reform Act, 19, 26
Municipal Society (London), 101
mutual self-help, see trade associations

National Cash Register Co., 66
National Chamber of Trade, 46, 76, 79, 99, 102
National Federation of Grocers' Associations, 64, 77, 82, 99, 121, 122
National Federation of Master Bakers' Associations, 77
National Federation of Meat Traders' Associations, 77, 142–3, 145
National Federation of Shopkeepers' and Small Traders' Protection Associations, 76, 95
National Insurance Act, 1911, 80, 103
National Union of Shop Assistants, 70, 71, 72, 94, 96
Nelson, James, 38, 142
Newcastle, 21, 52, 77, 88, 143
newsagents, 42, 45, 58, 68
Northbourne, 146, plate 24
Norwich, 143

O'Brien, Bronterre, 11, 24
O'Connor, Feargus, 24
off-licences, 94
old age pensions, 103
Oldham, 21–2, 24, 26, 101
opening hours, 57–8, 91, 94–9, 125, 127, 144, 147–8, 155, 163, 172, 187–8, 219. See also labour, conditions of; Shops Acts
Owenism, 37
ox muzzles, 178
Oxford Reform Club, 121

pavements, display on, 60, 65, 68, 157, 190–1
pawnbrokers, 182–98; numbers of, 14, 185–6; controls on, 64, 182–3; charges, 183–4, 189–90, 196; apprenticeships, 188, 194–8; social status of, 182, 186–7, 192–3, 195; associations of, 76, 182; criticisms of, 27, 182, 186; defence of, 184–5; domestic life of, 191–3; decline of, 185–6
Pearks, 126
Peek Freans', 124, 130, 212
Peel, Robert, 26
People's Budget, 103
pianos, 24, 194, plate 15
Place, Francis, 10, 20
Plymouth, 88
police, 26, 60, 79, 187
political influence, 19–30, 99–103. See also local politics, shopkeepers, voting
Polly, Mr, 40, 60, 68, 218
Poor Law, 19, 21, 26–7, 79, 103, 157, 163
Pooter, Charles, 54